FAITH AND POLITICS

- social theory — Catholicism — 145-6, 167-
- ecumenical conferences: Stockholm
  (1925) 172-174 ~~(1925)~~
  ~~London (14~~ Oxford (1937) — 175-7
  Amsterdam (1948) — 178
- a good eg. of RN's enthusiasm for Britain's
  historical accomplishment — 196.
- sources of the "ideology" in support democratic
  authority = the western world — 199-203
- obstacles to transporting this "ideology" to China + Corea 203
- ideological presupposition of Communist power — 203f
- a plea for stronger alliance with
  Britain — 210-211
- discriminating among various non-democratic
  regimes, between the "reversible" & the
  "irreversible" ones — 216-217
- the myth of a shared anti-imperialism as sum
  of US-USSR friendship [before Cold War] — 234-5
- did JFK play a part in overthrow of Diem? — 257
- solution of problem of civil rights our first
  priority — 261f

FAITH AND POLITICS

A Commentary on
Religious, Social and Political Thought
in a Technological Age

by
REINHOLD NIEBUHR

Edited by Ronald H. Stone

GEORGE BRAZILLER
New York

Acknowledgments

The author and editor wish to thank the following for permission to publish certain essays in this volume:

Christianity and Crisis for "Faith as the Sense of Meaning in Human Existence."

Harper and Row for "The Truths in Myths" from *The Nature of Religious Experience*, edited by J. S. Bixler, R. L. Calhoun and H. R. Niebuhr; for "God's Design and the Present Disorder of Society" from *Man's Disorder and God's Design*, Vol. III; and for "The Christian Faith and the Economic Life of Liberal Society" from *Goals of Economic Life*, edited by A. D. Ward.

Religion In Life for "Walter Rausenbusch in Historical Perspective." Copyright 1957 by Abingdon Press.

Shocken Books, Inc. for "Marx and Engels on Religion" from *On Religion* by Karl Marx and Friedrich Engels. Copyright 1964 by Shocken Books, Inc.

The Ecumenical Review for "Theology and Political Thought in the Western World."

Alumni Bulletin of the Theological Seminary for "The Spiritual Life of Modern Man."

World Publishing Company (Meridian Books) for "Freedom" from *Handbook of Christian Theology*, edited by Marvin Halverson.

Student Christian Movement Press, London, for "Do State and Nation Belong to God or the Devil?"

Charles Scribner's Sons for "Christian Faith and Social Action" from

Christian Faith and Social Action, edited by J. A. Hutchison. Copyright 1953 by Charles Scribner's Sons.

The Westminster Press for "The Development of a Social Ethic in the Ecumenical Movement" from *The Sufficiency of God,* edited by R. C. Mackie and C. G. West.

The Yale Review for "Liberty and Equality."

University of Notre Dame Press for "Power and Ideology in National and International Affairs" from *Theoretical Aspects of International Relations.*

The Annals (American Academy of Political and Social Science) for "American Hegemony and the Prospects for Peace."

Journal of International Affairs for "The Social Myths in the Cold War."

The New Leader for "Johnson and the Myths of Democracy," and for "Foreign Policy in a New Context."

Preface

This is a collection of essays on the religious, social and political philosophy of our time. Though the essays are on a variety of themes, they reveal a unity in that they attempt to establish the relevance of the Christian faith to contemporary political and ethical issues.

My primary purpose in this preface is to thank my young colleague and friend, Professor Ronald Stone. In addition to his many helpful services to an aging colleague, he has garnered all the occasional papers in the present volume, which were published originally in the popular and learned journals. His selections will I hope interest the general reader as they have interested me; indeed many of them were forgotten by their author until Professor Stone presented them for the volume of which he has kindly consented to be the editor.

My other purpose is to explain, or perhaps justify, the contrasting method in two of the major themes of these essays. The one theme is to validate the resources of biblical faith by applying its moral imperatives and its law of love, enjoining responsibility for the neighbor's welfare in a technical age. Today, social responsibilities must be guided by norms derived from all moral and empirical disciplines. A sacred text or a religiously sanctified tradition of past ages are inadequate guides to the ever-changing human relations of a secular culture.

The second theme is an explanation of the vitality of religious life in an age which expected the death of religion, after historical scholarship had discredited the legends in which the early life of religion abounds. The reason for this vitality is that religious faith is an expression of trust in the meaning of human existence, despite all the cross purposes, incongruities, and ills in nature and history.

It is one of the misunderstandings of modern culture that these ills make faith in God impossible. In fact they make it necessary. Faith in an ultimate and mysterious source and end of existence gives men the possibility of affirming life.

These ultimates do not belong to the category of prescientific myths. They represent the penumbra of mystery which surrounds a system of meaning. This mystery does not annul meaning, rather it is created by tangents of meaning which defy and transcend the ills of life. It must be one of the purposes of modern proponents of religious faith to combine acceptance of the cleansing effects of empirical disciplines with an understanding of the creative tasks of faith as the bearer of a sense of meaning.

The various papers in this book were written over a span of years, the earliest in 1930. I have not tried to bring them up to date, but have simply noted, at the end of each paper, the year in which it was written.

REINHOLD NIEBUHR

Union Theological Seminary
1968

Contents

PART THREE

FAITH AND POLITICS

Introduction

For more than half a century, Reinhold Niebuhr has contributed to America's self-understanding by analyzing its history, religion, and politics. Niebuhr has never found it easy to define his specific field of inquiry. His multifarious interests have taken him into the social sciences, philosophy, and theology, and his contribution to each has been significant. At various times he has been hailed as the foremost American political philosopher, moralist, or theologian of his time, although he himself has rejected the titles of theologian and philosopher and spurned the role of moralist. Traditional disciplines could not contain his inquiries, for he has confronted political scientists with theological issues and theologians with political problems. His own definition of his role, made in 1965, as that of a political and social philosopher teaching Christian ethics in Union Theological Seminary, brought together his three major concerns and implied a certain priority to political and social philosophy.

Niebuhr's mind was formed as a Protestant churchman and, though his writing was often in a secular style, it has been marked by his debt and continuing loyalty to his Protestant tradition. His major interest is not in theological problems per se, but rather in the social and ethical function of religion. He deals with the problems of Christology as they affect the formulation of an adequate doctrine of man or the development of a social ethic.

Believing deeply in the social relevance of religion to the problems of a technical age, he has not hesitated to demythologize and reformulate the Christian tradition to meet human problems of the modern world. Many, including admirers and critics, have not understood Niebuhr's use of religious symbols. His utilization of such symbols combines a loyalty to the tradition with a concern for the ethical and pedagogical integrity of the tradition. Concerned with the function of religious language, his method moves beyond analysis to the reformulation of traditional symbols to promote the integrity of the church in its confession and social action. Two essays in the first part of this book—"Faith as the Sense of Meaning in Human Existence" and "The Truth in Myths"—though written decades apart, reveal this twofold passion for the tradition and for contemporary meaningfulness.

For the longest part of his career, Niebuhr's official vocation was that of a professor of social ethics in Union Theological Seminary. There is a sense in which all ethics are social and the term *social ethics* contains a redundancy. The term points, however, to the contribution of the social gospel movement (See: "Walter Rauschenbusch in Historical Perspective") to Protestant theological education. Niebuhr stands in the social gospel tradition, which emphasizes the relevance of Christian faith to the social problems of the age.

Part II contains six of Niebuhr's longer essays which discuss the substance of Christian social ethics. They represent his concern that the Christian faith was relevant to the improvement of social life only when it took full account of all the factors which resisted the establishment of a more just order.

Since the time when he served as an adviser to George F. Kennan's Foreign Policy Planning Staff of the United States State Department, Niebuhr has devoted almost as much of his writing to international affairs as to more strictly religious issues. His work in the former sector combines analysis of issues of contemporary statecraft with reflection upon political philosophy. The essay entitled "Liberty and Equality" represents political philosophy in the classical tradition and reveals how deeply his thought is imbedded in liberal democratic theory. The essays on international politics in Part III discuss important facets of the contemporary struggle, while contributing to the philosophy of international politics.

Niebuhr's approach to an issue is characterized by his reliance upon history. In analyzing a political problem he indicates the major factors to be considered by emphasizing these in his recital of the problem's origins. In considering the validity of an ethical principle, he describes the evolution of the idea through various historical epochs. He challenges certain illusions of the American public and policy makers by reminding them of their history and particularly of its ironical aspects. His teaching and writing both reveal a preference for historical perspective to systematic construction; the contingency and irony in human affairs are not subverted to the uses of ideology. History is the art of interpreting the records of man's past, and Niebuhr relies more and more heavily upon this art in the post-World War II era.

As his thought became more historically oriented, it also grew more pragmatic. The results of the New Deal and Franklin D. Roosevelt's pragmatic foreign policy convinced Niebuhr of the dangers and irrelevance of ideology to the problems confronting the United States. The principles of social ethics were evaluated by their utility in promoting the common good in a given social situation. He had always had a great intellectual debt to William James, and in the post-World War II period he became one of the foremost exponents of Christian pragmatism. His influence in purging Protestantism of absolutisms in social ethics has been one of his most important contributions in American life. No man or political idea was good enough to be trusted completely; both had to be checked by other men and ideas and continually evaluated in the light of their contribution to the common good.

See p. 55

An issue which appears in many of the essays is the relationship of the ideal to the real. The relationship of man's hoped-for communities to the real communities in which he lives is the central problem in political philosophy for Niebuhr. Throughout his career, he has wrestled with the contradictory drives within himself toward political cynicism and Christian perfectionism. Neither pole prevailed, and his writing emphasizes the greatness of man in his freedom and the selfishness of man in his anxiety more thoroughly than any contemporary political philosopher of whom I am aware. The ideal of the love of Christ and the reality of Machiavellian politics are the poles within which he discusses man's social hopes and political strategies. Niebuhr's use of the dialectic denies neither altruism nor egoism, but shows how most of man's social life is a product of both self-giving and self-seeking impulses.

His work in Christian ethics has had a twofold purpose: (1) The Christian ideal of radical love must be protected from all particular cultural-religious corruptions of that ideal, and (2) The Christian faith must be expressed in symbols which inspire men to achieve the highest degree of social justice possible in their epoch. The ideal of love was defined for all time in Jesus' summary of the law of love and in his sacrifice. Particular expressions of this love, however, are relative to the contingencies of each situation. Christian love properly understood undergirds and promotes particular understandings of justice but always operates as a principle of criticism of particular realizations of justice. Love is the motive and justice the method of Christian action in society.

Niebuhr's ethic utilizes principles from the social philosophy of the West. Ethics is the study of principles and the development of their understanding for contemporary man. However, history reveals that all particular expressions of these principles are relative to a time, place, and world view. Niebuhr himself fits neither the natural law and casuistry camp nor the situationalist camp in the contemporary debate in Christian moral philosophy. Through dialectically relating principles (e.g., in "Liberty and Equality") and by emphasizing their pragmatic consequences (e.g., in "The Development of a Social Ethic in the Ecumenical Movement"), he transcends any narrow understanding of either school.

His social ethic was developed within the presuppositions of biblical faith. This means that the whole range of biblical ethics and Christian doctrine is a source which he has taken seriously and mined for ethical wisdom. The major presuppositions of the biblical faith are the reign and relevance of the will of God and the approach of the messianic age. Religious symbolism expresses the purposes and limits of man's history and promises its fulfillment. The Christian ethic is related to and enriched by the full panoply of Christian doctrine and is characterized in the Christian life by faith, hope, and love. Niebuhr has been criticized for reducing the Christian ethic to the love commandment. A more adequate understanding of his ethics is that for him Christian ethics comes to a focus in love but that the full Christian life is characterized by the other virtues as well.

The key to his social ethics is the dialectical relation between love and justice. Justice institutionalizes but never completely embodies the demands of love. Love increases the application and idea of justice, but it cannot be substituted for tolerable balances of justice. Underlying all of his reflection upon man's moral life is his secure trust in the meaning and purpose of life. Religious faith is the symbolic representation of this meaning and in this sense of meaning finally rests the motivation for seeking the moral life.

Niebuhr's understanding of history and man have not allowed him to remain satisfied with any structure of society. He always remains the critic of society, urging man to realize an ever higher degree of social justice. His critique of society does not drive him into utopianism nor to alienation from available political processes. Each society's patterns have to be evaluated in terms of the history of that society and in terms of that society's concrete needs.

Niebuhr's position of remaining always in tension with his society has not prevented him from combating totalitarianism in the forms of right-wing dictatorships, fascism, and Communism. Practically, he has participated in American left-wing third party movements and the liberal wing of the Democratic Party. Politically, he has always been a liberal in the classical sense of promoting the largest possible degree of liberty, even though his most bitter polemics have been directed against illusions of optimism which often characterized liberals. Niebuhr's career is that of the

Christian political man; if he refuses to accept the claims of any status quo settlement for final adequacy, he has never refused to face the hard task of ordering the society more justly through the political process.

His hatred of totalitarianism and his political realism have led him to urge responsible use of United States power on the international scene. He continually inveighs against the dangers of pride of power and argues that the United States guard against the blindness of imperialism. This country, in the post-World War II period, could hardly be an innocent nation free from responsibility, but neither should it become an arrogant nation pursuing "globalism." Between innocency and globalism Niebuhr saw possibilities of a responsible utilization of the capacity of the United States to encourage various experiments in nation-building while the stalemate of the cold war provided a tolerable degree of order. The essays of Part III indicate the character of his critique of American foreign policy in the 1960's.

May the act of collecting these essays be an installment on a debt that can never be paid to my teacher, Reinhold Niebuhr. They represent as deep a profundity as any I know, and I hope they will be useful to students of politics, ethics, and religion and to the increasing number of students of Niebuhr's thought. I would like to express my appreciation to Mrs. Ursula Niebuhr who, after graciously entertaining me as a student for years, assisted me in selecting these papers, and to my wife, Mrs. Joann Stone, who, after encouraging me as a student for years, supervised the typing and proofread the manuscript.

RONALD H. STONE

Columbia University
1968

PART ONE

Faith as the Sense of Meaning
in Human Existence (1966)

[handwritten: Christianity & Crisis]

[handwritten: the Death-of-God theology]

THE younger theologians who cheerfully, even blatantly, announced their discovery that "God is dead" do not seem to realize that all religious affirmations are an expression of a sense of meaning and that a penumbra of mystery surrounds every realm of meaning. Religious affirmations avail themselves of symbols and myths, which express both trust in the meaning of life and an awareness of the mystery of the unknowable that surrounds every realm of meaning.

The exertions of these men would seem to be futile. One reason is that they appear not to be concerned with the task of projecting alternative frames of meaning for the discarded faith. The prominent atheists of the past century, such as Marx, Freud, and Nietzsche, did project alternative schemes of meaning. The Marxist apocalypse presented a secular eschatology in which history's grand culmination was promised by a revolution that would usher in a classless and peaceful society. The poor would take vengeance on the wealthy in this secularized version of the promise "blessed are the poor . . . for theirs is the kingdom of heaven."

Freud's scheme was not a secularized version of traditional eschatology, but his distinction between the ego and the id seemed to echo Paul's pessimism about the power of the "carnal mind" over the "spiritual mind." Incidentally, both Freud's and Paul's estimates of human nature were strikingly similar to Plato's estimate of the *epithymeticon*, which only seeks immediate ends. Freud's analytical techniques have become a resource of modern therapeutic efforts to cure the mentally ill. Only in his *Civilization and Its Discontents* did he make an effort to explain human history in pessimistic terms. His techniques were usually confined to individual man's nature.

His atheism was, therefore, more individualistic and nonreligious, compared with Marx's apocalyptic vision, which constructed a scheme not only of historical meaning but of historical redemption. Thus Marx, particularly as amended by Lenin and more recently by Mao, gave the poor nations of the world both a new religion and a totalitarian culture.

It was Nietzsche, of course, who initiated the "death of God" phrase, interpreted the whole of human history as a ceaseless power struggle, and projected his vision of a "superman." This vision may or may not have been the basis of fascist politics. In short, the distinguished atheists of the nineteenth century gave alternative, partially contradictory, partially complementary, views of human nature and man's destiny. None of them were content to sweep the ground and purge culture of all traditional schemes of meaning.

Our current radical theologians have no apparent interest in the structures of meaning, traditional or modern, by which men seek to explain their nature and the complex history of mankind in its pathetic and even tragic proportions. These men seem not to feel an obligation to define a system of coherence or meaning.

One can only guess at their presuppositions. Sometimes these seem to be mystical, even Buddhist. Since the chief exponents dedicate their book* to the memory of Paul Tillich, one assumes that their outlook is influenced by Tillich's mysticism. If so, it may be well that Tillich is dead. He insisted in his lifetime that all propositions about the "existence" of God, either affirmative or negative, were irrelevant because God's "being" is beyond the categories of mere existence. He would have been horrified by the proposition "God is dead."

---

* Thomas J. Altizer and William Hamilton, *Radical Theology and the Death of God* (New York: Bobbs-Merrill, 1966).

Sometimes the presuppositions appear to be informed by the atheism of the French, pre-revolutionary *philosophes,* who worshiped nature and/or reason, assuming that the two concepts were identical. At other times they seem merely to be saying not that God is dead but that traditional images of him are dead or dying. If that is the case, they might have said so unmistakably. They would have achieved less notoriety but would have revealed themselves as responsible members of modern culture. That culture is, of course, informed by both religious and secular presuppositions.

They do not seem to realize, in any case, that our modern "open society" and pluralistic culture encourage cooperation between the traditionally pious and the secular humanists, so long as both partners understand the limits of both historical and contemporary symbols of meaning. The creative spirits in each group will know that it is pointless to clear the ground unless this spiritual purge is quickly followed by new and creative efforts to try to make sense out of life.

It will also become apparent that this partnership can cleanse both the pietists and the humanists of illusions. The partner who still clings to obviously religious symbols will be taught by the modern-minded partner that a literalistic interpretation of such symbols makes for obscurantism in culture and for confusion in moral and social standards. But the man of religious faith may convince the modern, i.e., the secularist, that the symbols of secularism are defective in expressing the penumbra of mystery.

This mystery may possibly suggest the various lacunae, the many cross-purposes and the incoherences that any tight and logical system of science or philosophy does not allow. Mystery in short is the shadowy realm of twilight where both coherence and incoherence are known or intimated, as well as the threshold of glory which gives light but does not reveal its nature.

Since the very word *God* represents both the unknowable "X" of mystery and the fullness of meaning—perhaps the "God the Father Almighty, Maker of heaven and earth" of the Christian creed, and the "King of the world" of Jewish faith—we might well begin our analysis of the relation of mystery and meaning

in the temporal order of the "created" world. Here traditional
faith includes the meaning, that is, the regularity and order (the
"seedtime and harvest, summer and winter, day and night"), in
this symbol or concept of God as well as the mystery of the
creative power that sustains these regularities.

The question is whether modern empirical sciences, Darwinian
theories of causal sequences, and theories of evolving forms and
structures have not made the temporal order self-explanatory, and
therefore the traditional conception of God irrelevant and implausible. Modern science certainly has made obscurantist views
of special acts and events in creation implausible, even as it has
refuted orthodox conceptions of "special providence," which pre-
suppose an arbitrary monarch whose caprice accounts for specific
events in the whole variegated drama of human history. In short,
is not the traditional creator God dead, or more accurately the
traditional conception of a divine creator?

To this question some modern humanist will venture a
confident affirmative answer. But it is advisable to consult a
metaphysical account of the temporal and natural process before
banishing mystery from the realm of either "creation" or "evolution." In Alfred Whitehead's memorable volume *Process and
Reality,* he posits God as the "principle of concretion" to account
for the fact that no previous cause is an adequate explanation
for a subsequent event. These events always reveal a relation to
previous causes and sequences but also novel features for which
there is no adequate explanation in the previous stream of events.

In short, there is a penumbra of mystery even if the streams of
historical or natural events be analyzed with empirical rigor. The
temporal order is not self-explanatory. The creation myths of the
great religions may be primitive in the light of modern evolutionary science. But the myth of creation, while prescientific, has
elements of permanent validity in the sense that the mystery of
creation hovers over any evolutionary chain of causes.

The Darwinian controversy of the nineteenth century is a vivid
example of the issues at stake. The emergence of the concept of
man as endowed with the radical freedom of reason and spirit in
the evolutionary chain gave the traditionally devout the oppor-

tunity to argue that a special act of creation must be posited in order to guard the dignity of man. But this special act without reference to the scientifically verified emergence of man in the chain of evolution, or to man's obvious relation to the brutes as a creature, or even his striking affinities of physiognomy with the monkeys, proved to be no more than a futile rearguard action by obscurantist defenders of the faith, e.g. Bishop Wilberforce and William Jennings Bryan.

But even the general consensus of an age of science about the doctrine of evolution, which made the ridicule of Bishop Wilberforce and Mr. Bryan almost universal, could not obscure the problem of the radical novelty of the emergence of human animals, whose freedom made them creators in the realm of history, though they never ceased to be creatures.

The puzzle about man's rational freedom even in the minds of secularists revealed itself in the long controversy about an alleged "missing link" between monkeys and man. The efforts of modern evolutionists to explain the emergence of mind through the natural or biological process of the "survival of the fittest" pointed to the realm of mystery and creation even in the most imposing structure of a scientifically validated evolutionary chain.

Thus the nineteenth-century Darwinian controversy established the necessary partnership between religious-mythical pointers to the mystery of creation and an empirical account of the evolutionary stream in the realm of natural causation.

It might be plausible to define the efforts of religious faith as futile and a pathetic rearguard action to preserve the tattered remnants of religion in an age of science. It certainly was inevitable that the creation myths of all religions would be seen as primitive notions of a temporal process, as indeed they were.

But meanwhile some nineteenth-century philosophers, analyzing the temporal world, still used notions such as Hegel's dubious concept of a supranatural rational and historical order to make a necessary distinction between the realm of nature and the realm of history. In the realm of history man was both creator and creature.

Here we confront the ambiguity of man's existence. Man is

a creature of nature; yet his freedom enables him to rise above
nature, to construct rational ends that transcend natural impulse,
and to make history in which he is both creator and creature.
Religious faith posits not only a mysterious creator God but a
mysterious divine providence, which somehow brings unity into
the incoherences and incongruities of man's individual and collective history; but only symbolic statements are possible. Faith looks
to an ultimate order beyond the incoherences, incongruities and
cross-purposes, and creates or accepts the presupposition of a
divine providence, related to the ultimate source of the temporal
process.

Such faith is bound to be expressed in symbolic and prescientific terms. And if spelled out, it is as primitive a notion as special
acts of creation. Yet such naïve notions as providence and creation,
progressively discredited by empirical sciences, are valid and necessary components of any scheme of meaning. They derive their
permanent relevance because they express a basic trust in the
meaningfulness of human existence. The Book of Job is the most
striking statement of this trust, which is affirmed despite, and
because of, the experience of confusion, cross-purposes and meaninglessness in human life.

Religious faith is permanently valid despite the discredit it
suffers because of its trust that the incoherences of nature and
history are finally overcome in a transcendent order. Though we
never experience this directly, we are prompted to believe because
instinctively we know that there is a universe and order and a
system of meaning.

Metaphysical systems by their rational nature are bound to
obscure the incoherences and ambiguities of actual life. Idealists
are more faulty in this respect than naturalistic philosophers. Hegel,
for instance, tried to comprehend both the natural and the historical order as a rational system. Two men who rebelled against
Hegelianism in the nineteenth century were Marx and Kierkegaard. Marx maintained that Hegel obscured the social tensions
of human history (the "class struggle"), and Kierkegaard felt that
Hegel's system obscured the incongruity of the "existing indi-

vidual." Kierkegaard posited a "leap of faith" to make sense out of life.

This leap of faith used the drama of Christ to give meaning to the incongruities that create anguish in the human soul, particularly the two facts of sin and death. Triumph over death is assured by the resurrection of Christ. Sin is accurately defined as the corruption of man's freedom rather than the inertia of his physical passions against the larger and more creative purposes of man's rational spirit.

Religious answers to the evils of sin and death are not to be fitted into a rational system. The Greek answer to the problem of death was the idea of an immortal discarnate soul, and the Hebrew answer was the equally nonrational concept of resurrection of the body. Both answers, although they outraged man's empirical experience of mortality, have stubbornly persisted even in a secular culture because men require a symbol of man's unique spirit that transcends the finiteness of his life as a creature of nature.

Thus the acceptance of suprarational symbols, on which both the pious and the unbelievers agree in the hour of grief over the death of a loved one, may be a testimony to the reality of the deathlessness of human personality. We experience this deathlessness most acutely in the hour of death, and we do so as "empirically" as we experience death. Our testimony to this reality is contained in the almost universal sentiment about loved ones: "I cannot believe that he is dead."

This lack of precision in the symbols of faith regarding the incongruity of man, as both mortal and immortal, is typical of all religious symbols about the mysteries of life. This holds whether they deal with the mysteries of the regularities of the natural world or the incongruities of human history, whether in individual or collective terms. We do not worry, unless we are devotees of precision, about the inexact and unscientific character of all religious and poetic symbols that express basic trust in the meaning of our existence or in the meaning of the total human historical enterprise.

Bishop John A. T. Robinson's plea in his book *Honest to God* for a "new image of God" agitated the dovecotes of the pious. He asked for a new, presumably more relevant, image of the divine mystery, and he is thus more relevant than the American theologians who insist that God is dead. If an outmoded image of God were dead, this fact would certainly not imply that the enigma of creativity and the mysteries of the world's beginning and end have ceased to be.

The Bishop of Woolwich's plea was strongly influenced by two eminent theologians, Rudolf Bultmann and Paul Tillich. Since Bultmann and Robinson are both New Testament theologians, the latter's tardy awareness of the former may be surprising. But in this context we should note that both Bultmann and Tillich must be criticized for obscuring the Hebrew, and therefore biblical, emphasis on the meaningfulness of history. This emphasis is the root of the Hebraic insistence on historical responsibility and, therefore, of the historical dynamism of our Western culture. In Bultmann's thought the prophetic sense of history becomes dissolved in an existentialist philosophy.

Tillich tried to fit biblical myths into a framework of mystic, Neoplatonic philosophy, which inevitably equates finiteness with evil. Bultmann makes no precise distinction between prescientific myths and those biblical symbols that are permanently valid in the Christian faith because they bear the very message of the Gospel. But he is concerned to purge the Bible of all prescientific myths, in fact the whole ancient cosmogony.

But his whole treatment of New Testament thought is to be explained in terms of the distinction between prescientific myths and those that carry the *kerygma*, the message of the Gospel presenting Christ as the savior from both sin and death. Bultmann is not concerned to discredit these essential myths and symbols of the Gospel; he is interested in rescuing the "kernel of truth" from the shell of contemporary imagination.

Thus he observes that the story of Christ's resurrection was not an account of a miracle or even of a "public event." In this, it has to be distinguished from the crucifixion, which was undoubtedly a "public event."

Tillich

The resurrection, on the other hand, was, in the original accounts, a spiritual experience of the disciples. It was, therefore, an expression of the faith of the early church that a crucified, rather than a victorious, messiah was indeed the real revelation of God's mercy, more exactly a revelation of the paradox of the divine mercy and judgment—a paradox that the Old Testament frequently expressed. But the new Gospel brought the atoning death of Christ into the center of the *kerygma* because only such an atonement would answer the question about the perennial sinfulness of all men—and the mixture of good and evil in all human striving.

Bultmann derives an existentialist philosophy from his interpretation of the message about Christ. For that message challenges men to transmute "unauthentic" to "authentic" existence. In short, a highly individualistic existentialism emerges in Bultmann's interpretation, which threatens the prophetic conception of mankind's collective history.

Bishop Robinson's discovery of the thought of Paul Tillich was also belated, and his reliance upon Tillich in his quest for a new image of God raises the serious question of the distinction between Neoplatonic mysticism and the historically oriented faith of Western culture. Tillich was an unusually erudite philosopher and theologian whose genius was to translate biblical faith into mystic categories. For Tillich, it was a foregone conclusion that if any modern Christian should reject the historical validity of the story of the fall of Adam in the primitive myth of Genesis, he would be forced to concede that "creation was really the fall." He translated the mythical idea of original sin so that it became a source of the distinction between essential and existential man. In this way, finiteness, creatureliness and, in fact, all historical phenomena were involved in evil.

Despite Tillich's genius, his total system was really a Neoplatonic version of Christianity, which includes the Hebrew and biblical myths. History and all temporal events were involved in evil. Hebraism's tremendous assertion of the "goodness of creation" was thus denied. Tillich believed that all definitions of God were metaphorical and symbolic, except, of course, his own mystic definition of the divine as "the Ground of Being" or "Being per se."

But this assertion obscures the obvious fact that men cannot have any experience of pure being, any more than they have an empirical experience of "God the Father Almighty, Maker of heaven and earth." In other words, a mystic "new image of God" is the image of an undifferentiated being and eternity, sans history and temporality. This new image may have been more sophisticated than the image of God "up there" or as an old man with a beard, but the question remains whether it is really, as Tillich asserts, the only truly metaphysical and nonmetaphorical definition.

The issue is important, particularly for faiths that include the dramas of time and history in the realm of meaning. Since these historically minded religions, such as the faith of the Hebrew prophets, emphasize historical responsibility, it may not be too farfetched to regard the myth of creation in particular as an indispensable mode of expression for faiths that do not follow Buddhism and other mystic faiths in equating temporality and finiteness with evil.

Within the limits of his Neoplatonic framework, Paul Tillich's genius was very creative in translating outmoded images and metaphors of religious history into current figures of speech and relating them to current problems of philosophy and depth psychology. Therefore, Bishop Robinson's search for a new image of God was legitimate, and his findings were suggestive for many. We must, however, be reconciled to the fact that all religions, particularly historically oriented faiths, must avail themselves of symbols, metaphors, and myths to point to the transcendent sources of meaning in the flux of the temporal and phenomenal reality.

The custodians of the ark of faith must not be too ashamed of these metaphors; but they must also not be too literalistic in defending their faith against all the empirical disciplines fortunately available in our pluralistic culture.

Ideally, a partnership between the guardians of faith and the secular disciplines will prevent extravagant errors of both partners. The guardians of faith will be saved from literalistic and obscurantist fallacies, which are the vices of all moribund religious traditions. But expressions of basic trust, though their symbols may be regarded as "primitive" by modern culture, will prevent the elimination of all interest in ultimate meanings and purposes. This empirical purge of culture usually results in barrenness or moral sentimentality in even the most impressive forms of humanism. The human story is too grand and awful to be told without reverence for the mystery and the majesty that transcend all human knowledge. Only humble men who recognize this mystery and majesty are able to face both the beauty and terror of life without exulting over its beauty or becoming crushed by its terror.

[1966]

The Truth in Myths

(1937)

I N THE lexicon of the average modern, particularly in America, a myth is a piece of fiction, usually inherited from the childhood of the race. The scientific outlook of our mature culture has supposedly invalidated the truth value of these primitive stories in which gods and devils, nymphs and satyrs, fairies and witches are portrayed in actions and attitudes which partly transcend and partly conform to human limitations. They are regarded as the opulent fruits of an infantile imagination which are bound to wither under the sober discipline of a developed intelligence. Science has displaced mythology. A careful observation of the detailed phenomena of life and history yields more credible explanations of life's mysteries than these fanciful accounts of the origin of life or the genesis of evil or these fantastic pictures of the universe. When we have the conception of evolution we do not need the story of creation, and when we see man's slow ascent toward the ideal we have no place for a mythical "fall" to account for the origin of evil in the world. The reign of law revealed by science invalidates the miracles which abound in all religions; and the insight into, and power over, his own future given to the modern man through his intelligence frees him of the need to seek salvation in the myths of religion. Such are the convictions which belong to the unquestioned certainties of the modern man.

Since mythical elements are irrevocably enshrined in the canons of all religions it has become the fashion of modern religion to defend itself against the criticisms of science by laborious reinterpretations of its central affirmations with the purpose of sloughing off the mythical elements, apologizing for them as inevitable concepts of infantile cultures, and extracting the perennially valid truths from these husks of the past. Unfortunately the protagonists of modern religion usually fail to placate the devotees of the scientific method by these diligent but not too dignified laborers. They are met by the contemptuous suggestion that they have been merely insinuating new meanings into ancient phrases, and that they have gained nothing for their pains but what might have been secured more simply by a scientific analysis of the known facts of life and existence. If science has the final word and authority about life, as many of those theologians who have been most anxious to adjust religion to the scientific world-view have assumed, this suggestion is plausible enough. Indeed some of the supposedly abiding truths which have been distilled from ancient myths by this process of reinterpretation have lost their religious essence so completely, have been flattened and deflated to such a degree in the process of adaptation, that the charge of the empiricists and naturalists seems perfectly justified.

The modern protagonists of religion made the mistake of retreating too far and too quickly when the exigencies of the cultural situation demanded a retreat. Their error was to disavow permanent myth with primitive myth. Religion had no right to insist on the scientific accuracy of its mythical heritage. From this position a retreat was necessary. That part of mythology which is derived from prescientific thought, which does not understand the causal relations in the natural and historical world, must naturally be sacrificed in a scientific age. But there is a permanent as well as a primitive myth in every great mythical heritage. This deals with aspects of reality which are suprascientific rather than prescientific. Modernistic religion has been so thin on the whole because it did not understand this distinction and thus sacrificed what is abiding with what is primitive in religious myth.

What are the aspects of reality which can be stated only in mythical terms?

The most obvious aspect of reality which can not be comprehended in terms of scientific concepts is the aspect of value. It is true that the value of things for a particular individual can always be stated in terms of aesthetic myths. The aesthetic myth (such as "Hail to thee, blithe Spirit! Bird thou never wert," in Shelley's ode "To a Skylark") makes no claim about the ultimate value of a thing in a total scheme of purpose. It merely asserts value in terms of the moods and purposes of an individual in a given instance. The purely aesthetic and nonreligious myth is therefore skeptical about values in the ultimate sense. "Poetry," declares Santayana, "is religion which is no longer believed."

The aesthetic myth becomes transmuted into a religious myth when it seeks to comprehend facts and occurrences in terms of their organic relation to the whole conceived in teleological terms. For only if things are related to each other organically in a total meaningful existence can it be claimed that they have value. Religion, to transpose Santayana's phrase, is poetry which is believed. Religion seeks mythically to grasp life in its unity and wholeness. This unity and wholeness can never be expressed in terms of complete rationality; for reason only observes and deduces. What it observes is concrete reality in its multifarious forms. Its deductions are based upon the sequences which it observes in nature and history. But these sequences reveal nothing of the internal unity in all organic growth.

For this reason scientific descriptions of reality always tend to a mechanistic interpretation of it. The facts of organic growth can be comprehended and described only by mythically transferring the inner unity of the human consciousness (where unity is directly experienced and apprehended) to the external world. A certain amount of primitive myth is always involved in this process (its analogy to animism of primitive mythology is apparent). But it is also permanent myth in the sense that it is permanently valid, since reality is actually organic and not mechanical in its processes.

A full analysis of the organic aspect of life reveals another quality of existence which can not be comprehended in terms of rationality and which might be defined as the dimension of depth in existence.

If the relatedness of things to each other is more than mechanical, the source of their unity lies beyond, behind, and above the observable phenomena. "The world of things as they are," to quote Professor William P. Montague, "is not self-explanatory; it bears the earmarks, if not of a manufactured product, at least of a thing which has been derived from something other than itself." Not only the secret of its unity but of its growth (the emergence of novelty) lies beyond itself. Sciences may carefully observe certain processes of life and history and describe how or under what concatenation of circumstances certain forms, biological or social, were transmuted into other forms. But it can only describe these processes after the fact, and it is forced to treat each new emergent as following necessarily from the forces which immediately preceded it. It is, therefore, constantly tempted to commit the logical fallacy of *post hoc*; *ergo propter hoc*. It is, in short, compelled to deny the idea of creation.

The idea of creation is a typical mythical idea. It relates the source of life to observable life in terms which defy rationality. The primitive myth speaks of God making man out of clay, and breathing the breath of life into him. But the idea of creation remains mythical even when the primitive myth is discarded. If the myth is completely rationalized the creator becomes the first cause. Insofar as he is merely a cause, among many causes, creation is denied and every new fact in history is explained in terms of previous facts. Insofar as he is a uniquely first cause the limits of logic in dealing with the problem of causation in history are recognized but the recognition is left in negative form. Thus when religion refuses to yield the idea of creation to the idea of evolution it is following an instinct for the truth. When, as has been frequently the case in modern religion, it apologetically declares that nothing but a difference in terminology is involved ("Some call it evolution and others call it God") it is erroneously yielding to the prejudices of a scientific age.

The myth of creation not only expresses dynamic and organic qualities in reality which can not be stated in rational terms, but paradoxical qualities which elude the canons of logic. The dimension of depth in life contains such a paradox. All life and existence in its concrete forms suggests not only sources but possibilities beyond itself. These possibilities must be implied in the source or they would not be true possibilities. God is, in other words, both the ultimate ground of reality and its ultimate goal. "Religion," to quote Professor Montague in a revealing phrase, ". . . is the acceptance of the momentous possibility—that what is highest in spirit is also deepest in nature, that the ideal and the real are at least to some extent identified, not merely evanescently in our own lives but in the universe itself."[1]

The myth of creation, in which God is neither identified with the historical world nor separated from it, offers the basis upon which all theologies are built in which God is conceived as both the ground and the ultimate fulfillment of a meaningful world, as both the creator and the judge of historical existence. This paradox is really the only ground of an effective ethic because it alone harmonizes ethical and metaphysical interests, and gives us a picture of a world which is really a universe, but not so unqualifiedly a meaningful world as to obscure the fact of evil and the possibility of a dynamic ethics. Every dynamic ethics depends upon the dimension of depth in life and upon a description of this dimension, which neither equates the metrical and mechanistic aspect of concrete existence with meaning and value, nor completely separates the world of value and ideals from the facts of concrete existence.

Efforts to describe the unity and meaningfulness of the world and existence in purely rational terms must ultimately choose between a metaphysics which inclines to monistic idealism (and may finally degenerate into a dualism) or a science which inclines to a mechanistic monism. Most of the modern efforts to arrive at a unified picture of life and reality have been under the direct influence of science rather than metaphysics. When science disavows both myth and metaphysics it has only two alternatives, in its attempt to construct a total world picture. It may picture the

[1] William Pepperell Montague, *Belief Unbound* (New Haven: Yale University Press, 1931).

world and life as a mechanism, held together by the mechanical processes which it believes to have discovered by its observations. But there is only superficial unity and no meaningfulness in such a world. There is no place in it for the kind of vital and organic unity which the self experiences in its own self-consciousness. The logical ultimate of such a world view is found in behavioristic psychology which denies the unity of consciousness as a reality. But such an ultimate is self-destructive because it invalidates the truth value of everything discovered by the conscious self about the world in which it lives. It is furthermore destructive of human vitality because it is impossible to live with zest if no purposes can be found worthy of our striving. A purely mechanical world is bereft of purpose and meaningfulness.

The other alternative (more generally followed) is to introduce mythical and transcendent elements covertly (usually unconsciously) into the supposedly scientific accounts of life and history. Our modern culture has maintained its spiritual life by such a covert myth, the idea of progress. It is possible to speak of progress in interpreting the endless changes of life only if some measuring rod of value can be found with which to gauge the process. But the rod must not be a part of the process. It must transcend it. The rod taken by modern culture has usually been some ethical ideal, inherited from religion. The confidence that the processes of nature support and contribute to the victory of this ethical ideal is really a rationalized version of the Christian myth of salvation. Unfortunately it is more optimistic and really less credible than the Christian myth. It derives its credulous optimism from the fact that it sacrificed the primary myth of creation prematurely and thus identifies the processes of history too uncritically with the transcendent ideal implied in these processes. It is only through the myth of creation that it is possible to assert both the meaningfulness of life and the fact of evil. To say that God created the world is to assert its meaningfulness; and to distinguish between the creator and his creation is to make a place for the reality of evil in the inevitable relativities of time and history.

Philosophy, before modern science made the futile effort to give a unified account of the world without metaphysical presuppositions, usually sought to comprehend the unity of life and the meaningfulness of existence by viewing all things from the perspective of the unity of human consciousness and bringing all forms of life under the categories of human reason. The world was declared meaningful because it is rational. While it is not exact to identify philosophical idealism with the method of philosophy as such and to equate naturalism with the method of science, such a distinction is roughly correct. Philosophy from Plato to Hegel was predominantly idealistic in interpreting reality in terms of rationality. The confidence that external reality conforms to the categories of human consciousness is itself a rationalized form of religious faith. It is true of course that men have partially validated this confidence by bringing the external world under the control of their practical purposes by acting upon their faith. But they would have been unable to do this if they had not initiated their efforts on the assumption that the structure of life is relevant to the forms of mind. Bertrand Russell is right, therefore, when he declares that philosophies which ascribe meaning and value to external reality are rationalized mythologies. He may be less correct in suggesting that the ascription of meaning to the world is always unwarranted.

The real difficulty with idealistic philosophies is that they are rationalized myths which lost their virtue in the process of rationalization. Idealistic philosophy is unable to do justice to either the heights or depths of life. It is unable to do justice to its heights because for it the transcendent source and goal of the meaning of life is still within the limits of human rationality. Thus the God of philosophical idealism is always less than a living creator. He is also less than the holy and perfect God of religious faith, though Plato overcomes this difficulty by frankly turning to myth and declaring "that the good is not essence but soars even beyond essence in dignity and power." The potentialities of life are in other words greater than can be comprehended in terms of the "essences" which are always the constructs of the human mind.

The God of philosophical idealism is always something more as
well as something less than the living creator (the source) and
the holy God (the goal) of existence. He is the totality of existence. Therefore idealism cannot deal adequately with the problem
of evil. By rationalizing reality it brings it into a premature
harmony; for a rational universe has no place for the incoherence
of evil. It discovers therefore that partial evil is universal good and
lames the energy of moral effort. The real fact is that mystery of
both good and evil in human life and in the world cannot be
completely comprehended or stated in perfectly rational terms.
Every sensitive human spirit is conscious of belonging to an order
of reality which embodies values beyond his achievements; but he
is also conscious of incarnating forces of evil which mysteriously
defy this order.

When philosophy deals with the problem of evil it either denies
the reality of evil by lifting all processes of history into the category
of the rational and the divine; or it reacts from this monism and
optimism, and culminates in an extreme dualism in which the
entire concrete, physical, and historical world are either relegated
to meaninglessness or equated with evil. This dualism is prompted
on the one hand by the failure of monism to do justice to the
dimension of depth in life (that is, to the contrast between the
real and the ideal) and on the other hand to the basic difficulties
of a rationalistic ontology. The totality of existence is first comprehended in rational categories; but since the facts of existence do
not conform to these categories, those which are not rational are
relegated to a lower order of existence. Finally this lower order
of existence is pronounced either evil or illusory.

This entire history is symbolized in the trend of thought from
Aristotle to Plotinus. In Aristotle the material world produces a
hierarchy of existence in which the pure being of God is the apex.
In Plotinus the pure being of God is the only real being; it
prompts emanations of mind, soul, and body, each with a lower
order of existence than the former. The logical culmination of
such rationalized religions is to be found significantly in Buddhism
in which the only reality is an eternal existence which has been

freed of all the characteristics of historic and corporeal life and therefore of every conceivable content.

Neither the vital thrust of life, nor its organic unities nor its disharmonies nor its highest possibilities can be expressed in terms of logic and rational consistency. The dynamic and creative energy of life can be described but not comprehended by reason. The unities of life are organic, and reason can only logically assemble after analytically dividing, thus reducing the organic to a mechanical unity. The disharmonies of life are paradoxically related to its harmonies, as mechanism is paradoxically related to the world of meaning and purpose and every rational scheme of coherence fails to do justice to the tragic realities of evil and to its paradoxical relation with the good.

The dimension of depth in existence has thus far been dealt with only as if it were a fact in the world external to man. But it is really man, with his capacity of transcending the world and transcending himself, who comprehends this depth in existence, and feels it within himself. Man is a creature of both necessity and freedom. He is inserted in the mechanisms of nature and bound by them. Yet he also gains freedom over them by his capacity to envisage purposes and ideals more inclusive than those to which he is driven by nature's impulses. For him the problem of evil is therefore also a problem of sin. His freedom endows him with responsibility and his responsibility spells guilt. The impulse of nature is not evil in the beast because it has no alternatives. But every human action is a choice between alternatives. An external description of the act may prove that a particular action was inevitable because a dominant impulse or set of forces actuated it. But an internal description of an act of choice can never escape a comparison between the act and a higher possibility. It is for this reason that religion, which has a grasp of this dimension of depth, deals with the fact of sin, while science, with its external descriptions, always inclines to deny the reality of sin and the fact of human responsibility.

In spite of the fact that the responsibility of freedom enters into every moral act, purely moralistic descriptions of human sin are as erroneous as purely deterministic and external descriptions of human conduct. The relation of man to freedom and to mechanism is paradoxical. His conscious self is never in complete control of the mechanisms of impulse with which nature has endowed him. Yet it is in sufficient control not only to check these impulses in the interest of a more inclusive purpose but to interfere with the harmony of natural impulses, and to transmute the harmless impulses of nature into demonic lusts and imperialistic purposes. It is, in other words, the nature of human sin that it arises at the juncture of nature and spirit and is as much the corruption of nature by spirit as the corruption of spirit by nature.

All this is darkly expressed in the myth of the fall in Christian theology, much more adequately than in rational explanations of human evil. In explanations which achieve full rational coherence, evil is either attributed to the ultimate source of being (as in various forms of monism), in which case the reality of evil is really denied; or it is attributed to the world of matter, nature and historical concretion (as in various forms of dualism) in which case the fall is equated with creation (in gnosticism for instance), and impulses of nature are regarded as the source of evil while the direction of mind is regarded as the source of all good. Modern liberalism, with its confidence in increasing virtue through increasing control of reason over impulse, is a particularly naïve version of this kind of dualism, though liberalism rests upon a metaphysical foundation of naturalistic monism.

Against these rationalistic versions the myth of the fall expresses these ideas: that an element of human perversity is always involved in human sin since a degree of freedom enters into every human action; that nevertheless sin is inevitable since all men are inserted into the paradoxical relation of freedom and mechanism and cannot escape the possibility of destroying the harmony of nature without achieving the ultimate harmony of spirit; and, finally, that this inevitability is not to be attributed merely to the fact of nature, finiteness, and the world of concrete mechanism and physical impulse. The fact that the fall came after creation, and is not synonymous or contemporaneous with it, in the Jewish-Christian myth, has always saved Christian orthodoxy from falling into dualistic heresies, no matter how strongly tempted it has been in various periods of Christian history. Modern theology has been scornful of the doctrine of original sin (a corollary of the myth of the fall in Christian orthodoxy), because in its moralism and optimism it imagined the possibility of escape from the paradoxical human situation of finiteness and freedom. Orthodoxy, leaning upon mythical insights, has been truer to the facts of the total human situation upon this point.

The real situation is that man's very self-consciousness and capacity for self-transcendence is not only the prerequisite of his morality but the fateful and inevitable cause of his sin. It is because man can transcend nature and himself that he is able to conceive of himself as the center of all life and the clue to the meaning of existence. It is this monstrous pretension of his egoism, the root of all imperialism and human cruelty, which is the very essence of sin. To recognize all this is not to accept the story of the fall as history. The modern dialectical theology of Germany calls it *Urgeschichte*, and that is perhaps as good a term as any. Whenever orthodoxy insists upon the literal truth of such myths it makes a bad historical science out of true religious insights. It fails to distinguish between what is primitive and what is permanent, what is prescientific and what is supra-scientific in great myths.

The religious myths of salvation spring from the same necessity as the myths of creation and the fall. The modern man thinks himself emancipated from the need of religious assurances of salvation. They seem to him theological and unreal. The only redemption in which he believes is moral redemption, the actual conquest of evil by the good. But he can regard the problem of salvation as so simple only because he has equated evil and sin with ignorance. Once the element of perversity in evil is recognized, salvation in the full sense is possible only if the will is changed (conversion), and if the guilt of the past is pardoned. In all genuine religious experiences of salvation there is a sense of new moral power and an assurance of pardon. This is in other words a transaction between a transcendent God, who is not bound by the iron laws of necessity in history, and a transcendent self, which also stands above these laws both in the evil that it has committed and in the moral will by which it overcomes its previous perversity. If sin is not merely imperfection and weakness but an act of the will, reconciliation is possible only through an act of the will of the Divine; and this can be revealed only if divine forgiveness achieves some form and symbol in history (the Incarnation).

The absurdity of theologies which try to define the two natures of Christ and to distinguish between the temporal and the eternal in the mythical God-man, prove how impossible it is to bring essential myth into the categories of rationality. A completely rationalized myth loses its virtue because it ceases to point to the realm of transcendence beyond history, or, pointing to it, fails to express the organic and paradoxical relationship between the conditioned and the unconditioned. That is why, as Clutton-Brock observed, religion is forced to tell many little lies in the interest of a great truth, while science inclines to tell many little truths in the interest of a great lie. The great truth in the interest of which many little lies are told is that life and history have meaning and that the source and the fulfillment of that meaning lie beyond history. The great lie in the interest of which science tells many little truths is that spatio-temporal realities are self-contained and self-explanatory and that a scientific description of sequences is an adequate analysis of causes.

It has been previously suggested that the myths of art are related to those of religion. It could be claimed, in further elaboration of this thesis, that great art is bound to be religious; for great art is more than the objectivization of a particular sentiment or sense of meaning. It is a symbolization of the universal in the particular, to use Goethe's definition of great art. Its analyses of particular situations or its objectivizations of particular sentiments contain suggestions of the total human situation. But the very quality in them which points to the universal or the transcendent makes them something more and less than a scientific description of the facts.

A portrait is mythical as compared with the scientific exactitude of a photograph. Though a wise photographer will try to catch the permanent and significant rather than the passing mood of his subject he is always limited by the physical facts. The artist, on the other hand, falsifies some of the physical details in order to arrive at a symbolic expression of the total character of his subject, this total character being a transcendent fact which is never completely embodied in any given moment of the subject's existence. A really great portrait goes beyond this and not only symbolizes the transcendent personality of the subject, but contains suggestions of a universal human mood. The artistic license of the artist belongs in the same category as the artistic license of religion. In both cases it is subject to abuses. The artist may falsify reality and produce a caricature of his subject rather than a true portrait; and religious myths may falsify the facts of history and experience. But at their best, both artist and prophet reveal the heights and depths of human experience by picturing the surface with something more and less than scientific exactness.

Critics of Greek literature are agreed that Euripides' *Electra* is inferior to the *Choephori* of Aeschylus and the *Electra* of Sophocles, all three dramas dealing with the same theme, the vengeance of Orestes upon his mother. But the prejudices of modern culture have made it difficult to give the reason for this inferiority as simply as it might be given. Euripides is the secularist among the three great dramatists. Under his pen the great myths are naturalized and secularized so that human actions and attitudes become the inevitable causes and consequences of succeeding and preceding actions. He thus dissipates the power of Greek tragedy; for at its best it fills us with a sense of the beauty and terror of life by suggesting that human destinies are woven by forces vaster than human wills. Greek drama at its best lies close to its source, Dionysiac religion. Like all great art, it shares with religion the intention and the power to illumine the facts of life and the course of history by pointing to sources of meaning which lie beyond the facts we see and the history we experience.

The ultimate problem of myth is always the problem of God. Myths may begin by picturing good and evil spirits and by personalizing the forces of wind and water, of sun and moon and the starry heavens. Since every natural phenomenon can be explained in terms of a preceding one the myth becomes useless when science discovers the chain of causation. But meanwhile mythical knowledge has been driven from the effort to seek the transcendent cause behind each phenomenon to the search after the ultimate source of the meaning of all existence.

The approach to the transcendent source of meaning confronts us with a problem which seems practically insoluble. If the meaningfulness of life points to a source beyond itself, how is it possible to say anything about that transcendence, and how can anything that may be said be verified as true? "The vision into the Absolute," declares Professor Morris Cohen, "is either into a fathomless depth in which no distinctions are visible or into a fulness of being that exceeds our human comprehension." Mysticism has usually insisted on the distinctionless aspect of the transcendent. By seeking the absolute through a progressive elimination of temporal distinctions it finally arrived at the knowledge of God; but the God it found was emptiness and void. It could say nothing about him but that he negated the reality of significance of temporal existence. The final logic of this method is consistently expressed in Buddhism in which the ultimate is a distinctionless reality which serves only to destroy the meaning of temporal existence. Something of the same logic is to be found in all mystic asceticism. Thus the search after meaning becomes self-devouring. An ultimate source of meaning is found about which nothing can be said except that it destroys the meaning of mundane existence.

Philosophical idealism has searched for the transcendent in terms of its "fulness of being"; but being jealous of the fullness which "exceeds our comprehension" it defined the ultimate in terms of totality and rationality. By defining the transcendent in terms of totality it obscured the fact that temporal existence reveals not only glimpses of meaning but suggestions of chaos which defy meaning and order. By defining the transcendent in terms of rationality it destroyed its transcendence; for human reason is a part and product of the temporal process, and a rational picture of the transcendent obscures the very qualities of transcendence and ultrarationality. Since, however, reason has its own transcendent perspective over the natural processes and even a degree of transcendence over its own processes (therefore a rational appreciation of the limits of rationality), the efforts of philosophical idealism to comprehend the meaning of existence are never without a measure of truth or without some suggestion of its own limitations.

The effort of modern naturalism to comprehend the meaning of existence by denying the reality or validity of any transcendence behind and beyond the temporal process, usually leads, as we have seen, to an unconscious ascription of transcendence to the processes of nature and therefore to an introduction of ethical meaning into the process. In ethical naturalism an ethical meaning is given to the historic process even more immediately and unqualifiedly than in philosophical idealism. Modern naturalism is thus an even more uncritical rationalism than philosophical idealism. Its fruits are invariably either despair in a meaningless world or sentimentality in a world too simply meaningful. Modern culture is torn by conflict between the two attitudes.

The inadequacy of purely rational approaches invariably forces a return to a purer mythical approach in which the transcendent is defined and ceases to be mere emptiness, but is defined in terms which insist that it is more (and therefore less) than mere totality. But the problem of religion is how it may define God without resorting to a dogmatic acceptance of whatever mythical definition a particular historic tradition has entrusted to a certain portion of the religious community. The modern reaction against naturalism and rationalism expressed in Barthianism fails, significantly, to escape dogmatism. It is superior to the older dogmatisms of orthodox religion in that it does not insist on the scientific and rational validity of the mythical details of its tradition. The fall and the resurrection are not conceived as historical in its theology. But the total truth of the biblical myth is asserted dogmatically with no effort to validate Christianity in experience against competition with other religions.

How is it possible to escape this dogmatism? It is possible only if it be realized that though human knowledge and experience always point to a source of meaning in life which transcends knowledge and experience, there are nevertheless suggestions of the character of this transcendence in experience. Great myths have actually been born out of profound experience and are constantly subject to verification by experience. It may be simplest to illustrate this point in terms of a specific religious doctrine, the Christian doctrine that God is love and that love is the highest moral ideal.

The ideal of love is not a caprice of mythology. It is not true because the cross has revealed it. The cross justifies itself to human faith because it symbolizes an ideal which establishes points of relevance with the deepest experiences and insights of human life.

The ideal of love can be validated as the ultimate moral ideal because it stands in a verifiable transcendent relation to all rational idealism. It is both the fulfillment and the abyss of the rational ideal of justice. Justice is the highest rational moral ideal because reason must seek to deal with human relations and moral conduct in terms of the ascertainable causes and consequences of action. A good act must be rewarded and an evil one punished. The interests of my neighbor must be guarded; but my own interests deserve protection as well. Yet all rational justice constantly sinks to something less than justice. Remedial justice fails to "do justice" to the causes which prompted an evil act because it is ignorant of the operations of mind and conscience in that secret place where actions are compounded. If reason should grow imaginative ("Love is justice grown imaginative," declares Santayana), and make shrewd guesses about the source of evil actions, it will result in a fairer justice. But if it should become so sensitive as to recognize that the evil in the other has its source in the self or the self's society it will destroy every form of remedial justice. "Let him who is without sin cast the first stone." Thus love is both the fulfillment and the denial of remedial and punitive justice.

Love is related to distributive justice in the same manner. It is "right" that I protect my own interests as well as those of my neighbor. But an imaginative regard for the interests of my neighbor will be concerned for his needs even if they are in competition

with mine. Such an imaginative concern for the neighbor's interests
transcends all ordinary conceptions of equity and enjoins actions
of generosity which no society can ever enjoin or regularize. But
this same tendency toward the fulfillment of justice in love leads
to the negation of justice by love. The neighbor's interests are
avowed rather than my own and no effort is made to protect
myself against the neighbor ("resist not evil"). Thus morality is
fed by a realm of transcendent possibilities in which the canons
of the good, established in ordinary experience, are both fulfilled
and negated. That is why Jesus could symbolize the mercy of God
through the impartiality of nature in which the sun shines on the
evil and the good and rain falls upon the just and the unjust. The
impartiality of nature is something less than human justice—and a
symbol of something more, the mercy of God.

The cross in Christian faith is the myth of the truth of the ideal
of love. The Christ of Christian faith is both human and divine.
His actions represent both human possibilities and the limits of
human possibilities. But the possibilities which transcend the
human are relevant to human experience and every moral experience suggests these ultimate possibilities. Therefore parental affec-
tion is a symbol of the love of God. ("If ye then being evil, know
how to give good gifts unto your children, how much more will
your heavenly Father give good gifts to them that ask him.")

The transcendent source of the meaning of life is thus in such
relation to all temporal process that a profound insight into any
process or reality yields a glimpse of the reality which is beyond
it. This reality can be revealed and expressed only in mythical
terms. These mythical terms are the most adequate symbols of
reality because the reality which we experience constantly suggests
a center and source of reality, which not only transcends immediate
experience, but also finally transcends the rational forms and categories by which we seek to apprehend and describe it.

[1937]

Walter Rauschenbusch
in Historical Perspective *(1957)*

Religio-Life

T HE book by Walter Rauschenbusch which shook the religious world of our nation, *Christianity and the Social Crisis*, appeared just a half century ago. So much has happened in that half century both to the world and to us as a nation, that it is not altogether surprising that a book which meant so much to American religious life and to the older among us personally should be so obviously dated. Perhaps that is the fate of any book or of any personality no matter how creative, for we are all little creatures in the great drama of history in which we are involved, partly as actors and partly as spectators; and even the most imaginative mind cannot anticipate the future which separates the wheat from the chaff in our meditations.

The pace of history has been so rapid that even those of us who are old enough to have lived through it have to remind ourselves of the historic situation in which Rauschenbusch both fired and guided the Christian conscience of the nation. America had gone far on the road to technical efficiency which makes her now the most powerful nation of the world. But the mechanics of justice lagged woefully behind and we were retarded by a half century in our social legislation behind the Western European nations. Even Bismarck's Germany had advanced social legislation immeasurably more than our country. The social distress in the nation at the turn of the century is accurately and vividly de-

scribed in the chapter entitled "The Present Crisis" in Rauschenbusch's famed book. "The rich are getting richer and the poor are
getting poorer," he declared. The latter statement was probably
not accurate except in the relative sense that the growing wealth
of the rich made the poverty of the poor more and more intolerable. Rauschenbusch devotes many pages to the idea of equality
as a regulative principle of justice and proves that our national
life violates this regulative principle. He quotes an economist who
estimated that in 1890 one per cent of the population owned half
of the wealth of the nation.

The result of this situation of poverty and wealth was that the
wealthy had the political power to protect their wealth against the
rising resentments of the poor. It is interesting that Rauschenbusch,
upon the basis of the facts of his day, adopts the Marxist thesis of
the primacy of economic power. While failing to define the government as the "executive committee of the ruling classes," he does
quote the dire prophecies of the eminent sociologist, Professor
Giddings, made in 1904, "What we are witnessing today is the
decay, perhaps the permanent decay, of republican institutions."

It is interesting that the whole generation identified injustice
with monarchial institutions or with "despotism," which were
regarded as identical. The possibility of despotism in the name of
the "people's democracy" had not yet loomed on the historical
horizon. "A class which is economically strong," wrote Rauschenbusch, "will have the necessary influence to secure and enforce
laws which protect its economic interest. . . . Politics is embroidered
with patriotic sentiment and phrases, but at bottom, consciously
or unconsciously, the economic interests dominate it always."[1]
Thus spoke the voice of realism at the turn of the century, and
Rauschenbusch's semi-Marxist version of the relation of economics
to politics seemed as true at the turn of the century in America
as it seemed in the middle of the previous century in Europe. More
than a quarter of a century was required to construct the proper
equilibria of power to refute the thesis of the importance of politi-

[1] *Christianity and the Social Crisis* (The Macmillan Company, 1907), pp.
253–254.

cal power. Rauschenbusch adduced the evidence in the failure to protect the workers against injury in the absence of pensions and unemployment insurance and in the unequal tax laws, for the pessimistic thesis that government was indeed in league with the rich.

Rauschenbusch's approval of Theodore Roosevelt's minor reforms and his gratitude for Roosevelt's stance against the "malefactors of great wealth" is a reminder of the ethos of an era in which none of the equalizing tendencies of modern European democracy had become operative in America and in which the present standards of social security were practically unknown. It was a strange world and one which well might have shaken the conscience of the nation earlier than it did.

The question of the reason for the moral and political complacency of the nation under these social injustices brings us to the equally strange moral and religious climate of the country at the turn of the century. We must remember that so much injustice had produced many forms of political revolt at the close of the century, that the Populist Movement prospered among the agrarians of the West, that Bryan had been nominated for the presidency after delivering his "Cross of Gold" speech (but had also been defeated in the subsequent election). The "Knights of Labor" had been organized and strikes were brutally suppressed in the budding steel industry. The poor were resistive, though their rebellion had never reached the organized political rebellion of the Marxist workers of Europe. The real mystery was the moral and political complacency of middle-class culture, and particularly of middle-class Protestantism.

Perhaps the reason for this complacency must be found in the fact that the nation was so much wealthier than Europe and social nobility was so much greater, both because of the constantly expanding economy and the advancing frontier, that social resentments had less provocation than in the Old World. The complacency of middle-class Protestantism had a special reason which Rauschenbusch seems never to have noted. He ascribed all of its blindness to its individualism, and he meant that kind

of Calvinism which believed it exhausted the moral demand of
Christianity in inculcating thrift, industry, and honesty. This was
indeed the main heritage of New England Puritanism. But the
additional social fact was that the nation's labor force was constantly recruited from Slavic and Latin and Irish peoples. It was,
therefore, Catholic in religion while the Anglo-Saxon ruling
minority was predominantly Protestant. The class struggle thus
had a particularly religious overtone which has never ceased to
influence religious attitudes to this day. For to this day, Catholicism has more intimate relations with the world of labor than
Protestantism; witness the significance of the Catholic Trade
Union League which, incidentally, has been so active in ridding
the unions of the menace of Communism.

But there were other cultural sources of middle-class complacency which operated at least to give that complacency some shreds
of rationalization to cover the nakedness of its moral position. Most
of these cultural influences may best be defined as "social Darwinism." It would be more accurate to say that the laissez-faire doctrines of classical economics, which became so popular after the
publication of Adam Smith's *Wealth of Nations*, were reinforced
by the application of the Darwinian idea of the "survival of the
fittest" to the realm of social policy, in which the idea supported
the already established theory that economic life had its own laws
which were to be interfered with at one's peril. One might
tentatively have a quirk of conscience about all the injustices which
Rauschenbusch and other reformers enumerated but one could
always hope that the operation of the free market, including the
free market of labor, would eliminate all these abuses.

Ordinarily, or rather normally, such a Spencerian doctrine which
equated human history with nature, and its "laws" with the "laws
of nature," might seem to be anathema to the Christian faith,
informed by the idea of man being made in the image of God.
But nothing can stop a powerful idea when it conforms to the
interests of the class which entertains it. The fact is that social
Darwinism even more than Calvinism made the Protestant middle
class complacent. It would be more accurate to say that the com-

bination of Calvinism and social Darwinism was the real source of Protestant middle-class complacency, so that Henry Ward Beecher could say that he had never seen an honest and thrifty man begging for bread.

It cannot be said that Rauschenbusch challenged these ideologically anchored illusions basically. His message was simply to insist on the social relevance of the Christian faith and the social responsibility of the Christian. He did this by a special emphasis or special application of the liberal interpretation of the Gospel which was regnant in the nineteenth century and which was, in a sense, the religious application of the idea of progress and of the perfectibility of man. In terms of secular ideologies, he set the voluntaristic ideas of Comte against the determinism of Spencer. It is interesting that even in his *Theology for the Social Gospel* he never clearly betrayed the religious rather than the secular source of his faith. For while on the secular side it was the idea of progress, on the religious side it was none other than the radicalism of sectarian Christianity which, as a Baptist, he had inherited from his father.

He closes his *Theology for the Social Gospel* with these words: "Before the Reformation, the Prophet had only a precarious foothold inside the church and had no right to live outside of it. The rise of free religion and political democracy has given him a field and a task. The era of prophetic and democratic Christianity has just begun." What is interesting about this observation is that even in the orthodox Reformation the prophet, as he or as we conceive him, had little place. Certainly Luther's doctrine of the two realms gave no room for anything which Rauschenbusch defines as prophetic Christianity. Nor are the limitations of the Calvinist theocracy with its conception of the "rule of the saints" discussed or the legitimacy of the Anabaptist radicalism analyzed. For in Rauschenbusch's estimation, the Reformation performed its significant task in emancipating the Church from the despotic and priestly regime of Catholicism. The whole history of Christianity is viewed as an evolutionary process in which the prophets first state the conditions of the Kingdom of God, which is then brought to a culmination in the life and teachings of Jesus. For "The fundamental first step in the salvation of mankind was the achievement of the personality of Jesus. Within Him, the kingdom of God got its first foothold in humanity. It was by virtue of his personality that he became the initiator of the kingdom."[2]

This position assigned to Jesus does not quite fit the evolutionary conception of history nor the role which he assigns to the prophets. It slightly obscures one of the genuine achievements of Rauschenbusch and the whole social gospel school of thought. That was to rediscover the prophets as teachers of social righteousness. One of the most eloquent chapters in Rauschenbusch's *Christianity and the Social Crisis* was the first chapter, entitled "The Historical Roots of Christianity: The Hebrew Prophets." In this chapter he calls the prophets to witness that the righteousness which God requires "was not merely the private morality of the home but the public morality in which the life of the nation was founded. They said less about the pure heart of the individual than about just institutions for the nation."[3]

One may question whether the social gospel fully understood Hebraic prophetism with its overtone of messianism, because the prophetic witness was coordinated too simply to their evolutionary conception of history. The whole tension of prophetism, with its demands upon the nation which neither that nation nor any nation can fulfill, was certainly obscured. But the errors did not prevent the social gospel from recognizing the importance of the prophetic insistence on social righteousness and on collective morality. That insistence makes the Old Testament a perpetual resource for a Christian social ethic, and raises the question whether in the history of Christianity ethics as distinguished from theology can ever develop an adequate social ethic if it neglects the Old Testament prophetism. For without the Old Testament witness, the moral tension between Christ and the world, as explicated in the New Testament, is always in danger of creating or of providing

---

[2] *A Theology for the Social Gospel* (The Macmillan Company, 1917), p. 151.

[3] *Christianity and the Social Crisis*, p. 8.

an escape for the tension in either the asceticism of the medieval church or the pietistic individualism of Protestantism.

Rauschenbusch, incidentally, erroneously ascribes asceticism solely to Greek dualism and does not do justice to the fact that the eschatological rigor of the New Testament, if translated into specific law, is bound to result in asceticism. One needs only to think of the influence upon medieval thought of the story of the rich young man on the one hand and of the critical attitude toward the family on the other hand. It is a question whether the social gospel fully understood the *agape* motif of the New Testament. This school would certainly have been surprised and outraged by Nygren's interpretation of *agape*—by which I do not imply that Nygren is absolutely correct in his conception of a fundamental contradiction between *agape* and all forms of natural love. For Rauschenbusch and his school, love is "the community building faculty." "Man," he declares, "is fundamentally gregarious and morality consists in being a good member of the community. Man is moral when he is social and immoral when he is antisocial." One of Rauschenbusch's disciples insisted that Christianity was foolishly exercised about the relation of love to justice, for that tension would not arise if one conceived all love as mutual love. Aristotle's *philia*, in short, contained the whole answer to the tension of love and justice.

Perhaps this brings us to the heart of the problem of the Christian social ethic as expounded by the social gospel. It did not understand either the height of the pinnacle of love or the base of justice. For the height of love is certainly more unprudential and uncalculating than mutual love and it contains universalistic demands which challenge any particular community. "If ye love them which love you, what reward have ye?" declared Jesus. About the family, that seedpot of all community, he made the critical judgment, "Whosoever loveth father and mother more than me is not worthy of me."

Furthermore, the motif of self-sacrifice and forgiveness are the pinnacles of the love which is expounded in the New Testament. It is obviously not easy to construct a social ethic from these nonprudential, heroic and ecstatic dimensions of the love ethic. That is one of the many reasons why Christianity in its various versions has not been too successful in guiding the collective morality of mankind; which is not to say that these pinnacles of the love ethic are irrelevant. They certainly describe the moral possibilities on the edge of the impossible for the individual life as it transcends collective possibilities. But the cross of Christ is a scandal in the field of ethics, and the social gospel obscured the pinnacle of the truth of the cross in the field of ethics by reducing love too simply to the dimension of mutual love.

Rauschenbusch's final chapter envisages social progress in the direction of an ideal communism which naturally did not have the benefit of our hindsight. He could not know that collectivism would, in the name of exalting (in his words) "people not things," create a power system which was blind not only to the sin of the wielders of power but to the indeterminate possibilities of both good and evil in the free play of individual freedom beyond the immediate necessities of the community.

This brings us to the other defect in the teachings of the social gospel. It did not understand the mechanics of justice though it contributed tremendously to the creation of a sense of justice. It did not understand justice because it did not measure adequately the power and persistence of man's self-concern, particularly in collective self-concern. Rauschenbusch, in his *Theology for the Social Gospel*, devotes a chapter to "Original Sin" in an effort to rehabilitate a doctrine which had become odious to his generation. He does this by attributing the universality of sin to the transmission of egoistic tendencies through faulty institutions. This leads inevitably to the Marxian hope of a radical change in the evil institutions, particularly the institution of property. Rauschenbusch never took the step toward Marxism except by implication. But many of his followers did, including many of us. A few even got caught in the toils of Stalinism. They did not realize that the nationalization of property would make for a monopoly of power for the oligarchy which managed the socialized property—a monopoly of power which the capitalist oligarchs possessed in the day when we were exercised about social injustice.

Meanwhile, a tolerable justice was established in all of Western civilization not by the wisdom of its wise men but by the wisdom which a free society was able to generate in separating truth from error in the warring creeds of Adam Smith and Karl Marx. This was done not systematically but pragmatically in actual political and economic history. Not only did the "New Deal" provide minimal social securities through the intervention of the state, in defiance of the individualistic creed which Rauschenbusch rightly criticized, but what is more important, organized labor began to set power against power. For justice in a sinful world demands an equilibrium of power. Power in juxtaposition with weakness is bound to cause exploitation. This basic fact cannot be obscured by the pathetic current developments in the labor movement with which that scoundrel, Hoffa, is related. These developments merely prove that every new advance in history creates its own problems on the new level of achievement.

We began by calling attention to the great difference in the moral and political climate of our day and the catastrophic mood of Rauschenbusch's generation. This difference was created not by the triumph of one philosophy over another or by the triumph of Comte over Spencer, but by the beneficent play of cultural and social forces in a free society. In this development, creeds and dogmas were transmuted into a wisdom better than that possessed by any dogma, and a free society was able to establish immunity against the corruptions of collectivism by overcoming the corruption of extravagant individualism. The progress which Western democracies have made in political and economic justice would seem to have vindicated the optimism which the social gospel shared with its generation and to have refuted the undertone of catastrophism which was the Marxian admixture in the utopianism of that generation. It did, indeed, refute the catastrophism but it failed to vindicate the historical optimism. That was the real common treasure between the secular liberalism and Christian liberalism at the turn of the century. Rauschenbusch expressed this optimism in familiar terms by identifying the "Kingdom of God" with historical progress. He suggested that the apocalyptic

note in later prophetism was merely the shell in which Jesus' more
adequate ideas of the kingdom grew.

Jesus [he wrote] had the scientific insight which comes to most men
only by training but to the elect few by divine gift. He grasped the
substance of that law of organic development in nature and history
which our own day at last has begun to elaborate systematically. His
parables of the sower, the net, the tares, the mustard seed, and the
leaven are all polemical in character. He was seeking to displace the
crude and misleading catastrophic conceptions with the saner views
of the coming of the kingdom. This conception of growth demanded
not only a finer insight but a higher faith.[4]

One reads this capitulation of a great theologian and a great
Christian soul to the regnant idea of progress of his day with some
dismay because it proves how vulnerable we are to the illusions
of our generation. In the light of our own more tragic experience
—which includes not only the progress toward democracy in the
nations of the West, but the Nazi horrors, two world wars and
the present contest with a totalitarianism (which is in some respects better but also in many respects worse than Nazism because
it is the corruption of a valid idea)—we know these hopes of the
nineteenth century to have been illusions. We also recognize that
the "catastrophism" of the prophets and what seemed to the
nineteenth century the "crude" messianism of the Old Testament
were, in fact, the consequence of the wrestle of a high faith with
the problem that the moral recalcitrance of man's collective behavior seemed to refute the idea of a divine sovereignty over the
whole of history.

Prophetic messianism insisted that in some way the injustices
of the world must yield to the divine power in the messianic age.
The course of history certainly did not prove that they would
yield out of conscience. The New Testament, by refuting the hope
of a triumphant Messiah and proclaiming instead a suffering
Messiah who took the sins of the world upon himself, certainly
did not substitute for the pessimism of the prophets its own conception of "the inevitability of gradualness." On the contrary, it

---

[4] *Christianity and the Social Crisis*, pp. 59–60.

was more deeply pessimistic about the moral capacities of man than the prophets were. That is why the Christian faith became so easily the ally of conservative politics, for conservatism traditionally rejected the utopian dreams of the liberals. Christianity was wrongly the ally of conservatism, however, because conservatism never fully recognized that the order in a sinful world, supplied by the rulers of the nations, was always paid for by too high a price in justice.

Thus even when the domestic history of the democratic nations seemed to vindicate the optimism which the social gospel shared with the Enlightenment, it certainly refuted the estimate of human behavior upon which that optimism was based. What progress in justice has been achieved has been won by a careful balancing of social forces. Love as "community building faculty" has been operative only as it availed itself both of the calculations of justice and of the mechanics of justice. This is to say that we cannot count on the "moral forces" nearly as much as the social gospel assumed. We must count on the humility of even the best men knowing that they are not sufficiently moral to be just if their power remains unchecked and their policy not under review.

If the optimism of the Enlightenment was refuted even in the area of domestic politics where an advancing justice seemed to vindicate it, it has been even more tragically refuted in the realm of foreign policy where it was hoped that history was moving toward "the parliament of man, the federation of the world." We indeed have that parliament in rudimentary form in the United Nations, but we also are involved in a cold war with a despotism built on the utopian illusions which the Enlightenment shared with the Marxist idealists. Nothing in the thought of either the Enlightenment or the social gospel even faintly surmised the tragic realities of the day which have become the daily bread of our spiritual existence.

In this situation we can pay our brief tribute to the heroes of another generation who defied malignant power and who tried to rescue the Christian faith both from irrelevance and from a conscious and unconscious alliance with evil, that is, with uncon-

trolled power. With the tools in their possession they did heroic
service. But they were prisoners of their own culture more than
they realized and they were, therefore, forced to counter a grave
error on the relation of Christianity to the social order by embracing or nearly embracing another error. Fortunately, we have
been saved from both errors not by the virtue of the Christian
church or any other virtue, but only by what we must define as
providential workings in history.

From these facts we cannot draw the conclusion that we are
wiser than they were, though we have experiences behind us which
they did not have. Nor can we draw the conclusion that we must
not seek to establish relations with a culture because these relations
so frequently turn out to be capitulations of the Christian truth
to some current illusion. Karl Barth, who has become a symbol
for this strategy, has become in these latter days a partial apologist
for tyranny. We have to hazard our ventures into the culture of our
day and hope that we will not make too many mistakes. We must
hazard them particularly when the problem of social responsibility
is at stake. For the Christian faith is not other-worldly, it always
commits us in a responsible relation to the community and bids us
to establish justice.

Yet the long history of the failures of Christian conservatism
and Christian liberalism in establishing tolerable justice in the community must prompt us to modesty. Conservatism has been too
complacent about the self-seeking of the rulers and the injustices
of the powerful. Liberalism, on the other hand, did not see that
idealists can be very dangerous the moment they have the power
to implement their "ideals" or to mix them with their self-interest.

We must not draw quietistic conclusions from the fact, but it
seems to be a fact that in that society which was originally so
unjust as to provoke a rebellion of the workers, both freedom and
justice have been established despite the power lusts of the rulers
and the illusions of the idealists. Thus God "maketh the wrath of
man to praise him" and we are reminded that our generation enjoys
the benefits of a social order which is more virtuous than the in-

sights of our fathers and our own achievements. To comprehend this is to see that the Gospel's interpretation of the human situation is superior to all realistic or idealistic versions of the Gospel.

[1957]

Marx and Engels on Religion (*1964*)

"FOR Germany the criticism of religion is . . . the premise of all criticism,"[1] declared Marx in a classical phrase which gives a key to many of his and Engels' observations on religion. In religion we have the final claim to absolute truth; Marx and Engels are social scientists, interested empirically in the way that the claim of the absolute is used as a screen for particular competitive historical interests.

Much of what Marx and Engels observed has become the object of attention of all social and cultural historians, if indeed it has not always been the true object of history. When Engels reviews the transmutation of Christianity from a little eschatological sect to an imperial religion, or from Augustine's rigorous separation of the "City of God" and the "city of this world" to the structure of papal power over political affairs constructed by Gregory VII in the Middle Ages, or when he analyzes the social forces and influences which made the Reformation radical in the sense that it used biblical authority to undermine ecclesiastical authority, and reactionary in the sense that it made the church subservient to the princes and ruthlessly opposed the Anabaptists, he is making observations on historical sequences which are the usual preoccupation of historians of culture and of political life.

[1] Karl Marx and Friedrich Engels, *On Religion* (New York: Schocken Books, Inc., 1964), p. 41.

It could be said that the observations of Marx and Engels validate the Marxist thesis that "the criticism of religion is the premise
of all criticism" because the absolute claim is used as a weapon
for various historically relative, and usually established, social and
political forces. Yet, their appreciation of the socially radical
peasants of the sixteenth century under Anabaptist religious leadership, revealed particularly in Engels' article on the peasant wars,
is not quite in agreement with Marxism's central thesis that religion is a weapon always used by the established social forces.
Later Marxists, Bernstein particularly, regarded the radical sects
of the Cromwellian Revolution in the seventeenth century, rightly,
as forerunners of the Marxist movement. The radical sectarians
appropriated messianism to make of it an instrument of social
revolt, while the more conservative religious forces used other-
worldly hopes to beguile men from injustices in history. Nevertheless, it must be realized that, with the exception of this
polemical quirk, the general order of Marxist observations on the
relation of the claim to the absolute to the relative forces of
history are unexceptionable. They would be accepted by any historian, religious or irreligious, who has an empirical grasp of
historical facts.

The writings of Marx and Engels on religion reveal the passion
for empirical observation and analysis, shared by them with many
moderns; moreover, there too are clues to that remarkable development of which many students have been made aware: of an
irreligion transmuted into a new political religion, canonized precisely in the writings of Marx (and the later Lenin) as sacred
scripture, and preached in notoriously practical and opportune
ways as the principles for a revolutionary reformation of the social
order according to an immutable dogma.

One of the most significant clues to the mystery of this ironic
transmutation is provided in these early writings. It consists in the
vagueness of both Marx and Engels about the problem of knowledge, and their consequent tendency to equate the epistemology
of empiricism with the metaphysical theory of materialism. This
tendency is revealed in Marx's attitude toward the medieval phi-

losopher Duns Scotus. Marx made this observation about Duns Scotus:

> Materialism is the native son of Great Britain. Even Britain's scholastic Duns Scotus wondered: "Can matter think?"
> In order to bring about that miracle he had recourse to God's omnipotence, i.e., he forced theology to preach materialism. In addition he was a nominalist. Nominalism is a main component of English materialism and is in general the first expression of materialism.
> The real founder of English materialism and all modern experimental science was Bacon.[2]

Thus nominalism, the first form of empiricism, and the whole empirical tradition is equated with the metaphysical position of materialism. The reason for this identification is obvious. Marx rightly observes that idealism in epistemology leads to metaphysical idealism which leads to "theological prejudice." About Locke and Condillac, Marx observes:

> Locke's immediate follower, Condillac, who also translated him into French, at once opposed Locke's sensualism to seventeenth-century metaphysics. He proved that the French had . . . rejected metaphysics as the mere bungling of fancy and theological prejudice.[3]

It is clear that the ex-Hegelian and anti-Hegelian Marx rightly equates metaphysical idealism with religion. But he wrongly equates empiricism, and epistemological theory, with materialism as metaphysical doctrine. We know, of course, that empiricism in epistemology and naturalism in metaphysics, are akin outside the orbit of Marxism. But non-Marxist empiricism abhors all dogmas, while Marx's metaphysics without a solution of the epistemological problem, the problem of knowledge, becomes the basis of a great religio-political dogma.

The path which is traveled becomes clear in Engels' essay on "Feuerbach and the End of German Classical Philosophy." Engels agrees with Feuerbach in their common anti-Hegelianism. He asserts that the young Hegelians were driven back to Anglo-French materialism by the practical necessities of their fight against positive religion.

[2] *Ibid.*, p. 63.
[3] *Ibid.*, p. 66.

This brought them into conflict with their school system. While materialism conceives nature as the sole reality, nature in the Hegelian system represents merely the "alienation" of the absolute idea, so to say, a degradation of the idea. At all events, thinking and its thought-product, the idea, is here the primary, nature the derivative, which only exists by condescension of the idea. And in this contradiction they floundered as well or as ill as they could.

Then came Feuerbach's *Essence of Christianity*. With one blow it pulverized the contradiction in that without circumlocutions it placed materialism on the throne again.[4]

The logic of the Marxist viewpoint is clear. Any theory which takes the problem of knowledge seriously enough to distinguish between the self as object and the self as knower is potentially idealism; it ends by giving primacy to the theoretical "copies of reality" rather than to reality itself. An empirical approach to epistemology on the other hand is identified with "materialism," that is, a philosophical naturalism and a vaguely conceived epistemology which guarantees the primacy of "reality vis à vis the fanciful copies of reality." Thus we arrive at absolute truth in the name of science against absolute pretensions in the name of religion and idealism.

Marx distinguishes between two forms of French materialism. He affirms that Cartesian materialism merges into natural science. But the other branch, concerned with historical problems, "leads directly to socialism and communism." He then proceeds to prove deductively, not empirically, how this comes about. He writes, in *The Holy Family, or Critique of Critical Criticism*:

There is no need of any great penetration to see from the teaching of materialism on the original goodness and equal intellectual endowment of men, the omnipotence of experience, habit and education, and the influence of environment on man, the great significance of industry, the justification of enjoyment, etc., how necessarily materialism is connected with communism and socialism. If man draws all his knowledge, sensation, etc., from the world of the senses and the experience gained in it, the empirical world must be arranged so that in it man experiences and gets used to what is really human and that he becomes aware of himself as man. If correctly understood interest

4 *Ibid.,* p. 224.

is the principle of all morals, man's private interest must be made to coincide with the interest of humanity. If man is unfree in the materialist sense, i.e., is free not through the negative power to avoid this or that, but through the positive power to assert his true individuality, crime must not be punished in the individual, but the anti-social source of crime must be destroyed, and each man must be given social scope for the vital manifestation of his being.[5]

In this breathtaking series of propositions, Marx, the revolutionary humanist, pretends to draw self-evident deductions from the mere presupposition of metaphysical materialism—which for Marx meant essentially Lockean empiricism. All the propositions dear to a revolutionary and apocalyptic idealist—universalism, collectivism, humanism, and socialism—are drawn, like so many rabbits, out of the hat of materialism.

If one remembers that for Marx materialism and empiricism are practically identical, and realizes that all his criticisms of either orthodox religion or Hegelian idealism and all his refutations of their pretensions to "eternal" validity avail themselves of empirical analyses of their claims, one can only regard this passage, and similar passages, as the ladders on which the empirical critic of the status quo climbed up to the heaven and haven of a new religious apocalypse which made him the revered prophet of a new world religion, as potent in the twentieth century as was Islam in the seventh.

In his climb up the ladder Marx obviously left behind his passion for empirical observation and analysis. His humanism was taken from the humanistic tradition of the West, but his collectivism, the assignment of a messianic role to the "proletariat," and his doctrine of a climactic revolution in which the kingdom of universal justice would be ushered in as a heaven on earth were all highly speculative, even more so than all historical generalizations usually are. Marx deduces these doctrines from "materialism" without bothering to establish them by refuting the democratic and individualistic doctrines of his fellow empiricist, John Locke, or the political absolutism of his fellow materialist, Thomas

[5] *Ibid.*, pp. 67–68.

Hobbes. The latter's political absolutism, incidentally, had strong affinities with the doctrines of Hegel, whom Marx, with the aid of Feuerbach, had summarily dismissed.

Evidently even a scrupulous empirical method fails to achieve common conclusions in the complex field of historical causation, in which causal sequences on many different levels intertwine. Marx, as an empiricist, would have been just another learned man. As an apocalyptic dogmatist, he became the founder of a new religion, whose writings would be quoted as parts of a new sacred canon.

The most interesting portion of this transformation of an empirical observer into a religious prophet who appropriated the messianic visions of Jewish and Christian faith, was that from the beginning the common humanism was subordinated in Marx's vision to the purposes of a revolutionist who wanted not so much to understand the world as to remake it. In his *Theses on Feuerbach*, Marx makes this criticism of previous materialism: "The chief defect of hitherto existing materialism—that of Feuerbach included—is that the thing, reality, sensuousness, is conceived only in the form of the object or of contemplation (*Anschauung*), but not as human sensuous activity, practice."[6] Reality must be studied for the sake of transforming it. Here speaks the revolutionist and religious prophet, rather than the scientist and philosopher.

A modern school of post-Marxist Marxism is celebrating Marx's "early humanism" as if it were an original purity which has since been corrupted by political polemics. But the historic evidence reveals this humanism to have always been a subordinate part of his political revolutionary propaganda. Thus the theme of the "alienation" or "estrangement" of the worker from his humanity transmutes the Hegelian idea of alienation to make it mean that modern industry, by treating the worker as a commodity, has alienated him from his humanity. Marx writes:

We have considered the act of estranging practical human activity, labor, in two of its aspects: (1) the relation of the worker to the product of his labor as an alien object exercising power over him. This

[6] *Ibid.*, p. 69.

relation is at the same time the relation to the sensuous external world, to the objects of nature, as an alien world inimically opposed to him. (2) The relation of the worker to the act of production within the labor process. This relation is the relation of the worker to his own activity as an alien activity not belonging to him; it is activity as suffering, strength as weakness, begetting as emasculating the worker's own physical and mental energy, his personal life, indeed what is life but activity?—as an activity which is turned against him, independent of him and not belonging to him. Here we have self-estrangement, as we previously had estrangement from the thing.[7]

This indictment of the dehumanizing effect of modern industry is indeed an expression of Marx's humanism, but the argument about man is strictly subordinated to the polemical purpose of an antibourgeois revolutionist. The words and the dialectic mode of thought remind one of Hegel, rather than Locke, whose empiricism Marx frequently cites but whose convictions he never quotes. Thus the anti-Hegelian materialist speaks in terms of Hegelian dialectic to project a materialistic version of an even more traditional religious apocalypse.

What is lacking is a discriminate and truly empirical analysis of the effects of modern technical civilization on the humanity of the working person, so as to determine to what degree the deleterious effects are inherent in the technical process itself and to what degree these effects are due to the profit motive in modern industry. Undoubtedly the indictment was relevant to the historic facts of early nineteenth-century European industrialism. This relevance made the Marxist dogma effective in the nineteenth century but implausible in twentieth-century European culture where an open society had taken innumerable steps to guard the rights and the essential humanity of the person.

Insofar as some of the dehumanizing effects are inherent in the technical process itself, they are, of course, symptomatic of the rapid process of industrialization throughout the world in which a Communist and capitalist bloc of nations are ironically competing. Unfortunately Marx's celebrated humanism, belatedly dis-

[7] Karl Marx, *Economic and Philosophic Manuscripts of 1844* (Moscow: Foreign Languages Publishing House), pp. 73–74.

covered by certain intellectuals and allegedly purged of Leninist and Stalinist corruptions, does not serve us in making the necessary empirical distinctions about the effects of industrialism, whether inherent in the technical process or in a social order.

It was from the very beginning too indiscriminate, too lacking in empirical precision, too much the weapon of the "class struggle" and the instrument of the revolutionary prophet who had transmuted atheism into a new religion. The priests of this religion are now the priest-kings of an empire based on utopian illusions, of a culture in which materialism has become the canonized philosophy. The vaunted affinity between empiricism and materialism has been transmuted into a new dogma.

The irony of these developments is complete. But preoccupation with the irony of these developments cannot obscure either the original humanistic passion of Marx's enterprise or the dogmatic uses to which it was put and the dogmatic atrophy in which it has now been enmeshed. That atrophy was not a corruption, introduced by later Marxists, whether Lenin or Stalin. It was inherent in Marx's transmutation of empiricism to materialism to revolutionary religious apocalypse.

[1964]

Theology and Political Thought in the Western World

Ecumenical Review (1957)

T HE assertion is not too hazardous that the ecumenical movement has achieved more telling results in the field of Christian political and social ethics than in any other field of thought and life. These results may be briefly defined as the dissolution of traditional dogmas which Christian thinkers had inherited from the political right or the political left and a gradual elaboration of what Dr. Visser 't Hooft has designated as "Christian pragmatism." "Pragmatism" has been a *Schimpfwort* in Christian circles for some time. How then do we arrive at a "Christian" pragmatism? One can answer that question very simply by the assertion that Christian pragmatism is merely the application of Christian freedom and a sense of responsibility to the complex issues of economics and politics, with the firm resolve that inherited dogmas and generalizations will not be accepted, no matter how revered or venerable, if they do not contribute to the establishment of justice in a given situation.

Consider for instance the state of Christian social thought at both the Stockholm and Oxford conferences. The first of these at Stockholm was still laboring under secular illusions, which we would now define as "liberal." One thinks for instance of the extravagant hopes which were placed in the League of Nations. At Oxford the atmosphere, in keeping with the mood of the time, when the second world war already cast its shadow before it, was

more realistic. But it was still necessary to entertain ideas which
were derived from the right and the left in politics and to ask
whether or not they were "Christian."

We have now come to the fairly general conclusion that there
is no "Christian" economic or political system. But there is a
Christian attitude toward all systems and schemes of justice. It
consists on the one hand of a critical attitude toward the claims
of all systems and schemes, expressed in the question whether they
will contribute to justice in a concrete situation; and on the other
hand a responsible attitude, which will not pretend to be God
nor refuse to make a decision between political answers to a
problem because each answer is discovered to contain a moral
ambiguity in God's sight. We are men, not God; we are responsible for making choices between greater and lesser evils, even
when our Christian faith, illuminating the human scene, makes
it quite apparent that there is no pure good in history; and probably no pure evil either. The fate of civilizations may depend
upon these choices between systems of which some are more,
others less, just.

This Christian "pragmatism" has dissolved the certainties of
Christian Marxists and Christian conservatives. Perhaps it would
be more modest to assert that it has profited by the refutation
of claims and counterclaims in actual historical experience. It has
been Christian only in the sense that it drew upon Christian insights which were long obscured in the minds of even the most
pious, but which have been clarified by historical experience even
as they have clarified that experience.

There were those, for instance, who were so outraged by the
injustices of a "capitalist" system that they were ready, though
usually with some reservations, to embrace that part of the Marxist
creed which promised a higher degree of justice through the
socialization of property. Experience has proved that socialization
does not remove economic power from the community. The
nationalization of property may on the other hand merely cumu-
late both economic and political power in the hands of a single
oligarchy. We know the baneful effects of this policy in the

realities of contemporary communism. But even the more moderate and democratic socialism no longer offers the attraction to the Christian conscience which it once did. For it has become apparent that the measures which it may take to establish a minimum of justice in the community are in danger of destroying the freedom and spontaneity which its economic life requires. In the effort to correct unjust inequalities such measures may bind the community in a static equalitarianism. This will remind us that equality is the regulative principle of justice but that it is, like liberty and love, no simple possibility in any political community.

Other illusions of the left have been dispelled. Nationalism was once thought to be the product of capitalism and idealists embraced socialism for the sake of its alleged internationalism. Now the Socialist Parties are all tempted to espouse nationalistic interests partly because socialization means nationalization (a fact which throws many European socialists into opposition to such supranational institutions as the European Coal and Steel Community) and partly because socialists find the liberal Catholic parties espousing the cause of international cooperation. How strangely history dispels our illusions and punctures our pretensions!

It would, however, be quite wrong to espouse economic conservatism because of this disillusionment of the left or with the left. Conservatism in America and in some parts of Europe means the anachronistic espousal of physiocratic theories, which promise justice through the emancipation of economic life from every kind of political and moral control. It rests on the illusion that there are "laws of nature" in history, that there are "pre-established" harmonies in nature, and therefore presumably in history, which is equated with nature.

These physiocratic theories lie at the foundation of what has become the "philosophy" of the "free enterprise" system on which the whole bourgeois world has consistently prided itself, and which did indeed emancipate economic enterprise from irrelevant political restraints and encourage productivity through economic incentives.

But naturally the basic theory was as heretical, from the Chris-

tian standpoint, as Marxism. The self-interest was not as harmless
as the theory assumed; and the trusted "pre-established harmonies"
did not exist. Ironically enough, the static disharmonies of history, due to the disbalances of social power characteristic of an
agrarian civilization, were transmuted into the dynamic disproportions of power of a commercial civilization at the precise
moment when they were so confidently proclaimed.

The social consequences of this miscalculation were catastrophic
in the early days of industrialism. The social distress among industrial workers was responsible for their defection from the hopes
of the democratic world, and for a rebellion which ultimately led
to their adoption of the Marxist creed, in its various versions.

The social history of the Western world could be summarized
as the gradual refutation in experience of both dogmas, which
inspired the political activities of both the middle classes and
the workers. In the healthiest of the nations of Western civilization, each of the dogmas or presuppositions contributed something
to the extension of both freedom and justice; and contributed
the more certainly because neither political force was able to gain
a clear victory over the other.

The political and social history of Great Britain is perhaps a
classical symbol of the social history of the whole Western world.
For in Britain (and possibly in the British Commonwealth of
Nations), the dogmatic distance between the two contending
parties consistently narrowed; and no party has been able to gain
a secure dominance over the other. This is the historical expression of the paradoxical relation of freedom to equal justice, which
makes it impossible to sacrifice either value to the other. Christians
will recognize this history as one evidence of the providential workings of God in history, generating more wisdom than the proposals of the human agents in the social struggle, the wisdom
of each being clouded by interest to such a degree that it cannot
see the obvious facts. Thus the social history of the Western world
has been the gradual attainment of wisdom and justice through
the inconclusive contest between two social forces, informed by
equally heretical dogmas and partially true presuppositions.

Christian thought must not pretend that what we have described as its growing pragmatism has not been influenced by this general history in Western thought and life. But we must also recognize that what has been wrought out has actually been a view of life and the establishment of justice in a community which could have been elaborated originally if we had had a clear biblical insight into the nature of history, the freedom of man, and the corruption of sin in that freedom, and had therefore realized that history cannot be equated with nature; nor can the political judgments which we make about our and each other's interests be equated with the judgments which a scientist makes about natural phenomena. In other words the process we have described has been the gradual extrication of our thought from the baneful effects of heresies about man and God which have infected it ever since the French Enlightenment.

It would be wrong however to suggest that our civilization gained nothing from this conflict of heresies, for they established precisely that contest of political and social forces which was the prerequisite of justice in our society. These developments were not anticipated in the traditional "Christian" societies before the rise of these heresies. If we ask why they were not anticipated we will learn why it was necessary to challenge "Christian conservatism" before either political or economic justice could be established. We are now speaking of "Christian conservatism" in the traditional sense, and not in the sense which it has acquired in America and some continental countries. For, according to that connotation, this conservatism is only the religious sanctification of laissez-faire economics.

This older conservatism may be defined as the religious sanctification of established authority, which made it difficult to resist such authority and to correct the injustices which arose from permitting an unchallenged authority in the human community. We must humbly confess the limitations of this conservative approach to political problems, for they prove that Protestant Christianity is not as directly related to the rise of free societies as we would all like to believe. Ever since the Reformation this

Christian conservatism has made the mistake of interpreting the Christian reverence for orders in society, providentially established beyond the contrivance of men, as the uncritical acceptance of a particular authority and a particular order. We must remember that it required a whole century for later Calvinism to add the proper discriminations to the thought of Calvin and Luther, so that it was possible for Christians both to accept the providentially established order of a nation, and to resist a particular government for its injustice.

Upon this distinction between the principle of order and a particular government, established by seventeenth-century Calvinism in Scotland, Holland, France and England, the health of our whole free world depends. It is important to establish this point, because it contains both the resources of the Christian faith in the political sphere and the limitations of a conventional interpretation of that faith. The resource is a proper reverence for providential order and justice, established beyond the resources of the human agents, and not to be lightly challenged. The limitation is an undue and uncritical respect for any particular authority and a consequent disinclination to challenge it. Secular idealists are therefore right in drawing attention to the contributions which rational discrimination made to the creation of contemporary democratic institutions. But they are wrong when they conceal the fact that the worship of "reason" was as fruitful in generating modern tyrannies as the veneration of established authority was in preserving ancient tyrannies.

If we fully analyze the complex relation which exists between religious and rational factors in the establishment of justice, we must come to the conclusion that two elements are equally necessary for the solution of the problems of the human community. One is a proper reverence for factors and forces which are truly absolute; and the other is a discriminate attitude toward relative and ambiguous factors and forces. As Christians we insist that there be a proper reverence for the absolute factors, which might be enumerated as: (1) The authority of God beyond all human and historic authorities, enabling us to defy those authorities on

occasion with a resolute "We must obey God rather than men."
(2) The authority of the moral law embodied in the revelation
in Christ, which is to be distinguished from any particular version
of that law which may have evolved historically, including the
different versions of "natural law." (3) The insistence upon the
"dignity" of the person which makes it illegitimate for any community to debase the individual into a mere instrument of social
process and power and try to obscure the fact of his ultimate
destiny, which transcends all historic realities. This acknowledg-
ment of the "dignity" of man must be accompanied in Christian
thought by a recognition that this precious individual is also a
sinner, that his lusts and ambitions are a danger to the community; and that his rational processes are tainted by the taint of
his own interests. (4) Reverence for the "orders" of authority and
social harmony which have actually been established among us,
beyond the wisdom of man and frequently by providential workings in which "God hath made the wrath of man to praise him."

Every one of these "absolutes" is in danger of corruption; which
is why we cannot speak so simply of Christian "civic virtue."
Reverence for the will of God may degenerate into a too-simple
identification of our interests with the divine will, a fact which
may make conventional Christianity a source of confusion in the
community. Reverence for the historical dignity of the person may
degenerate into a "bourgeois" individualism in which the individual is falsely exalted above the community and the cause of
justice. The moral law may be falsely interpreted from the standpoint of the interests of any portion of the community, and more
particularly of the pious section of the community. Reverence for
the principle of order may degenerate into an undue respect for
a particular order, a form of degeneration which Calvinism, and
later Lutheranism, overcame only at the price of bitter experience
with tyranny.

If we summarize these developments we must recognize that
the same faith which prompted reverence for the absolutes, which
transcend the relativities of history, may also confuse the picture
of the human community in its political and economic perplex-

ities by imparting religious sanction to one of the relative factors
and removing it from the wholesome challenges which have been
discovered to be necessary to prevent any power in the human
community from becoming pretentious in its pride or vexatious
in its power. In short we must face the fact that the Reformation
did not draw sufficiently rigorous conclusions from its principle
Justus et Peccator simul. For according to that principle the
redeemed man could not be trusted to exercise power without sin.
Therefore the checks upon his power were necessary, even if it was
the power of government which was involved. It required a full
century to gain the necessary discrimination for the distinction
between the principle of order and the providentially established
political order of a given nation, and a particular government,
upon which close check must be placed and its power, in the words
of Sam Rutherford, "measured out ounce by ounce."

To this failure in discriminate judgment in our Reformation
heritage one must add all those indiscriminate judgments which
result from deriving political judgment from analogies between
historically contingent social norms, embodied in the canon, and
the contingent circumstances of contemporary life. After all, the
original error in regard to government was due not only to a failure
to distinguish between the majesty of government and the majesty
of a particular government; it was also due to an excessive emphasis upon St. Paul's admonition in Romans 13, an admonition
which obviously had the immediate purpose of arresting "eschatological unrest" and which would, taken alone, disturb the scriptural "consensus" upon the attitude toward government. For that
consensus includes two motifs. The one is appreciation of government as divinely ordained, and established by forces greater than
the conscious contrivance of men. The other is a critical attitude
toward government as inclined to usurp the divine majesty by its
pretensions of pride and the injustices of its power.

The problem of relating scriptural insights to the flowing stream
of human events is a very important one to this day. We cannot
deny that frequently scriptural insights are falsely related to highly
contingent situations, in such a way as to bring confusion into

our judgments. We children of the Reformation pride ourselves on freedom from the inflexible standards which Catholics draw from their conception of "natural law." But it must be confessed that an indiscriminate biblicism is as much a source of confusion as Catholic natural law theories.

In the history of the slow development of justice in the free societies of Western civilization, the secular section of our civilization claims that it provided exactly those discriminations which the religious elements found such difficulty in achieving. This is partly true but partly false. For modern secularism obscured its rational discrimination between constant and variable factors in the problems of the community by its worship of human "reason" as a source of virtue. This worship, which had its rise in the eighteenth century, failed to take account of the sinful corruption of reason, which made the "checks and balances" of justice as necessary in an "enlightened" as in an ignorant community. The observer of history will note that all the illusions which lie at the foundation of modern Communist tyranny had their inception in the eighteenth century worship of "reason" or "nature." These illusions were insensible of the unique character of human freedom, and consequently of human history. Above all, they obscured the fact that sinful self-assertion might rise from the same human capacities which were praised as "rational."

If the secular part of our culture derived grave errors from its worship of reason and nature, rather than the worship of God, it compounded those errors by its extreme voluntarism, which was blind to the workings of providence in history and thought that men could create both governments and communities by the "social contract." This mistake, of imagining that men are in complete control of their historical destiny, reveals itself today in the secular proposals for "world government," which our secular idealists press upon us, and they are disappointed when we refuse to share their illusions.

But we would do well to note that even the errors of the social contract theorists served some purpose when they were brought into contact with truth, which removed their evil effects. Thus the principle of government "by consent of the governed" is a legitimate political principle of democracy, drawn from the illegitimate illusions of social contract theorists. In this way error contributed to truth and served to counteract the error in the Christian truth. For it was true that God established order in human society beyond the contrivance of men; and it was an error to give particular governments an undue reverence and deny the citizen the political power involved in the right of suffrage.

The manner in which the errors and truths of Christians and secularists, of later Calvinists and sectarian Christians, of Catholics and Protestants, have been used for the attainment of justice in a technical age, is itself a remarkable display of providence as contrasted with the wisdom and the foolishness of men. For it is quite apparent that no single force, whether pious or impious, could have accomplished what has been done.

The political and economic sphere, as a realm of relative and contingent realities and of ambiguous moral choices, makes discriminate judgment so necessary, because it is always important to distinguish between the constant and the variable factors, and between the ultimate and the proximate moral norms. This fact has led to one type of Christian politics, which merely asserts the moral ambiguity of all political positions and exhibits its Christian transcendence by refusing to make a choice "which the Pope or Mr. Truman could make just as well." There is no particular wisdom in this kind of neutrality. It leads, in fact, to the political confusion before Nazism, which led to Nazism. Nor is it very helpful to introduce discriminations into the fields of judgment which are supposed to be uniquely Christian but which detract from consideration of the main problems of justice. The judgment, for instance, that Communism is preferable to Nazism because it is not morally nihilistic, or not militaristic, or that it does not intend to corrupt the Christian faith (its only purpose being to annihilate it), or that it is not anti-Semitic. All these judgments obscure the very significant fact that utopian illusions may be as fruitful of tyranny as moral cynicism. This fact is one of the most significant experiences of our day. Observers, whether theologians or rationalists, who obscure this fact do our generation a disservice.

Incidentally, it would be well for theologians and religious people generally to recognize that when they claim to make political judgments on hazardous issues from the standpoint of their faith, their knowledge of the Bible or their theology, they run exactly the same danger of seeking absolute sanction for their frail human judgments as our secular friends run when they claim "scientific" or "objective" validity for their judgments. Every judgment is hazardous and corrupted in the realm where we judge each other. Theologians are just as tempted to obscure that fact as "social scientists."

In the contest between the free world and Communism, for instance, we have all the perplexities which have confused the consciences and minds of men through the centuries. If we become obsessed with the distinction between our righteousness and the evil of Communism we may reduce the conflict to one between two forces which Professor Butterfield has defined as "two organized systems of self-righteousness." If on the other hand we insist that this struggle is merely one more illustration of the fact that all historic struggles are between sinful men, we run the danger of conniving with a vicious tyranny and playing traitor to the God of justice.

The sum of these considerations is that we have an obligation as Christians to establish and extend community and justice as far as lies within our power. We must obey the law of love under conditions and within limits which make no simple application possible. It is not possible because the sins of men, the persistence of individual and collective self-interest, force us to maintain order by coercion and may make resistance and war a necessity of justice. We assume our responsibilities in this community with many other citizens who do not share our faith. We assume them from the standpoint of a faith which discerns a mysterious divine sovereignty over the whole drama of human events, which ought not be surprised by any manifestations of evil history but is not prepared to yield to any evil for motives of self-love. We believe that this majestic God who created the world and sustains it by his providence is finally revealed in Christ our Lord. We are protected by this faith from many aberrations into which the "children of this world" perennially fall: hope of gaining purely human mastery over the drama of history; hope that evil will gradually be eliminated from the human community by growing human goodness or by more adequate instruments of justice; trust in the power of human reason and blindness to the corruption of that reason.

These resources give us some treasures to contribute to the community in its struggle for justice. Among them are an understanding of the fragmentary character of all human virtue; the tentative character of all schemes of justice, since they are subject to the flow of history; the irrevocable character of the "moral law" transcending all historical relativities; and the hazardous judgments which must be made to establish justice between the competing forces and interests. We can tolerate all these hazards, relativities and tentativities because we "look for a city which has foundations whose builder and maker is God."

But we must also accept in all humility the fact that this Christian faith is mediated to the community by sinful men and that our sins frequently obscure the wisdom of the Gospel and interfere with the course of God's grace to men. We must therefore also acknowledge that the community needs protection against our religious aberrations, against our tendency to fanatic intrusions into the tolerance which the community requires for its harmony, against our inclination to indiscriminate judgment.

In short, the health of any of our communities is best served if Christians try at one and the same time to bear witness to their faith, humbly accept treasures of wisdom which may be mediated to the community by those who do not share their faith, and welcome those policies of communal justice which are designed to correct the aberrations of men.

[1957]

The Spiritual Life
of Modern Man (1930)

Alumni Bulletin of the Theological Seminary.

MEN'S highest aspirations do not greatly change from generation to generation, but each age has its own perils and opportunities. What unites us with the aspiring souls of every age is our desire to be whole, to fulfill every capacity and develop every potentiality of the human spirit, and to bring abundance and wholeness of life to our fellows. Now, as always, the spirit of each individual is set in a society and in a universe, and the development of its capacities depend upon the adjustment of its life to both the world of men and the world which is at once more and less than man.

What distinguishes our life from that of our fathers is the fact that our sense of organic relationship to society and to the universe has been destroyed. We lack inner unity and spiritual vitality because we are not organic to our world. We are isolated souls who can find no inner peace partly because we are not at home in our universe and partly because we lack that natural relationship to our fellow men in which our fathers were prompted to the social passions and purposes which disciplined their lives. In our relationship to the universe we vacillate between megalomania and despair, lifting ourselves proudly and defiantly above the world of nature in one moment and sinking in confusion before her inexorable and blind fortunes in the next. In our relations to our fellow men only a small portion of our generation has achieved that combination of intelligence and social energy which is adequate to express ethical passions in terms relevant to the needs and the circumstances of a complex civilization. The rest, left to drift in a sea of social complexity and mechanical relationships, can find no goal to steer for except as caprice sets some immediate end. Some impulse of nature becomes the organizing center of their lives; they live for sex or for greed or by the lust for power; or perhaps they can do no better than to obscure the confusion of their lives by hectic work and hectic play.

The tragic aspects of our modern life are not the result of any deterioration in the human mind or any retrogression in the human enterprise. We are the victims of our achievements. Beginning with the seventeenth century our race has made steady progress in understanding the detailed phenomena of the world which surrounds us. Becoming ever more precise in analyzing, weighing, and balancing the various forces and factors which enter into the total harmony of things, we have substituted for the crude magic, by which our fathers tried to bend cosmic forces to the human will, an exact and potent science which brought ever larger areas of nature under the dominion of human purposes. It would be idle to minimize and futile to enlarge upon these achievements of modern civilization. Science has not only increased comfort and well-being but it has contributed to the ethical progress of the race by offering the means, through its instruments of commerce and communication, for wider and more effective human cooperation and by putting man into a fuller understanding and control of the emotions and impulses which are the motive power of his multifarious activities.

The losses which we have suffered by this development can be put into two categories, one cultural and the other social and moral. We have lost our sense of organic unity with the universe and we have created a mechanical civilization in which our organic relationship to our fellow men has been destroyed.

The scientist alone cannot recapture either one of these relationships. He can conquer nature for us, but there are limits to his conquests. He can aid us in the development of the kind of social intelligence necessary for the ordering of our common lives, but he cannot revive the social passions by which we will that our common life be ordered. Ultimately neither our cultural nor our social problem is one which pure rationality can solve. Neither our ultimate faith by which we adjust ourselves to the universe, nor our moral will through which we find ourselves in our society can be expressed in terms of pure reason. The energies of life are not rational. Reason may guide them but it cannot create them. The adjustment of man to his universe, toward which he must maintain an attitude of both filial piety and heroic rebellion, involves too many paradoxes to be expressed in terms of pure rationality.

Man comes to terms with his universe only by heroic and poetic insights, and he is nerved to undertake them only as he gains sufficient self-respect in his moral relationships to his fellow men to feel that the human spirit must be taken into account when the effort is made to penetrate the ultimate mysteries. Religion, which is the whole of man adjusting himself to the whole of life, involves precisely these two elements—poetic insight and moral vigor. Inextricably united, each is cause and each effect in the whole. We cannot solve our cultural problem without first creating the kind of moral integrity in our social life which will prompt us to be heroic in our ultimate insights about the character of the universe and we will not develop new moral energy if we cannot support it by the sublime assumption that our moral struggle is more than an effervescence on the surface of reality, that it is integral and organic to the character of the universe. So the poet leans on the prophet and the prophet on the poet in guiding the spirit of man.

In the heart of every true and vital religion, as for instance in the religion of Jesus, the two are one. If it seems difficult to us to face at once the social and cultural problem, we who call ourselves disciples and followers of Jesus would do well to return for inspiration and guidance to one who based religious insights on moral experience and moral aspiration on religious insights, who

asked men to practice love because he saw the love of God revealed
in the impartiality of nature (the rain descending upon the evil
and the good and the sun shining upon the just and the unjust),
and who strengthened his faith in the love of God because he
saw and appreciated the glimpses of love which are revealed even
in imperfect human life ("if ye then being evil know how to give
good gifts unto your children, how much more will your heavenly
Father give good gifts to them that ask him").

If we begin with the social and moral problem of modern man
as intrinsically the more important, we cannot be long in discover-
ing that what disturbs the inner unity of man's life and vitiates
the once robust quality of his spiritual life is the mechanical
civilization in which he lives. The civilization is too vast and
intricate to be brought under ready control and its relationships
are too indirect to excite the social sympathies which are needed
to establish true brotherhood. Your modern man is related to more
and more people in this world of mechanical interdependency,
but he is not related to them spiritually. Human sympathy which
flows at the touch of human hands ceases to flow where men
feel only the bonds of steel which hold them together in artificial
societies. The cooperative societies in which our fathers lived were
small compared to ours and their loyalties were correspondingly
narrow, but they were potent. We are challenged by many
loyalties but none of them is potent enough to offer us true self-
fulfillment in terms of brotherhood.

Modern means of communication relate us intimately to people
all over the world who are spiritually strangers to us, and modern
means of production relate us mechanically to people who were
once our neighbors. Our neighbors have become strangers and
strangers have become neighbors. We do not have the intelligence
to make social goodwill effective in the intricacy of these relationships and the mechanical character of the relationships makes the
generation of goodwill difficult. The result is that our common
life is ordered by the impulses of nature, greed, and the lust for
power, which have achieved a new and awful potency by the

advance of science; and our individual lives, lacking the discipline of a great social passion, are not ordered at all.

Living in a civilization which he has not conquered morally, and in which life feeds on life in ruthless fashion, it is not surprising that man should be bereft of moral self-respect and should have neither the moral energy nor the spiritual imagination to come to terms with his ultimate problems. Modern man is not immoral because he is irreligious; he is irreligious because he is immoral. Lacking essential self-respect, he tries to bolster his waning pride by the quantitative achievements which modern technology has made possible. The big city and the skyscraper have long since exceeded economic feasibility, except for the real-estate man. In these vast metropolitan conglomerates of ours the law of diminishing returns has set in. They are monstrosities from an economic standpoint. They are built for psychological reasons. The same may be said for our worship of power and bigness in the nation. Lacking moral self-respect we try to impress ourselves, and the universe perhaps, by power. The splendor of the New York skyline and the venality of the political life of our city put in juxtaposition are a perfect symbol of the spiritual state of modern man.

Clearly the spiritual leadership which our generation needs must come from prophets who know how to insist that man cannot be whole until he lives again in organic unity with his fellow men. All civilization is a peril to brotherhood. The Hebrew prophets warred against a civilization much simpler than ours in the name of their ideal of brotherhood. No authentic moral idealism will ever live in perfect peace with a civilization which is bound to disregard human values for the sake of its secular ends of power, wealth, and efficiency. But it is idle to protest against the inevitable in the name of an ideal. Your modern prophet must be a technician who knows how to transmute realities in terms of his ideal. He must be a pedagogical technician who knows how to create the kind of social and spiritual imagination which will overcome the mechanical and indirect relationships which modern life has produced and help man to feel with and for his brother in this sort of society. He needs to be a social technician who knows how to create social organisms which can come into control of the mechanical world that moves now without social intelligence to match our engineering skill. Certainly our prophet-technicians must be more than engineers. Intelligence may be able to solve the problem which intelligence has created, but it will have to be more than engineering intelligence.

If we admit that in the modern world the aim of the prophet is to create moral energy and social intelligence in equal proportions, and that his ambition is to generate and direct moral good will to socially useful ends, we arrive inevitably at our cultural problem: How can we maintain the energy and the intelligence at one and the same time? Are not our schools, which ought to be producing young men and women with the capacity to deal with the intellectual problems of our era, developing instead a rather large number of young people who are going to wait with Mr. Joseph Wood Krutch for "the influx of a simpler people not yet ripe for despair"? Is it not true that many people of our generation who are intelligent enough to make their ideals effective are also too intelligent to believe in the efficacy of any ideal or the validity of any great purpose?

The fact is that we have no clear intellectual right to believe in any solid purpose or any value which has ever claimed the loyalty of men. If value schemes have as their basis on the one hand the self-justifying vitality of moral and social experience, they are rooted on the other hand in the soil of man's religion, in his rational and yet reason-defying faith that the highest purposes he can conceive have cosmic support and are but refractions of cosmic destiny. The various faiths by which your modern man, who has not capitulated to despair, lives are clearly vestigial remnants of another day of more robust faith when man felt himself organically related to his universe and worshiped a God who was in nature and yet above nature, a God who related man and his ideals to the universe.

Standing before these ultimate problems and ultimate mysteries pure science is clearly at a loss. It has a method for dealing with detailed phenomena but not meant for meanings which are revealed in totalities of relationships. Its intellectual instruments, its precise scientific concepts, are moreover hardly designed to capture or to express what man feels about life and about his organic relationship to the whole of life. These instruments of precision have gained such a prestige by their immediate triumphs and achievements that your modern man is unable to see what he cannot see through these instruments and is afraid to confess that he feels unities and relationships which cannot be expressed in their terms!

Obviously there are areas of experience and profundities in reality which can be expressed and discovered only in intuitions, presentiments, insights, and volitions that escape the bounds of pure rationality. They need to be, it goes without saying, constantly under the discipline of reason. They need to feed on reason but reason must also feed on them. Both self-consciousness and consciousness of the world have in them something of a direct perception which we cannot catch or express in a category of science. The fact that I am a self-conscious individual, that in my brief moment of consciousness I comprehend all time, surveying the past and planning the future, the fact that my conscious moment is dwarfed by the world's immensities and infinities and yet stands above them insofar as it comprehends them more than they comprehend it, the fact that I am both the world's child and the world's rebel and that I must find something in nature to explain my organic relationship to it and something above nature to explain my rebellion against it, these facts can never be adequately experienced in pure rationality nor stated in terms of pure science.

Philosophy can help me to understand and to express this experience but it is filled with too many paradoxes for philosophy. Without the philosopher the poet will let his imagination degenerate into free fancy just as without him the scientist will draw unwarranted conclusions from his little fields of experimentation. So we need the discipline of philosophy with the imagination of poetry and mysticism for the solution of our cultural problem.

But ultimately man's cultural problem, the problem of making two worlds one, of achieving a sense of unity with his world, requires a heroic logic to which men are nerved only by a robust moral vitality and which they can express only by poetic symbols.

What we try painfully to recapture in our modern day, this wholeness of life, this organic relationship of man to his fellow men and to his world, existed, as we have already suggested, as the unexamined possession of simpler people of another day—of the peasant, for instance, who had grown sufficiently intelligent to be fully self-conscious but not so intellectual as to be separated from his world and his fellows. The complexities of life destroyed that simple unity of thought and feeling and it cannot be reestablished on its old basis. Religion which grew naturally out of the heart of the peasant can live in a more complex era only by collaboration of prophets who are also technicians with poets who are also philosophers. Only by their combined insights and achievements can we restore man to unity and wholeness. Even at best we may fall short of some of the virtues which were generated in this original simplicity.

Perhaps, as Spengler thinks, each civilization pays for the achievements of its ripened intellect by the enervation of its vital capacities. We will console ourselves with the thought that the high price which we have paid for our complex world has not been altogether in vain, for few of us would be willing to return to that simpler world. But while maturity is inevitable, there is no reason why we should not mitigate its limitations by preserving as well as we know how the graces of childhood. Religion is in fact the spirit of childhood eternalized.

We have a good authority for placing a premium upon the insights of the child, holding with Jesus that the simple intuitions which spring from the unspoiled unity of its spiritual life have the grace of ultimate wisdom in them. This too is our justification for holding so resolutely to the inspiration and the guidance of Jesus himself, in defiance of the moderns who fear traditions of every kind, religious traditions and loyalties most of all. These loyalties may on occasion betray us into error but anyone who has the wit to realize that intellectual maturity is not only a mark of growth but also a mark of decay will try resolutely, in defiance of modernity, to appropriate and profit by religious revelations and insights which our age could not produce but cannot afford to dispense with. If it is our task to create moral vigor and spiritual imagination, and if the cooperation of poet and prophet are needed for this task it might be added in conclusion that there is no easy way of uniting these two functions. It is difficult enough for the prophet to add the function of technician and for the poet to acquire the circumspection of the philosopher, but it is still more difficult for prophet and poet to be one. The prophet must try to come to terms with our civilization and the poet must try to come to terms with our culture. But the world of culture is, in terms of our civilization, a world of privilege. When the prophet inveighs against social injustice he is striking at least in part against inequalities which make the world of culture possible. The poets and the mystics have the time to discipline their imaginations and to say their prayers in a leisure which, in our kind of world, is bought at the expense of other men's toil.

We cannot come to moral terms with our civilization without standing outside of it, and we cannot come to terms with our culture without being a part of it; and being a part of it means profiting by our civilization. Confronting that problem no one can make rules for another. But we can give at least this warning, that any religious leader who is not conscious of this situation and who does not try to reduce its inconsistencies to a minimum will sink into moral impotence and will find himself in the end in the absurd position of worshiping a God of love without really loving his brother. That is unfortunately the sorry state in which professional religion is frequently enmeshed. We may well remind ourselves continually, one might say by fasting and prayer, that the prophet can stand alone more easily than the poet can in the final crisis. Moral vitality may become a substitute for poetic insight since it can generate the latter; but there is no substitute for it. If that was true in the past it is doubly true for us; for we live in a narrow world and there are many of us.

If we cannot recapture some organic unity, some sense of brotherhood with our fellows, in which the saps and juices of a spiritual organism can replenish the easily exhausted resources of the individual, we will have no vitality to claim our kinship with the stars and make our ultimate adjustment to life itself. "If," said Jesus, "thou offerest thy gift at the altar and rememberest that thy brother hath aught against thee, leave there thy gift at the altar and first be reconciled with thy brother." Without the refreshment of authentic moral experience, your poet becomes priest and your priest a mere magic monger. Goodness, and in our day, socially adequate goodness, is still the one sure way to the knowledge of the divine. "Blessed are the pure in heart for they shall see God."

[1930]

PART TWO

Freedom

BOTH human and natural history enter into the formation
of events, in that both the free actions of men and natural
necessities are involved.

The distinguishing mark of human history is that men super-
impose their desires, ambitions, and ends upon the limited ends
of nature. They have the freedom to do this because they possess the conceptual capacity to apprehend not only single events
and objects but to comprehend the flux of events in its general
patterns and essential character. Consequently they can lift themselves above the immediacies of events and project ends more
inclusive than those for which the creatures of nature strive. Another facet of human freedom is man's capacity to retain past
events in his memory. He is thus delivered from the immediate
course of natural events and is able, by remembering history, to
affect history. His memory enables him to record not only natural
recurrences but the unique and contingent events which, by virtue
of man's unpredictable freedom, constantly occur.

Man, despite his unique freedom, never ceases to be a natural
creature, driven by natural hungers and necessities. But human
freedom can enlarge, for both good and evil, the scope of every
natural desire. Insofar as man is a creature and his actions are
determined by previous events, they are subject to scientific analysis. They can be sorted out in categories and can be predicted as

natural events can be predicted. But insofar as human freedom is woven into the events of history, historical events are not exactly predictable. Even a scientific analysis of the motives which prompt human action cannot become the basis of a prediction, for of many motives and of many causes, it is impossible to prove which is the determining or dominant one in a given situation.

The historical sciences are in a different category from the natural sciences. Since historical events produce an endless variety of configurations and patterns in which the historian may discern, at best, inexact analogies and recurrences, he is inescapably preoccupied with the problem of distinguishing invariable from variable factors. The good historian is therefore half artist and half scientist. He is a scientist in that he may analyze causes and historical trends. He is an artist in that he must interpret the meaning of an historical structure according to a general system of meaning, which his imagination partly imposes upon them and partly elicits from them.

Since the ultimate freedom of the person beyond all psychological, economic, political, geographic and other determining factors is always hidden and can be known only introspectively, and since every event or action, once having taken place, can be plausibly interpreted as the inevitable consequence of a previous event or action, there is a natural temptation for all students of historical events to be more deterministic than the facts warrant. The freedom of persons, which is evident particularly in the biographical pinnacles of the mountains of history, remains a threat to every scientific account of historical events. It cannot be charted and remains a mystery to the observer of the drama of history, who must be content with statistical averages for the description of the main currents of history. Yet the endless variety and unpredictability of the historical drama are proofs of the reality of that freedom, supporting the introspective evidence of the actors themselves, who know that they make free and responsible decisions, though they are also conscious of all the determining factors which prompt and occasion decisions.

The social and political freedoms which modern democratic

communities accord the person express the belated convictions of modern communities, gained after desperate struggles, that the community must give the person a social freedom which corresponds to the essential freedom of his nature, and which enables him to express hopes and ambitions and to engage in interests and vitalities which are not immediately relevant to the collective purposes of the community, but which in the long run enrich the culture and leaven the lump of the community's collective will and purpose.

The unique and radical freedom of man, and the resulting endless variety of historical configurations, which can only be partially reduced to rational systems of meaning, give validity to the biblical account of history and of the relation of the individual to the divine source and end of meaning, which transcends the coherences of nature and history. The biblical account assumes a divine providence over individual and collective destinies, which establishes meaning on the vast panorama of history without annulling human freedom. The alternative methods of establishing meaning by coordinating historical events into systems of natural or rational coherences, tend to create excessively deterministic or equally excessive voluntaristic interpretations of historical events in which either the freedom or the finiteness of men is obscured.

On the other hand, it must be admitted that versions of the Christian faith frequently interpret the idea of providence so that the freedom of man is annulled or imperiled and God appears to be an arbitrary despot of the historical drama who creates meanings by special providence, that is, by interference with the natural causalities and coherences which always furnish the foundation upon which human freedom erects the various pinnacles of history. Calvinism has been particularly guilty of the primitive interpretation of the legitimate biblical idea of the sovereignty of a mysterious divine power who is both the creator and providential preserver of the human and historical enterprise.

[1958]

Do the State and Nation Belong to God or the Devil? *(1937)*

BOTH the nations and the states, through which the life of nations is organized and their wills articulated, have made the perennial claim of being divine throughout human history. The states of the early Babylonian and Egyptian empires were priestly states, whose rulers were god-kings. Perhaps they were so successful in maintaining a semblance of unity and cohesion in a vast heterogeneous population because religious reverence for majesty is a more potent force of subjection than fear of power. The priest who subjugates the soul is a more successful ruler than the soldier who coerces the body. Yet neither priest nor soldier can achieve perfect success alone. The most potent government is one in which the functions of priest and soldier are combined. Stated in other terms, reverence for majesty and fear of force are the two most effective motives of obedience to government. The element of rational consent, which has become a third element of government in modern times, is even now not as potent as rationalists assume. The giving and withholding of rational consent may make and unmake particular governments within a given state, but it will hardly destroy the state and create a new state structure. It may prompt the choice of Tory, liberal and labor governments, but only as long as the general presuppositions of a given state are maintained by these governments.

The claim of divine majesty on the part of a state and nation always involves fraud. But the rationalists and moderns who imagine that this fraud is the calculated deception of a designing priesthood have not looked very deeply into the mysteries of human social life. The fact is that both the nation and the state are large enough and powerful enough to impress the simple subject as the very source of life itself; yet they are too partial and relative to deserve this reverence. Majesty is a reality which involves both power and goodness. The majesty of a nation, state or ruler is derived on the one hand from the idea that a particular government or social order is identical with social order *per se.* A particular society claims the reverence of its citizens because it seems to them to be society itself. While rulers and priests may accentuate this pretension, they do not create it. The claim is really generated in the simple imagination of the common man, who may on occasion even go to the length of regarding his state as the source of the bounties of nature with which he is surrounded, beneficences which no government has created.

There is consequently a religious overtone in all political loyalties; that is, conditioned, relative and partial human institutions tend to make unconditioned claims upon the lives of individuals and to secure the acceptance of such claims. What the modern totalitarian state is doing in this direction is merely an accentuation of what has been an element of political life since the very beginning. To a certain degree modern totalitarianism involves a primitivistic effort to reconstruct the simple religious loyalties of primitive society and of early civilization. The idea of a sacred blood brotherhood is derived from primitive society and the idea of a sacred ruler is reminiscent of the priest-king of early civilization. Even in a highly rationalist Marxian state, Stalin is beginning* to ascertain the proportions of a priest-king, who demands and receives religious reverence in terms of the religious presuppositions of his particular politico-religious cult.

The unqualified (divine) majesty of state and nation is doubly dubious. No nation deserves the unconditioned devotion of man, because it is not the universal community or the absolute value.

* Written in 1937.

The fact that it is able to transmute such unconditioned devotion into a force of international anarchy reveals the tragic character of modern patriotism. It also suggests that the nation is as much the servant of the devil as the servant of God. The nation may be the incarnation of the principle of order within the community, but it is also the incarnation of the principle of anarchy between communities. This very simple fact completely refutes the pretentious claims of idealistic philosophy for the nation-state. Hegel's and Bosanquet's metaphysical theory of the state is no more than a rationalized version of tribal, that is, pre-prophetic religion.

The national community is thus ethically ambiguous. Its very claim to unqualified moral worth is the basis of its demonic character. In other words, it belongs to the devil precisely because it claims to be God. On the other hand it could not make such claims if it were not the bearer of genuine values. Human beings do not live in abstract universal societies. They live in historic communities; and the peace, order and justice of such communities, such as it is, is the product of ages of development, a fact which justifies Edmund Burke in regarding historic rights and duties as more important than abstract rational rights and duties. The same historic process which makes the community partial and relative also endows it with a religious aura. The social peace of a community is never as completely a rational contract between free individuals as bourgeois rationalism, from the day of John Locke to the present, has supposed. It is the product of vast natural and historical forces.

The state is even more ambiguous, ethically, than the nation. The state is the bearer of power in the community. This power is compounded partly of coercive force and partly of the prestige of the community itself. The coercive force may be of varying types. It may be purely military power, as in the older feudal societies. It may be the power of economic ownership, which in feudal society was derived from military power but which in modern capitalism is more basic than the latter and bends it to its purposes and will. But no state governs purely by coercive force.

A state is able to gain obedience by direct coercion only when it can assume the loyalty of a majority and proceed against a recalcitrant minority. The possibility of a tyrannical oligarchy maintaining itself against the will of the majority, purely by the use of coercion, is not excluded. But the obvious lesson of history is that such efforts, usually made in a period of decline of a particular political and social system, are subject to a law of diminishing returns. A state, or even a government, which has lost the respect of the populace finds itself in a vicious circle if it seeks to substitute fear for implicit consent as the motive of loyalty. The more it increases fear of force the more it sacrifices the respect and implicit loyalty of its subjects.

It is wrong to assume, however, that the ambiguous ethical position of the state is due primarily to its use of physical force. The real cause of its questionable moral worth lies in the fact that the power which it wields (composed of both force and majesty) is ostensibly derived from the total community and justified by its service to the community. But practically this power is always in the hands of a particular oligarchy, of some group which possesses the most significant form of social power, whether priestly, military, economic, or political. If such a ruling class possesses sufficient power to place itself in charge of the government, it is able to appropriate the reverence of the populace for the principle of government as such and to profit from its grateful remembrance of historic glories of the nation. Every ruling class pretends that its interests are identical with those of the nation. This is never exactly true. If it is not partially true the ruling class cannot maintain itself. Unqualified incompatibility between the interests of a ruling oligarchy and the national community is the proof of the decay of a social system. Thus for instance it has become a question whether the modern capitalistic oligarchies are not so inevitably driven into conflict with the best interests of their national communities that their doom as effective oligarchies is not sealed.

But even at best the oligarchy is always driven by self-interest to exact a larger share of the community fund for the service which it renders than the service is worth. The possession of power is a constant temptation to exploitation. A ruling class is thus subject to the same moral equivocation which we have discovered in the nation as such. Power is always partial. It always has a particular locus. Yet power would degenerate into naked force if it could not pretend that it is universal and not partial and particular. Even the development of democracy does not change this situation. Democratic institutions may give the total community frequent opportunities to review the policies of a government and to check the expansive tendencies of a ruling oligarchy. But democracy does not initiate a new state structure. There is a power of referendum but not a power of initiative in democratic masses. Masses do not organize themselves. A democratic revolutionary movement can be successful only if its will is formed and articulated (and formed before it can be articulated) by a new oligarchy.

Just as the national community is a particular community which claims the unconditional loyalty which only a universal community deserves, so the state is a particular ruling class which claims the unconditional loyalty which only the total community deserves. In other words, a religious pretension is involved in each instance; and the success of this religious pretension is a necessary force of government.

Until the rise of the Hebrew prophets this ambiguous character of both state and nation was never seriously challenged. Greek philosophy certainly did not challenge it. Both Plato and Aristotle accentuated the moral pretensions of oligarchs by assuming that the class structure of society was justified by an innate difference in the capacity of human beings. Plato's ideal society merely envisaged an oligarchy which would be prevented from selfish use of its power by ascetic discipline. The challenge of the Hebrew prophets to both state and nation came from the vantage point of faith in a God in whom power and goodness were truly one because he was the creative source of all life.

In the name of this God tribal religion was challenged. The Hebrew prophets envisaged the tremendous possibility that their nation might be destroyed and their sense of the meaningfulness of human existence would not be destroyed with it. In other words the meaning of life transcended the relation of the individual to his national community. From the standpoint of his faith in a God who was the Lord of all history, the Hebrew prophet saw the vicissitudes of nations, the rise and fall of national communities as strands in the fabric of a total history. The most significant fact in this judgment was the belief that it was the very pretension of the nation to be God (that is, the center of unconditioned loyalty) which would ultimately destroy it. This pride violates the law of life because it makes what is not the center of life into a spurious center.

Inevitably this pride is also the cause of injustice, for it seeks to subject all life to a false center. Isaiah expresses the idea of God's jealousy of a nation which makes false pretensions in the words, "Woe to the crown of pride, to the drunkards of Ephraim, whose glorious beauty is a fading flower. . . . The crown of pride, the drunkards of Ephraim, shall be trodden under feet. . . . In that day shall the Lord of hosts be for a crown of glory, and for a diadem of beauty, unto the residue of his people." This prophetic conception of the self-destruction of power, because it lacks the goodness which it pretends, is a rather exact description of the actual processes of self-destructive imperialisms which all history records.

The state does not fare any better than the nation under prophetic strictures. The injustices of the ruling class, the unevenness of their justice, whose "treading is upon the poor" (Amos v: 11), who "turn aside the needy from judgment" (Isa. x: 2), who live in luxurious complacency (Amos vi: 1-6) and place grievous tax burdens upon the poor, are consistently excoriated. The Majesty of God is set against the false majesty of the rulers. "He bringeth the princes to nothing and maketh the judges of the world as vanity" (Isa. xi: 23). The critical attitude of prophetic religion toward the rulers is maintained throughout all biblical religion, both Old and New Testaments. In the "Magnificat" God is praised for putting down the mighty from their seat and exalting them of low degree (Luke i: 52). Jesus speaks of the "kings of the gentiles" who "lord it over them" and admonishes his disciples, "but ye shall not be so, but he that is greatest among you let him be as the younger; and he that is chief as he that doth serve" (Luke xxii: 26).

This critical attitude toward the centers of power in society is informed by both religio-moral and socio-moral considerations. From the standpoint of religion the rulers are judged because their pride offends the majesty of God. From the standpoint of society they are judged because their power leads to injustice. Even St. Paul, who does not always stand fully in the prophetic tradition, maintains the religious criticism of the men of power. He declares,

For ye see your calling, brethren, how that not many wise men after the flesh, not many mighty, not many noble, are called. But God hath chosen the foolish things of the world to confound the wise; and God hath chosen the weak things of the world to confound the things that are mighty, and base things of the world and things which are despised hath God chosen, yea and things that are not, to put to nought things that are (1 Cor. i: 26-28).

This idea of the self-destruction of power, which pretends to divinity in spite of its partiality, is accompanied in prophetic literature by the more positive messianic hope of the ultimate establishment of justice. In early prophecy this is to be accomplished through a Davidic king who will combine both power and goodness. This conception of a shepherd king who "will not judge according to the seeing of the eye or the hearing of the ear," that is, who will not judge superficially but imaginatively, is earlier than Hebrew prophecy. It appears in the earliest messianic literature of Babylon and Egypt. There is a curious pathos in this hope. For the complete compatibility of power and goodness is an impossibility. Only in God are power and goodness one, since only he is both the transcendent source and transcendent unity of existence. In actual history power always endows the individual or the collective agent with the possibility of infringing upon other life. Thus the same power which justifies itself as the principle of unity must be judged as the cause of oppression.

Every power in history has a particular locus in an individual group or nation. If it unites life beyond itself it also makes undue claims upon the life which it has unified. Hosea was the first prophet to see this partiality of power. He declares in God's name: "I will be thy king. Where is there another who will bring salvation to all your cities?" (Hosea xiii: 10). This prophetic recognition of the inevitability of injustice in the use of historic power finally transmutes messianism into a hope for a completely redeemed world which will be ushered in by the "son of man," the man from heaven in the visions of Daniel and the Similitudes of Enoch. This apocalyptic literature has not received much attention in recent philosophies of history. But it is the bearer of a profound insight which modern utopians lack. It knows that the problem of power is a perennial one in historic existence. The problem could be put in terms of a simple paradox: There is no peace without power and there is no justice with power. There is no peace without power because larger societies can never be unified purely by voluntary association. There is no justice with power because power tempts every mortal man to gratifications beyond the requirements of his service to the community.

The fact that there is no peace without power justifies a qualified religious reverence toward historic centers of power which maintain a tolerably just relationship to the community. The fact that there is no justice with power requires an unrelenting critical attitude toward all government. It is in this latter function that traditional Christianity played truant to its prophetic insights. It forgot St. Paul's word about the wise, the noble and the mighty, and remembered only his fateful sanctification of government in Romans xiii:

Let every soul be subject unto the higher powers. For there is no power but of God; the powers that be are ordained of God. Whosoever therefore resisteth the power, resisteth the ordinance of God; and they that resist shall receive to themselves damnation. For rulers are not a terror to good works but to the evil.

The most charitable judgment about this Pauline dictum is that it is inexact. There have been many rulers of history who have been a terror to good works. St. Paul might have remembered another word of his in which he declares that the "princes of this world" did not understand the wisdom of God or they would not have crucified "the prince of glory." The fact is that all governments tend to crucify the prophet and the criminals on the same Calvary. They find difficulty in distinguishing between the prophetic and the criminal minorities, both of which threaten their mediocre social peace, their uneasy compromises between justice and injustice.

As the church established itself in the world and made alliances with government it found the Pauline word most convenient. The theologians were not altogether wrong in their realism, in terms of which they asserted the necessity of government in a sinful world. But their realism was incomplete. The same realism which sees the necessity of power for the sake of maintaining social order must also see the necessity of resistance to the exactions of power for the sake of justice. Catholicism at its best was able to criticize the injustice of governments from the perspective of its ideals of a natural law which transcended any given historic law. But it was never able to implement this moral criticism with a justification of political rebellion. In Protestantism the sanctification of government was even more complete. "It does not help the peasants," declared Martin Luther, "to claim in Genesis i and ii that all things were created free and equal. For in the New Testament Moses counts for nothing, but there stands our Master Christ and casts us body and possessions under the Kaiser and the worldly law." "There are two kinds of rebels," declared John Calvin in writing to the Duke of Somerset. After enumerating sectaries and Catholics as such rebels, he continues: "Both deserve to be repressed by the sword which is committed to you, since they not only attack the king but strive against God who has placed him on the royal throne."

In this word of Calvin we see the whole danger of a too unqualified and uncritical religious reverence for government. Not only did orthodox Christianity fail to deal realistically with the dangers of injustice in government; it also tended to sanctify a

particular type of historic government rather than government
per se. Thus throughout the medieval and early Protestant period
hereditary monarchy was accepted as the divinely sanctioned government. Kings were assumed to rule by divine right. Such a
doctrine finally resulted not only in the sanctification of a particular type of government but of a particular ruler within such
a scheme of government. Orthodox Christianity never heeded the
nicely cynical advice of Peter Crassus, who said, "Render unto
Caesar the things that are Caesar's, but not unto Tiberius the
things that are Tiberius'; for Caesar is good, but Tiberius is bad."

It must be admitted that both Catholicism and Protestantism
allowed a few exceptions to this general counsel of acquiescence
in injustice. Catholicism could be quite critical of secular government if it judged the state from the perspective of the higher
claims of the church, a more universal government than the nation.
Nor can it be denied that the papacy at its best represented a
universal force which mitigated the anarchy of conflicting nation-
alisms. But this very virtue of Catholicism betrayed it into a new
error. It forgot that the papacy as a supernational political system
was subject to the same difficulties which beset every seat of
power. The Pope claimed to be the vicar of Christ. But he was
also a Caesar. The papacy was in fact a kind of ghostly aftermath
of Caesarism. The Pope claimed to rule by spiritual rather than
physical power. Though this was not always the case, abstention
from the use of physical coercion is not the certain guarantee of
moral superiority that the church supposed.

This is a lesson which pacifists, who take the moral superiority
of "spiritual" over physical force for granted, must still learn. A
Pope who used the weapons of interdict and excommunication
might possess more potent instruments of coercion in a religious
age than the man who carried the sword. Nor were these instruments inherently more social than other weapons. Any kind of
power is a temptation to selfish aggrandizement. The church was
more universal than the nation; but it was not as universal at it
claimed to be; and the Pope was a human being, presiding over
a priestly oligarchy, no matter how great his achievements and

his greater pretensions as "vicar of Christ." The church at its best was also the church at its worst. It built a universal European civilization; but the civilization was European and not universal. It ruled this civilization in alliance with the feudal landlord, a fact for which contemporary Spain is the most vivid example.

The papacy in its greatest triumph succeeded in establishing a government in which the soldier was the ally of the priest rather than the priest the ally of the soldier. Since reverence for majesty is a more effective motive of loyalty than fear of force, such a government achieved both a stability and a universality which transcended the governments of the man with the sword. But whether its virtues and achievements greatly transcended the similar achievements of Babylonian and Egyptian priest-kings is an open question. A telling indication of its inadequacies is furnished by the history of the modern period. When the businessman arose to contend with the landed oligarchy for supremacy in the modern state, he was under the necessity of destroying the hierarchy with the aristocracy and the Christian religion with the feudal social order, because the former was so intimately linked with the latter. In Catholic Christianity, in other words, the prophetic protest against and criticism of all temporal majesty had become completely domesticated and corrupted. The God who transcends all nations and brings all princes to nothing, including ecclesiastical princes, was made the servant of a particular political system.

While Protestantism has always been more servile in its attitude toward nation and state than Catholicism, it also allowed a few exceptions to its general counsel of acquiescence to the power and pretensions of the state. It allowed rebellion against princes and kings if the latter violated the law of God. In this sense Protestantism maintains a truly prophetic characteristic of its Hebraic-Christian heritage. At its best it enables the Protestant church to offer heroic resistance to the religious pretensions of the totalitarian state, as revealed in Germany today.* But it accepts the qualified religious pretensions of nations, states and rulers with reverent respect. It has thus been quite unable to guide the

* 1937 (Ed. note)

conscience of men in the relative problems of justice which determine the qualities of government.

At its worst Protestantism regarded the ruler's violation of the
law of God purely from the standpoint of theological dogma.
A ruler who professed a religion different from the one held by
the Protestant theologian or who sought to violate the religious
convictions of his subjects, was held to be disobedient to God
and therefore unworthy of the obedience of his subjects. "We
must obey our princes, but if they rise against God they must
be put down and held of no more account than worn-out shoes,"
declared Calvin, a sentiment which might seem to be in perfect accord with the prophetic tradition. Unfortunately, however,
Calvin's idea of the ruler's rebellion against God had a purely
theological connotation. It was not the ruler's violation of the
law of justice which justified rebellion against him, but rather his
unfortunate adherence to a wrong religion. Toward the injustice
of a ruler, Calvin had a complacent attitude: "Therefore if we
are vexed by an inhuman prince or robbed and plundered by an
avaricious one, let us first of all remember our offences against
God which are doubtlessly chastised by these plagues."

If we sum up this record of orthodox Christianity, both Catholic
and Protestant, we are forced to the conclusion that it has consistently failed to maintain the prophetic criticism against both
the nation and the state which inheres in a prophetic religion's
faith in a God of transcendent majesty, who judges the pretensions
of majesty, inevitably made by temporal rulers and particular
human communities. This failure of orthodox Christianity has
two sources. On the one hand the prophets of religion tend to
become transmuted and corrupted into auxiliary rulers. The king
knows how to bargain with the prophet. He gives him particular
privileges and advantages which increase his stakes in the particular social organization in which he functions. Consciously and
unconsciously these advantages tempt the prophet to forget the
words of judgment against power and injustice implied in his
religion and to accentuate the counsels of reverence for temporal
majesty and acquiescence in its inevitable injustices. Thus every

new political movement which seeks a higher justice is forced to contend against the priestly allies of an older system of justice.

But the religious sanctification of power has another source, which the critics of the priests are usually unable to discern. Modern proponents of a more equal justice, whether eighteenth-century radical bourgeoisie or contemporary proletarians, have usually been rationalists who sincerely believed that the priestly sanctification of injustice was purely an artifact of rulers. In this Diderot and Marx were in perfect agreement. They regarded religious conservatism as the simple fruit of priestly fraud. They did not realize that the religious sanctification of power, though fraudulently accentuated by priestly classes, springs inevitably out of the heart of simple men. Insofar as Christianity assumed a subservient and uncritical attitude toward nation and state it merely capitulated to the natural religion which expresses itself in every age.

The basic characteristic of all natural religion is self-glorification. The most common mode of expression of such self-glorification is to revere the collective self and to discover in its majesty a compensation for the weakness and frustration of the individual. This glorification of the self through the collective ego is compounded with reverence for something greater than the self. The national community is the most natural symbol and focus for something which is revered both because it is a glorified "I" and because it is actually more than the ego. It is society itself, the very principle of social order, in relation and subordination to which the ego finds life meaningful.

Natural religion, in other words, finds a God who is majestic, but not majestic enough to threaten human self-esteem. The gods of natural religion are both greater and no greater than the "I." That is why the prophets call them demons. They subject the individual to something greater than itself and manage at the same time to glorify the self. That is what determines their equivocal character. Insofar as they actually unify life and relate the individual to a community they must be regarded as lesser divinities, angelic forces, which have a right to exist even in a prophetic religion. Insofar as they express human pride and defy the limits of human finiteness and creatureliness they must be regarded as demons.

It is naturally difficult for the imagination to envisage the national community. A proper symbol for such comprehension is necessary. The most logical symbol for this purpose is the ruler. So potent is the personal symbol, as against the more impersonal symbols which rationalistic democracies seek to construct (as for instance the American Constitution) that the slogan "for king and country" maintains its efficacy in a nation as advanced as Great Britain. It is instructive, moreover, that the symbol seems to gain, rather than suffer a loss, in potency if the ruler is stripped of all actual power so that he incarnates the religious majesty of the community and not the political power of the ruling oligarchy. In this respect there is only a slight difference between the constitutional monarchy of Great Britain and the absolute monarchy of Japan. The Japanese emperor ostensibly exercises both sovereignty and power; but the latter claim is a transparent fiction and the emperor is saved from the resentments which accompany the exercise of power in political disputes by the device of never holding him responsible for any specific policy. The real difference is that in the one case the symbol of sovereignty is manipulated by an undemocratic oligarchy (in Japan the army and navy) and in the other case it is manipulated by an oligarchy under a greater degree of democratic control.

In all cases, whatever the merits and the inevitability of such symbols, the reverence shown the ruler is quite obviously compounded of the same ingredients which determine devotion to the nation. Every man sees himself glorified in his sovereign; but he also sees the symbol of a majesty which transcends his own little life. The fact that such symbols have proved their capacity to outlast the cynicism of a rationalistic age reveals the human heart of any age as a perennial source of natural religion. It was an illusion of a rationalistic age to believe that it could reduce human society to a rational social contract and eliminate all religious overtones from it. This is impossible both because the community is a source of meaning which men are bound to revere and because pride is an inevitable sin which men are bound to betray.

The fact that the sources of natural religion are in the heart of the common man does not justify all the consequences of such religion in social life. It expresses not only a sinful national pride but also prompts dangerous abuses in government. The royal symbol of national unity, even when divorced from power, is never as completely impartial as the common man believes and the government pretends. It need not be consciously dishonest to give the weight of its influence to particular social groups in a nation. It is not only manipulated by the dominant oligarchy of the contemporary period but it is also partly determined by the historic forces out of which it grew. A constitutional monarchy, for instance, favors feudalism on its monarchic side and bourgeois capitalism on its constitutional side. The aura of feudalism is able to maintain itself through the prestige of the monarchy beyond its day, while the dominant capitalistic oligarchs of the contemporary period exploit its prestige in immediate situations.

The obvious dangers of a natural religion which prompts undue reverence for both the particular nation and the particular government and state, persuaded eighteenth-century democrats and modern proletarians to attempt a completely rational political order. But the mere will of rationalists is not powerful enough to destroy a permanent force in social life. Pure rationalism leads to tentativity and finally to cynicism and meaninglessness. In Germany a rationalistic democracy gave way to the demonic fury of a new political movement, explicitly affirming the divinity of nation and ruler. The primitivism of such unqualified affirmations prompt one to a new appreciation of the Christian ages in which the prophetic element in religion at least partially qualified, though it did not sufficiently criticize, the pretensions of nations and rulers.

In America, which began its national enterprise with a completely secular state, a religious reverence for the Constitution and the Supreme Court has gradually emerged which serves some of the same purposes and exhibits the same perils with which the history of sacerdotal states has made us familiar. Even the creation of a classless society in Russia under Marxian rationalism has not been able to overcome this element of natural religion in politics. André Gide's recent booklet on Russia is particularly concerned with the uncritical reverence of the average Russian for the Russian dictator; and in Trotsky's *Betrayal of the Russian Revolution* he charges that this reverence is an instrument of a bureaucracy by which it is establishing a tyranny in defiance of true Marxism. He even includes the charge in his indictment that this bureaucracy is constantly increasing its privileges beyond the necessities and deserts of its social functions. If only half of what Trotsky says is true we are confronted with irrefutable evidence that the Communist hope of the withering away of the state, of an ultimate anarchistic millennium is a delusion. This is not to say that a Communist society does not offer immeasurably higher possibilities of social justice than a capitalistic one.

Old social systems, which have outlived their usefulness, must give way to more adequate social and economic organizations, even though the latter do not guarantee us a millennium. Oligarchies based upon the power of property have become the chief cause of social anarchy in our day. They must give way to a new social system, even though it is romantic to assume that a new society, which socializes property and thus rids society of the primary source of injustice in our day, will be able ultimately to dispense with power completely. Society cannot dispense with power because coercion is a necessary element of social cohesion; nor can it reduce power to naked physical or military force, even if that were desirable, because reverence for the majesty of authority is a natural inclination of the human heart.

The inevitable abuses of power have prompted idealists of every age, particularly Christian idealists, to attempt to construct a powerless type of politics. Such pacifism may take one of two forms. It may disavow the use of physical force but assert the necessity of nonphysical and nonviolent types of power. Or it may aspire to a complete powerlessness and nonresistance. The latter is a form of pure individualistic perfectionism. Since politics is inevitably a contest of power, and justice is always the consequence of some tolerable equilibrium of power, it is clear that consistent nonresistance must be politically irresponsible and ascetic. Nonresistance is, in fact, spiritually dignified only if it understands that individual perfection requires disavowal not only of political responsibilities but of any social responsibilities by which the individual is drawn into the relativities of society. In such a pure ascetic form nonresistance may perform a high function in society by reminding those who do accept responsibilities for the always dubious relativities of political life, of the perils of opportunistic compromise in their strategy.

The more popular contemporary form of pacifism is not the classical religious nonresistance but the espousal of the ideal of nonviolent resistance and coercion. Such a strategy of nonviolence does not withdraw the idealist from the pressures and counter-pressures of social life. It may arm the individual or group with a very effective instrument for gaining a particular social end. But no instrument which is effective in gaining a social end can prevent such an end from being corrupted by selfish ambition. The power-ful man, whether he be priest or soldier, propagandist or property owner, is under the temptation of using his power for selfish rather than social ends. There is therefore no reason to suppose that the substitution of nonphysical for physical, and nonviolent for violent, forms of coercion will make a permanent contribu-tion to the problem of power, though any intelligent society will seek to increase nonviolent forms of social pressure and discourage violence. Pacifism, in short, cannot cut the Gordian knot of the problem of power.

There is in fact no simple moral solution for this problem. An intelligent society will keep its centers of power under the highest possible degree of democratic control. It may even seek to prevent too large or high centers of power from arising. But since a com-munity cannot organize or articulate its life without them, such equalitarianism faces definite limits in actual history.

The real question is how a society is to maintain a permanently critical attitude toward government and how it is to express its sense of an authority which transcends the authority of the nation. There are two possible answers to this question. The one is offered

by rational analysts who would subject the pretensions of governments and of nations to such a searching scrutiny that their
unjustified demands will not be able to maintain themselves.
This method is an actual necessity of social life to a certain degree.
Since power is always dangerous, the power of both nation and
state should be subjected to the analysis of cool critics, who must
qualify the reverence of religious devotees. Cynical realism is a
necessary antidote for the extravagances of religious reverence.
Unfortunately, however, the critical temper can only destroy and
not construct. If consistently applied life would sink into anarchy
and meaninglessness, since natural religion enters into every form
of social cohesion and religious presuppositions are the foundation
of every sense of meaning of life. The natural religion of state
and nation cannot be destroyed, even if it were desirable, because
it is a perennial expression of permanent forces of human spiritu-
ality. Yet the pretensions of such religion will grow to insufferable
proportions if they are not placed under the scrutiny of a higher
religion; of a religion which finds the center of life's meaning
beyond the nation and believes in a Majesty which transcends
all temporal sovereignties.

When the universalism of the Christian religion is corrupted
into subservience to nationalism and the majesty of God is fashioned into a crown for some puny human potentate, the effect
is worse than that which results from the less pretentious claims
of more primitive religions. A genuinely prophetic religion speaks
a word of judgment against every ruler and every nation, even
against good rulers and good nations. It speaks in the name of a
jealous God, who is necessarily jealous because so much in history
which is not God seeks to preempt divine prestige and preroga-
tives. In that sense a prophetic religion must be revolutionary in
every age. Its revolutionary temper will have no political effect
in the heyday of a social system in which its sins have not yet
brought forth death. But it will not be without political effect
in the day of disaster in which history has proved the correctness
of the prophetic judgment that power always destroys itself
ultimately by its injustice.

Such a religion will consequently have a vital relationship to the building of a new society in which a more perfect justice will prevail. But it will naturally have an ambiguous relationship to this new society, and that will never be understood by the secular devotees of the new society. It will insist that a new society stands under the judgment of God as well as an old one; that classes in society which were the instruments of God yesterday may become the enemies of God tomorrow. It will, to borrow a phrase from Marxism and to amend it, insist that the dialectical processes of history do not end with any revolution, either with the immanent revolution or one a thousand years off. It will know that as long as man lives upon the earth the basic character of his sin is to glorify himself and that he can commit this sin most successfully when his glorification of self is related to something which is better than self-glorification. It will therefore be particularly critical of those areas of human life in which man is tempted to worship God and the devil at the same time, to transcend himself and to aggrandize himself. Consequently it must speak in the name of a divine Majesty to every monarch, whether he be called king or commissar; and must bring every national community under judgment. This word of judgment will not eliminate the sins in which natural religion is always involved; but it can mitigate them.

It is naturally not to be expected that any established religion will ever mediate the word of divine judgment unequivocally to its own society. In any established society the prophet is easily transmuted into a priest who insists, as did Amaziah to Amos that "this is the king's chapel and this is the king's court." In actual history the king's chapel and the king's court are so intimately related to each other that the priest who functions in the one is hardly to be distinguished from the courtier who functions in the other. Nevertheless, biblical religion is founded upon the insights of the prophet Amos more than upon the circumspections of the king's chaplain who castigated him. One may therefore confidently hope that the insights of Amos will never be completely denied in the Christian faith. Periodically they may even achieve a new and creative potency in the life of the world.

[1937]

God's Design and the
Present Disorder of Civilization
(1948)

O UR civilization has been engulfed in obvious and widespread political and social confusion since the second decade
of this century. One world war has followed another; and the
second conflagration has left the world in even deeper distress
and less assurance for the future than the first. While Western
civilization has been the center and source of the world's disorders,
the social confusion and political tumult has spread from this
center into the whole world.

The most immediate cause of our distress could be defined as
the inability and unwillingness of modern men and nations to
establish and reestablish community, or to achieve and to reconstruct justice under conditions which a technical civilization has
created. We know, of course, that no human society has ever been
free of corruption, of injustice and domination. As Christians we
are particularly aware of the fragmentary and imperfect character
of all human communities. But there are periods of history in
which conflicting and competing social forces reach a state of
comparative equilibrium and nations arrive at comparative con-
cord. While we cannot, from the standpoint of a Christian interpretation of history, make too sharp a distinction between these
periods of calm and of tumult, it is nevertheless important to
consider the specific causes of the more explicit forms of disorder
from which our generation is suffering and see how they are

related to the general and perennially operative causes of injustice
and confusion in the human community.

The favorite Christian interpretation of our present distress is
to attribute it simply to the secularism of our age. It is an interpretation to which Catholicism is particularly prone but which
many Protestants also make. According to this thesis the world
fell into confusion when modern civilization disavowed faith in
God, an apostasy which had the moral consequence of destroying
the authority of God's law over the recalcitrant and competing
wills and interests of men and of nations. While it is worth noting
that the sanguine hopes of a humanistic age have been cruelly
disappointed in the harsh realities of our own day, we must resist
the temptation to throw the whole responsibility of our present
distress upon "secularism."

The fact is that the "Christian" medieval civilization against
which modern secularism revolted had not so simply achieved
"God's order" as it pretended. It was in fact incapable of making
place for the forces and interests which a commercial civilization
had developed; and its own uncritical identification of the ambiguous moral realities of a feudal society with the will of God
was one of the causes of the secularist revolt. Furthermore, modern
secularism was not primarily involved in the moral nihilism of
denying any law beyond human interests. It was blinded by
another error. It believed that it would be a comparatively simple
matter to define the laws of justice by which human affairs were
to be regulated, and an even simpler matter to achieve an accord
between competing and conflicting human wills and interests.

A truly Christian interpretation of our present distress must be
able to appreciate the necessity, or at least the inevitability, of
revolts against the pretensions of so-called "Christian" civilizations
even while it seeks to correct the illusions which led modern secularism astray. We must beware lest we fall into the sins of the
elder brother in our Lord's parable, gloating over the discomfiture
of the prodigal son who is not yet prepared to return to the house
of his father but who has certainly wasted his substance in that
"far country" in which he hoped to achieve independence.

The interpretation of our present disorder which attributes it primarily to the evils of secularism is usually also involved in the error of assuming that it is possible to define the order of God in detailed and specific laws and rules of justice. But God's order can never be identified with some specific form of social organization. It is very important to arrive at concepts of justice which draw upon the common experience of mankind and set a restraint upon human self-interest. But it must be recognized that insofar as such principles of justice are given specific historical meaning, they also become touched by historical contingency.

There are basic conditions set by God to which human life must conform. But these cannot be identified with any particular social or political organization. For these are all tentative and ambiguous methods of preserving a tolerable harmony of life with life, sin presupposed. Among man's God-given gifts are the unique freedom which enables him to create human communities, wider and more complex than those which natural cohesion prompts. Insofar as man is a limited creature his forms of social organization are determined by natural compulsions. He lives in communities in which the kinship of family and tribe and geographic limitations set the bounds of his society.

Insofar as man is a unique creature who can break the bounds and transcend the limits of nature, forms of communal organization and structures of justice are subject to endless historical elaboration. The natural limits of geography, language, and ethnic affinity always remain as one factor of cohesion in the human community; but they are determinative only in the negative sense. Positively the law of human existence for man as free spirit, who transcends natural limitations, is the law of love. Only in the free giving of life to life and the uncoerced relation of personality to personality can full justice be done both to the unique individuality of every person and the requirements of peace for the whole community. Various schemes of justice must be devised to give the law of love practical effect amidst the complexities of human society and to approximate under the conditions of human sinfulness its ideal harmony of life with life. But all such structures and schemes of justice must be regarded as relative; for they embody egoistic and sinful elements in the very structure intended to set bounds to sin. For the Christian the love which is revealed in the suffering and self-giving life and death of our Lord is the only final and authoritative definition of the "order of God."

Our actual human communities are always shot through with disorder and confusion; for the same freedom which enables man to build wider and more complex communities also gives him the power to make his own will, whether individual or collective, the perverse center of the whole community, whether the whole community be defined in national or international terms. The domination of the weak by the strong and the conflict between various wills, interests, and forces are the inevitable corruptions of human self-seeking in all historic communities, though tremendous differences may and do exist between forms of justice which preserve a tolerable degree of harmony and those which embody domination or conflict.

While there is thus no perfect peace or order in any human community there are times and seasons when a tolerable justice, hallowed by tradition and supplemented by personal discipline and goodness, gives society a long period of social stability. There are other times when the sins of the fathers are visited upon the children; and new social forces rise up as the "vengeance of the Lord" against traditional injustice. We are living in such a time. This is a period of judgment in which the structures and systems of community which once guaranteed a tolerable justice have themselves become the source of confusion and injustice.

We are witnessing, and participating in, the decline of a European civilization, together with a wide confusion in a world community. The immediate occasion for the social and political confusion of our day is the progressive development of technics. Technical advance first created a commercial civilization which could not be contained within the static forms of the agrarian-feudal economy of the medieval period. Subsequently a further development of technics created an industrial civilization which could not achieve or maintain a tolerable justice, within the liberal presuppositions which a commercial civilization had complacently accepted. These same technics increased the possibilities of world community; but the first impetus of a technical society toward world community was an imperialistic one. The European nations, armed with new technical-economic power, used their power to establish their dominion in Africa and Asia; and came in conflict with each other over the spoils of their imperial thrusts.

More recently the African and Asiatic world has risen in rebellion and opposition to this dominion. Their first resentment was against economic and political injustices, resulting from this new expansion of European power. More recently they have felt the pretension of ethnic superiority, which the white races expressed in establishing their power, even more keenly than the economic and political injustices. The missionary enterprise, emanating from the Christian portion of the white world, has been, on the whole, a counterweight to this evil. But this enterprise was seriously embarrassed by the fact that the European world (in which we must include America and the British dominions as well as other nations with a European heritage) was not only the source of the Christian missionary impulse but also the basis of the thrust of imperial dominion.

Thus the development of new technical power created a potential, but not an actual, world community. The new power was exercised too egotistically to establish world-wide community. Some of the imperial powers gradually developed a sense of imperial responsibility which mitigated the exploiting tendencies of imperialism. Nevertheless the total effect of the expansion of technical power has been to give international tensions a world-wide scope and to involve the world in two conflicts of global dimensions.

The introduction of technics into the various national economies also tended to destroy the more organic and traditional forms of community on the national level. Urban life produced atomic individuals who lacked the social disciplines of the older and more organic societies and industrialism substituted dynamic inequalities and injustices in place of the more static inequalities of an agrarian society. The new liberal society which developed with modern commerce and industry did establish many individual rights and liberties which did not exist in the older society. It created democratic political institutions, extended and even universalized popular education, prompted many genuine humanitarian reforms, granted the rights of citizenship to women, and used many new scientific technics for alleviating human misery.

But all these gains could not hide the fact that modern industrial society was unable to establish a tolerable justice or to give a basic security to the vast masses involved in modern industry. Consequently a virtual civil war between the new industrial classes and the more privileged and secure classes of landowners and owners of industrial property destroyed the unity of industrial nations. The healthiest modern nations are those who either (like America) have been sufficiently privileged to be able to avoid a desperate struggle between the industrial and middle classes; or who (like Britain and some of its dominions, as well as some of the smaller nations of northern and western Europe) have been able to mitigate this conflict by religious and moral resources of a special order. Nevertheless the total effect of the rise of modern industry has been the destruction of community on the national level and the extension of conflict on the international level.

To attribute the social confusion of our era to the introduction of technics is, however, to give only the negative cause of our discontent. The more positive cause has been the failure of men and nations either to desire or to achieve a tolerable justice within the new conditions created by expanding technical power. This moral failure cannot be attributed merely to ignorance and sloth. Everywhere there are evidences of the positive thrust of the sinful pride and will-to-power of old oligarchies and new social forces, of old cultures and new ideologies. Every one of the social, cultural and religious forces involved in the readjustments of modern society has contributed to the failure of modern society. We must seek most rigorously to avoid the temptation to interpret our disaster as the consequence, primarily, of the sins of the classes, nations, and forces with which we are not allied.

Amidst the vast social and cultural movements of modern life it is possible to isolate and define three broad forces, each of which must bear a portion of responsibility for our present situation. The first is the old power of the landlord who dominated the agrarian society; the second is the newer commercial and industrial owners; and the third the rising industrial classes. The Catholic faith had historic affinities with the first class, though in some predominantly Protestant nations established or state churches tended to maintain as intimate an embrace with the older agrarian aristocratic classes as did Catholicism. This affinity gave the Catholic Church a certain freedom from the prejudices of the rising commercial-industrial culture which sometimes enabled it to establish contact with, or maintain the allegiance of, the new industrial laborers. This was an achievement which was beyond the moral and religious competence of most Protestant groups. But this affinity also placed Catholicism in frequent alliance with feudal-agrarian conservatism and in opposition to both the liberal-democratic forces and Marxist-labor forces. The political situation in Spain and some South American countries exemplifies this tendency with particular vividness. Sometimes efforts to reconstruct the older authoritarianism under modern conditions betray Catholicism into active alliance with fascism, as in Italy, Spain, and Austria.

Furthermore, Catholic moral and political theory, which makes a "natural law," with fixed and specific content, the norm of political and economic justice, is an inadequate guide for regulating the complex relations of a modern industrial society.

In general, churches, both Catholic and Protestant, are inclined to prefer the social forms of an established order and fail to recognize that new conditions may change an old justice into a new injustice. Thus they are heedless of the divine judgment which challenges every historic social order insofar as it incorporates injustices. Thereby they tend to give religious support to the moral complacency of established and privileged classes.

The new commercial-industrial society was informed partly by secular-liberal and partly by Protestant religious and moral viewpoints. The modern liberal culture assumed that a free expression of all forces and interests in society would automatically make for justice. In its most consistent form modern liberalism believed in a preestablished harmony in society, akin to the harmony of non-historical nature which would guarantee justice if only governmental controls were reduced to minimal terms. This laissez-faire theory did not realize that human freedom expresses itself destructively as well as creatively, and that an increase in human freedom and power through the introduction of technics makes the achievement of justice more, rather than less, difficult than in nontechnical civilizations. The liberal culture of our era believed, either that the egoism of individuals, classes and nations was limited and harmless, or it hoped that the expression of self-interest was due to ignorance which could be overcome by growing social and political intelligence. This optimism misread the facts of human nature, as they are known from the standpoint of the Christian faith and as they are attested by every page of history. It therefore led to pathetic illusions which might have been refuted by contemporary history. Thus the political principles which were to guarantee justice actually contributed to ever greater concentrations of power in modern society and to resulting injustices.

While some Protestant churches capitulated to the moral sentimentalities of this secular creed of progress and became uncritical allies of the commercial and industrial oligarchy in modern society, others failed to preserve a prophetic independence of modern middle-class culture, even where they maintained a more biblical faith. Sometimes (and this was the special temptation of Lutheran churches) they sought to be apolitical because they recognized that all political positions are morally ambiguous. But they failed to recognize that an ostensibly nonpolitical position tends to become political by supporting the established, against the advancing or challenging social classes. Also they did not always see that although it may be impossible or unwise for the church as such to engage in the political struggle, it is the duty of Christians to engage in it. For the political struggle is the means of achieving a tolerably just social order. However morally ambiguous every political position may be, Christians cannot disavow the responsibility of making political choices and decisions.

Sometimes (and this was the particular temptation of Calvinist churches) the new problems of justice in a technical society were approached legalistically. The biblical legalism was frequently irrelevant to the issues raised and tended to support an uncritical individualism against the urgent demand for community in an industrial society.

Both the Catholic and the Protestant forms of the Christian faith were thus involved in the decay of our civilization and were partially responsible for the rise of new secular religions, which promised the establishment of a more integral community and which rose in revolt against both the Christian and the secular forms of the liberal society.

Every form of community in human history only approximates to the obligations of the love commandment; for communities are kept in order partly by power and partly by natural impulses of cohesion, such as a common language, a geographic limit and a common history. But the achievement of a tolerable harmony of life with life is always related to the love commandment. Historic Christianity failed to implement the moral imperatives of the love commandment under the new conditions of a technical age. Thereby it helped to give rise to political religions which sought either cynical or utopian methods of achieving community. Traditional Christianity expressed that side of the Christian truth which appreciates the perennially fragmentary character of all historic achievements and realizes that our final fulfillment is possible only through God's forgiveness. But it neglected the possibility and necessity of achieving community under the new conditions which each age sets and which were particularly challenging under the new conditions of a technical age. The new political religions on the other hand had no sense of the divine judgment and the divine fulfillment which stands against and over all human history. They promised the fulfillment of life either in an idolatrous national community or in an international classless society, conceived in utopian terms.

The two forms of political religion which have aggravated the social confusion of our day, in their very effort to arrest it, are remarkably different in principle. The one is morally cynical and the other morally sentimental and utopian. The one worships force and the other hopes to establish an anarchistic millennium by using revolutionary force to eliminate the need of force in a pure and classless society. The one worships a limited national community. The other hopes for world-wide international community. That they should turn out to be so similar in practice is one of the most instructive aspects of our contemporary situation. It proves that the self-righteous fury of a consistent Marxism may be as dangerous to the establishment of community as the cynicism of a consistent fascism. This similarity in practice, despite differences in principle, can only be understood from the standpoint of a Christian interpretation of life and history; for only from that standpoint is it possible to see how quickly human virtue turns to evil when men forget the sinful corruption in every expression of human interest.

It is nevertheless important to emphasize the differences in principle between the two. Fascism was immediately responsible for plunging the world into the second world war. Its consistent moral cynicism destroyed all moral restraints and disciplines of a Christian and a humanistic culture. It developed forms of cruelty and inhumanity which plumbed hitherto unimagined depths of evil and sowed seeds of vindictiveness from which European civilization still suffers. Marxism, on the other hand, when stripped of its religious illusions and of its false promises of redemption may well contain proximate solutions for the immediate problems of social justice in our day. It is wrong to regard the socialization of property as a cure-all for every social ill; but it is no more wrong than to regard such socialization as of itself evil.

There is even now no possibility of bringing social stability and a measure of justice to an impoverished world if this conflict between Christianity and Marxism is not resolved. In the whole of Europe there are forms of socialism which dread and abhor the totalitarian consequences of a consistent Communism. They do not always recognize that this totalitarianism may be, not so much a corruption of the original Marxism, as the inevitable consequence of consistent Marxist principles.

The socialism in the Western world, which abhors the totalitarianism of Communism, has difficulty in achieving a pragmatic attitude toward the problem of property because remnants of a utopian religion still infect its thought. But a conservative Christian culture bears a large measure of responsibility for this confusion. It also has not freed itself from a too-dogmatic negative attitude toward socialization. It is significant that the healthiest Western nations are those in which this conflict was mitigated by various cultural and religious influences. In these nations the impulse to achieve justice through socialization was partly generated by the Christian faith and was therefore not in opposition to the whole Christian heritage. In some of the smaller continental nations, particularly in Scandinavia, the socialist impulse stands in competitive, but not uncreative, relation to the more traditional Christian culture. In Britain Marxism was always qualified by Christian perspectives. Therefore a pragmatic form of socialism gained political victory without any obvious rent in the national community or in the texture of an historic Christian culture. In America, on the other hand, the technical achievements and the natural wealth of the nation have prevented the socialist impulse from achieving any success. This fact prevents sharp social conflicts but it also places the nation in the grave peril of a too-uncritical devotion to the principles of classical liberalism. Therefore it may deal too tardily with the problem of adequate moral and political control over the dynamics of a technical society.

The problem of how to maintain freedom under the intense and complex forms of social cohesion in modern technical society and how to achieve justice when freedom is maintained cannot be solved by any neat principles. It must be approached pragmatically from case to case and point to point. We know that it is possible to buy security at too great a price of freedom; and to maintain freedom at too great a price of insecurity for the masses involved in the modern industrial society. The Christian faith as such has no solution for this problem. It ought, however, to be possible for a vital Christian faith to help people to see that both freedom and order are facets of the love commandment to which we must approximate; and also that such approximations under conditions of sin and law are bound to be imperfect in all human history. The conflict between order and freedom is perfectly resolved only in the kingdom of perfect love which cannot be completely realized in history.

The possibility of avoiding another international conflict depends to a large degree upon the measure of health which can be achieved in that part of the world which is not under the dominion of the Communist totalitarianism. Such health in turn requires a new and more creative relationship between the Christian faith and the problems of justice and community in national life. But the peril of international anarchy is broader than the dangers thus far discussed. The internal confusion within the life of nations has aggravated, but is not solely responsible for, the new situation which we face in the community of nations. Even without the particular forms of social chaos in European culture previously analyzed, we would have faced the difficult problem of organizing the global community, which modern technical civilization had created by the new interdependence of modern means of transport and communication. Contrary to the assumption of our secular culture that this new interdependence would automatically create a new international accord, the increased intimacy of nations actually accentuated the evils of both imperial dominion and international conflict. Modern technics have, in short, created a potential, but not an actual, world community. Nor have the hopes of our secular culture been realized, that the fear of mutual annihilation would persuade nations to adjust their institutions and loyalties to the wider ends and responsibilities which this worldwide interdependence requires. Furthermore, the hope, expressed by many secular utopians, that the peril in which we stand would persuade nations to create a world government out of whole cloth, has also proved false. We have seen how the fear of mutual annihilation through atomic destruction is easily transmuted into the fear that the foe may annihilate us.

On every side we see in the life of nations that it is more difficult for man, particularly for collective man, to do the things he ought to do than modern secularism had imagined. All human actions betray the fact that though "we delight in the law of God after the inward man, there is a law in our members which wars against the law that is in our mind." We see, furthermore, that even the most terrible judgments do not quickly shake men and nations from the paths of self-seeking or from vindictive passions, which aggravate the evils caused by war. The words of the prophet Jeremiah apply to our generation: "Thou hast stricken them but they have not grieved; thou hast consumed them but they have not received correction" (Jer. v: 3). The general tendency of men and nations is either to minimize the depth and breadth of the crisis in which they stand or to be driven into hysteria by it. As St. Paul observes: "For they that sleep, sleep in the night, and they that be drunken are drunken in the night" (I Thess. v: 7).

In this situation the first task of the Christian church is to interpret our sorrows and distresses, the agonies and pains through which the world is passing, and to recognize the hand of God in them. We must, as Christians, neither fall into complacency by evading the gravity of our experience, nor into despair and hysteria by interpreting the distress of our day as merely confusion without meaning. There is a divine judgment upon our sins in this travail of the nations and in this fall of nations and empires, in this shaking of historic stabilities and traditions. If this divine judgment is perceived it can transmute the despair (the sorrow of this world which leads to death) into the "godly sorrow which worketh repentance" (2 Cor. vii: 10).

The prophets of Israel saw no possibility that the entire nation would thus interpret the vicissitudes of history. They hoped that the renewal of life would be possible through a "saving remnant" which would understand them from the standpoint of faith. St. Paul rightly insisted that the Church had become the "Israel of

God," the saving remnant, with this function in society. But the Church, too, must not presume that it has this redemptive relation to society unless it fulfills the conditions of contrite faith. The measure of our creative relation to the perplexities of our time depends upon the knowledge of our own involvement in the guilt of the nations. It is not our business to defend a "Christian" civilization which was never Christian in ethical achievement, or to justify ourselves against the mistakes of secularists and utopians. We must, of course, bear witness against the illusions of a secular culture which have developed from the rejection of the Gospel of Christ. But we must also know that "judgment" begins "at the house of God," and that the judgment of God is upon all the institutions and traditions of religion as well as upon the political and economic arrangements of the nations.

While we must inevitably make careful and considerate judgments upon men, nations, and institutions according to the relative degree of justice and community which they embody, we cannot afford to make such judgments final. Neither the Christian church nor a Christian civilization is called upon to judge the world, but to mediate divine judgment and grace upon all men and nations and upon itself. However terrible the evils which the Nazi rebels against civilization achieved, our resentment against these evils must not obscure the common sin and guilt of all nations, out of which this specific evil emerged. This insight of biblical faith must persuade the church to bear testimony against the vindictiveness of nations toward their vanquished foes. They foolishly imagine that their victory is the proof of their righteousness and therefore vainly imagine that the destruction of an evil foe will eliminate evil from human society. Thus, heedless of the truth our Lord taught in the parable of the unmerciful servant, they accentuate evil in trying to overcome it.

This Gospel warning against self-righteous vindictiveness is as relevant to our relations with possible competitors of today as with the fallen foe of yesterday. A democratic civilization will take the wisest possible steps to prevent the new spread of totalitarian creeds; and if it is truly wise it will know that economic and political health is a better barrier to the spread of totalitarianism than purely strategic measures.

The Christian faith is, of course, unable to promise, as do secular creeds, some final historical redemption from all social evil. The revelation of God's judgment and mercy in Christ negated both the pre-Christian and the post-Christian expectations of an early paradise; and has taught us to look "for a city which hath foundations; whose builder and maker is God" (Hebrews xi: 10). The kingdom of God always impinges upon history and reminds us of the indeterminate possibilities of a more perfect brotherhood in every historic community. But the sufferings of Christ also remain a permanent judgment upon the continued fragmentary and corrupted character of all our historic achievements. They are completed only as the divine mercy, mediated in Christ, purges and completes them. Our final hope is in "the forgiveness of sins, the resurrection of the body, and life everlasting."

Applied to our present situation this means that we must on the one hand strive to reform and reconstruct our historic communities so that they will achieve a tolerable peace and justice. On the other hand we know, as Christians, that sinful corruptions will be found in even the highest human achievements.

We ought as Christians to strive more, and not less, earnestly for the peace of nations. We ought not to be indifferent to the problem of what technical-political instruments are best suited to maintain a tolerable peace and to express man's obligation to his neighbor. On the other hand, our faith ought to supply us with a resource which secular idealism lacks. We must learn to do our duty in the peace of our security in God, which is not disturbed by the alternate furies of unjustified hopes and unjustified despair. Knowing that "neither life nor death . . . can separate us from the love of God which is in Christ Jesus our Lord" we will not be surprised to discover that all historic security is imperfect.

There is a tendency among Christians, as well as non-Christians, to retire to the security of law, and to forget that even the best laws may become the servant of interest and sin, and that even the most hallowed institutions must be submitted to the test of whether they achieve the best possible accord between a man and his neighbor under prevailing conditions. The rapidly changing conditions of a technical society require that our sense of obedience to law shall be expressed primarily in terms of our obedience to the law of love. We have been tempted to forget not only St. Paul's warning against the impotence of law (Romans ii: 17-23) but also our Lord's warning that our righteousness must exceed the righteousness of the law. Unless divine grace flow into the heart, men will not only fail to obey the law but will use it as an instrument for their own advantage. Christian legalism has helped to sow confusion into the chaos of our day. The cure for modern lawlessness is not more emphasis upon law or efforts to define specific laws more sharply. The cure of modern lawlessness is to bring the idolatry and self-worship of all men and nations under divine judgment and to free men from both law and sin so that all things may be theirs if they are Christ's. In that spirit they can create not an anarchistic millennium but communities, and constantly renew and refresh them by the spirit of love.

Whether the nations and empires, the cultures and institutions of our day will bring forth fruits meet for repentance and thereby escape the wrath which overhangs them we do not know. Our business must be to mediate the divine judgment and mercy through word and sacrament so that men may know God as the author of both their death and their new life, of both the judgments under which they suffer and the new health which they may find as men and nations by his grace.

[1948]

Christian Faith and Social Action

(1953)

THE Frontier Fellowship was originally concerned to establish a viable Christian social ethic. It conceived its task to require refutation of four alternative positions. These positions were: first, the standpoint of Protestant pietistic individualism, according to which there is no obligation or necessity to change the social and political structures in the interest of a higher justice. It was regarded as unnecessary partly because these structures were interpreted as eternal "laws of nature" which make for justice, and partly because right individual conduct is supposed to be more important than any social structure. This position was judged the most indefensible of all allegedly Christian positions because it combined a naturalistic version of human society with a highly individualistic version of the Christian faith. It was, nevertheless, the dominant attitude of American Protestantism until the social gospel rescued the church from its influence. It has achieved a new relevance in this latter day, when war and post-war armament expenditures have been able to obscure the inherent problems of a free economy and have thus encouraged the American business community to a new complacency. Yet it does not hold this position with a completely good conscience, and it seeks whatever support, religious and otherwise, it can find for it.

The second position which the Fellowship challenged was a vague Christian or secular moralism, which was uneasy about the

social realities of an industrial society but assumed that any injustices could be cured by persuading the society to govern its
relations by the "ideals of love." This position was really the
moralistic wing of the social gospel and was not very distinct from
secular moralism. Frequently it expressed itself in terms of pacifistic
socialism. It hoped to achieve collectivism without the class struggle or without any serious dislocations and conflicts. It was against
this position that the Fellowship emphasized the Christian doctrine of original sin. In terms of social theory, this implied the
inevitability of tensions of interest and conflict in human affairs.
The idea of the progressive perfectibility of man was rejected as a
secular corruption of the Christian faith and in manifest conflict
with the realities of history.

The third Christian position to which the Fellowship felt itself
in conflict was that of historic Catholicism's idea of a "Christian
civilization" and of "Christian politics." According to this position,
the Christian Church made the pretension that it was not merely
one among other political forces in the world, but a redemptive
overarching force. The Fellowship felt that such a pretension was
theologically and religiously unsound, for it created an idolatrous
force in the name of Christianity. We also believed that its political unsoundness was proved by the realities of Latin politics,
whether in Italy or Argentina.

A fourth position deserves special consideration, for thereby
hangs our tale. It was the position which the Fellowship espoused
and from which it gradually retreated, though the degree of the
retreat is still a matter of debate. It is, broadly speaking, the
socialist alternative in politics. In an original statement of principles the Fellowship declared that it was "committed to the belief
that the social ownership of the natural resources and the basic
means of production is a primary requisite of justice in a technical
age." It justified this conviction by the fairly orthodox Marxist
analysis that "capitalism in its inevitable contracting phase subordinates the needs of the masses to the preservation and enhance-
ment of a steadily narrowing class of owners." Those words were
written twenty years ago and give a fairly accurate picture of the

convictions of the socially sensitive part of the Christian Church of the early days of the New Deal.

It must be added immediately that the Fellowship did not espouse Marxism or even socialism without reservation. It called itself a Fellowship of Socialist Christians to emphasize by its use of adjective and noun the primacy of its Christian, rather than socialist, convictions. And it insisted that it objected to socialist philosophies on "empirical grounds as well as on Christian grounds because of the danger of collectivism, mutilating organic forms of social life by coercing them into mechanical moulds." It also repudiated the optimism of the Marxist belief "that a new mechanism of ownership will eliminate all conflict in the world and solve all the problems of the human spirit." In short, it rejected Marxism as a guaranteed solution of the socio-ethical problem and objected even more to the religious pretensions of Marxism. These reservations could be regarded as fairly shrewd anticipations of what history actually proved to be the monstrous errors of Marxism. Yet the anticipations were not too profound, and the Christian understanding of the relativity of all socio-political systems not too discerning. The depth and degree of corruption which Communism would create on the basis of orthodox Marxism was not fully anticipated, though the Fellowship followed this disillusioning development with clear eyes and challenged the poor deluded Christian Stalinists who confused the conscience of the church with their loyalty to the tortuous processes of Stalinist politics, step by step.

More significantly, however, the weaknesses of parliamentary or democratic socialism were not fully understood. It was not realized that even a democratic socialism might face problems of preserving incentives in a completely collectivist economy and would betray the perils of the concentration of economic and political power in the hands of a bureaucracy even when held in a democratic framework.

In a revision of its Statement, issued in 1946, the Fellowship declared: "Our understanding of socialism has undergone progressive modification due to a deepening of our theological convictions, a gradual assimilation of European experience through our émigré members, a close observation of the Soviet development, and our experience with the American communist party." While still believing that "most strategic centers of economic power must be socialized," it nevertheless expressed fear of too great concentration of power "through state intervention" and therefore asked for the creation of autonomous public agencies such as the TVA. "We are deeply aware," the statement continues, "that economic collectivism may be achieved at the price of losing democracy in the social and political sphere." Here we have the consequence of our tragic contemporary history upon the Christian conscience, as indeed upon the conscience of the modern world. What seemed to be a fairly clear alternative to the injustices of a free economy has turned out to be not only worse than the disease for which it was meant to be the cure; but a disease of such virulent proportions as to threaten our whole world with disaster.

Thus the fact that socialism could not be unequivocally espoused, which the Fellowship hinted at even in its earliest years, became a certainty in the present situation. This certainty has not only called any intimate relation between Christianity and socialism into question. It has also made the whole question of a Christian social ethics more problematic. We cannot doubt that Christians must make their decisions about political and economic alternatives with a sense of responsibility to the divine will as revealed in Christ. But the question is whether there are any criteria whereby we can judge between alternative movements. The love which is the final criteria is obviously a principle of criticism applicable to all political and economic realities, since it reveals the sinful element of self-seeking and of coercive restraint in all forms of human community. But does it help us to arrive at discriminate choices between alternative systems when all of them have morally ambiguous elements in them? In the field of economic life, self-seeking, about which one must have an ultimate scruple, must be immediately used and harnessed for proximate purposes. In the field of politics, power which may be provisionally useful in establishing tolerable harmonies of life may become, if unrestrained, the instrument of tyranny and oppression.

Since there is moral ambiguity in every possible political and economic position (derived from the fact that self-interest and power must be used and manipulated despite the perils to justice and to order which they may bear within themselves under certain conditions) it would seem that the first duty of Christian faith is to preserve a certain distance between the sanctities of faith and the ambiguities of politics. This is to say that it is the duty of a Christian in politics to have no specific "Christian politics." The Christian politics based upon concepts of justice derived from an eternal natural law have been a source of error because relative historical judgments, prompted by interest and passion, have been insinuated into the sanctity of eternal law.

The Christian politics of Protestant individualism is even more unsatisfactory because it has regarded the competitive struggle in a modern bourgeois-capitalistic society as a simple instrument of justice and obscured the disproportions of power and resulting injustices in the system. The Christian politics of a moralistic socialism, on the other hand, hid the power-realities of a collectivist state behind the concept of "cooperation" interpreted as Christian love. In every case religious sanctities confused rather than clarified the picture. Sometimes they are the screen for particular interests, as, for instance, when a feudal nobility or a modern business oligarchy appeals to the eternal standards of natural law or natural rights to justify its power and privilege. Sometimes they are meant to hide the tension between the purity of the ultimate and the complexity of the immediate situation, as, for instance, when a coercive political arrangement is pictured as an embodiment of the principle of love.

But this exclusion of the religious element from pragmatic decisions is only a negative determinant of a Christian approach to the economic and political order. How shall we find a positive answer?

The basic presupposition of a positive answer must lie in a Christian understanding of the realities of man's social life. It is wrong to interpret these realities in purely cynical terms or in purely idealistic ones. It is important to recognize an admixture of self-seeking in every form of human togetherness and also in every strategy of government required to prevent competitive self-seeking from degenerating into anarchy. We cannot (as does classical liberalism) regard the self-seeking which a bourgeois-liberal economy permits as completely harmless; and we cannot, as does orthodox Protestantism, particularly Lutheranism, be uncritical toward the coercive power of government on the ground that God ordained it to prevent anarchy. For both the economic power which competes in the market place and the political power which sets restraints upon the competition are tainted by motives other than the desire for justice. On the other hand, it would be wrong to be too cynical about this admixture of self-interest in all the vital forces of society. Men do have a residual capacity for justice. Government does express the desire of a community for order and justice; and not merely the will-to-power of the oligarchy which controls the engines of power in government. An attitude which avoids both sentimentality and cynicism must obviously be grounded in a Christian view of human nature which is schooled by the Gospel not to take the pretensions of men at their face value, on the one hand, and, on the other, not to deny the residual capacity for justice among even sinful men.

If this be the general attitude of circumspection it follows that no political decision can be reached in terms of merely broad principles, whether of "freedom" or "justice" or "planning." The evils which have developed from Communist pretensions are a reminder and proof of the fact that the worst evils of history are derived not from pure selfishness but from self-interest clothed in the pretensions of ideals. Western society has been in virtual civil war between the middle-class proponents of free economy and the proletarian proponents of a collectivist one. Each creed obviously contains a mixture of truth and error. Property is not as simply the servant of justice as the liberal creed assumes and not as simply the basis of all evil as the Marxist creed avers. The power of the state is not as dangerous as the liberal creed imagines and not as beneficent as collectivist theory assumes. The damage to society is being done by general programs, serving as weapons of warring groups and classes.

It is important to understand this baneful effect of general and abstract programs upon the social life of man. Two reasons may be given why evil flows from these too inclusive and abstract programs: (1) These generalizations fail to take the endless contingencies of history into account; (2) General programs and panaceas are stubbornly held and not easily amended by empirical data.

General programs tend to be a screen for particular interests in society and as their weapons in social controversy. Thus medieval conceptions of natural law were used by the aristocratic classes to put the rising middle class at a moral disadvantage; and modern "natural rights" concepts were used with similar purpose by the bourgeois classes to prove that a system of "natural liberty," which would be to their advantage, was in accord with the "laws of nature" and of "nature's God"; and the modern industrial classes are generally inclined to view processes, defined as "historical dialectic," as giving a kind of cosmic support to their particular struggle in society.

Panaceas do not, however, merely hide special economic or social interests. They may have another purpose which is of particular concern for students of morals and religion. They tend to obscure the tension between individual and social morality. This tension is a serious problem for all religiously sensitive individuals. The social order is involved in collective forms of egotism, in injustices, in conflicts of self-interest, and in subordinations of life to life which are an affront to the sensitive conscience. There is, therefore, a strong tendency to develop "ideologies of conscience" as well as ideologies of interest. The middle classes eased their conscience by the conviction that the "natural system of liberty" would make for justice in the long run even if in the short run it manifested obvious injustices. When this failed to materialize it was a natural inclination of the religious conscience to invest a collectivist alternative with more moral capital that it did not deserve. This was done primarily by contrasting the "motives of service" which were supposed to rule the collectivist order as against the "motives of profit" in the old order.

A certain taint of this moral ideology is evident in the earlier

pronouncements of our Fellowship, and indeed in all pronouncements of the Christian left. The ideology obscured the fact that
no form of social organization could eliminate the "profit motive"
insofar as it stood for particular interest as opposed to "general"
or universal interest. What was defined as the profit motive was,
as a matter of fact, not purely individual interest but usually concern for the family. Not only were particular interests likely to
include concern for the family rather than the self but they were
also not purely economic since they might express desire for
prestige and power rather than gain. Furthermore, the "general"
interest is not simply universal. It is most generally national. Certainly the Marxist doctrine that the socialization of property would
destroy national self-interest has been refuted not only by Russian nationalistic imperialism but by the display of national self-
interest in the mildest social European states. Thus it is obvious
that this moralistic ideology of the Christian as well as the secular
left tended to obscure moral perplexities in man's social life which
are perennial and not merely the fruit of capitalism or any other
form of social organization.

The rational, moral, and religious defects of general political
and social and economic programs, does not justify the conclusion
that no moral choice between general programs is possible and
that only pragmatic approaches to detailed problems of justice
are legitimate. General decisions must be made at particular points
in history. It was, for instance, morally right as well as historically
inevitable that the rising middle classes should have challenged
the organic cohesions and the traditional authorities of monarchial
absolutism in the early part of the modern period. The bourgeois
movement destroyed the monopoly of political power by espousing democracy against monarchism. And it released vast new
energies by supporting a system of "natural liberty" against mer-
cantilism and other forms of political restraint upon economic life.
It is just as right and inevitable that the sensitive conscience
should now support programs for bringing economic power under
state control and for insisting upon certain minimal welfare

standards in housing, social security, education. The fact that it has been necessary to shift from the emphasis upon liberty to the emphasis upon mutual responsibility and political restraint upon economic power, proves the historical relativity of all socio-moral choices. The "sweetest things turn sourest by their deeds" and the virtues of one era become the vices of the next. The shift in emphasis was necessary because justice did not flow as inevitably from liberty as the earlier bourgeois creed assumed. It did not do so because modern industrial society develops more serious disproportions of power in the economic sphere than had been anticipated; and these disproportions of power are more destructive of justice than had been assumed by a creed which understood the relation of power to interest and justice so little. But by the same token the creed by which this shift in emphasis was accomplished must also be re-examined in the light of historical experience.

Nothing is more important and tragic in contemporary history than that the Marxist alternative to capitalistic injustice should have generated so much more terrible evils than capitalism itself. But these Communist evils are only vivid revelations of a general defect in collectivist theories. If the libertarian creed failed to anticipate the disproportions of power in modern economic society, the collectivist creeds failed to anticipate the moral perils in a system which compounded political and economic power in a single oligarchy. It also failed to provide for sufficient local and immediate centers of initiative in both the economic and political life of the community.

Thus it is clear that significant decisions between competing systems and political philosophies must be made; but also that they must be constantly reviewed empirically and amended in the light of new evidence. Some of the resources for these procedures have nothing to do with our Christian faith, at least not directly. They are the resources of an inductive rather than a deductive social science. Such a science will not speak vaguely about general concepts such as property or planning. It will ask what the institution of property is in an agrarian as against an industrial situation. It will recognize that a peasant's relation to the soil is of a different order than the relation of either an owner or a worker to a factory. It will study the effects of socialization of property and will probably conclude that there were important economic as well as social reasons for Britain's socialization of coal which do not necessarily justify the plan for socializing steel. It will recognize the necessity of guaranteeing human wants as, for instance, in housing and medical services. But it will not assume that human desires are naturally ordinate and that they can be satisfied by government agencies without the necessity of some restraint upon inordinate, or at least disproportionate, demands. It will not assume that all government interference in economic process is either good or bad; but it will study the effect of each type of interference.

In Professor Tillich's brilliant chapter, in which he analyzes the conflicts between human personality and the realities of a technical civilization, we have evidence of another ironic historic transmutation of good into evil which must be pragmatically analyzed. For technics originally came as an emancipating force, creating flexible and mobile forms of property, and individual forms of skill by which men were freed of the dead weight of a traditional society as well as from the slavery of poverty.

Yet gradually the elaboration of technics has created a mass society in which men are held together mechanically, and in which their tastes are standardized and vulgarized by mass means of communication. There could be no better symbol than that of the meat of one generation turning into the poison of the next. We need not elaborate upon the spiritual strategies required to counteract the deleterious effects of a technical society, particularly not since that is done so ably by Professor Tillich. It is worth observing, however, as he himself points out, that some of the spiritual animus directed against an allegedly capitalist society by modern reformers was really more applicable to the growing dangers of technics as such. The elimination of the property system, which was intended to cure the evils, actually accentuated them in modern totalitarian regimes. Nothing could be more ironic than the contrast between Marx's early visions of creative personality in an ideal society and the sorry realities of a totalitarian community.

But the problems of social ethics are not solved merely by an empirical and pragmatic approach to the complex issues. Or perhaps it would be more accurate to say that something more than wrong traditions of science prevent men from applying their intelligence empirically to the problems of their common life. The real fact is that a religious problem underlies this persistence with which general ideals, laws, and systems are used either as weapons of special interest or as efforts to hide the hiatus between the demands of a sensitive conscience and the morally ambiguous realities of man's social life. There can, therefore, be no genuine empiricism without a religious correction of this tendency.

The relevance of a genuine and vital Christian faith is that it unmasks the errors of a false and abstract idealism by two forces, one negative and one positive. The negative force is the contrite recognition in the Christian faith, as expounded in the New Testament, that the law is not redemptive but may be the servant of sin. This recognition belongs to the radical Christian understanding of the persistence of sin in the life of man. It is able, as Kant recognized in a rare moment of evangelical insight, to corrupt the standards themselves. The laws and ideals which we regard as guarantors of justice and bearers of our goodness can be persistently used as instruments of the ego. The knowledge of this fact is withheld from all secular idealism, and this ignorance is responsible for the fact that an age which prides itself on its humanity becomes so inhumane, and not merely among the exponents of a totalitarian creed. It is also withheld from Christian idealists. Its absence is always proved by the complacency with which Christian businessmen or labor leaders or any other group in society hold to and propound their ideals without fear and trembling, that is, without a contrite recognition of the ambiguity of all human laws and ideals.

It must be observed that democracy at its best rests upon a

recognition of this truth because it provides that no laws, ideals, structures, and systems should exist without the criticism which may disclose their ambiguous character and thereby prevent the evil in them from destroying the good. Without this contrite recognition of the double character of all human ideals even a democracy can degenerate into a tyranny of the majority. The weakness of what is now generally defined as "liberal Christianity" is that it does not rigorously subject the admixture of interest in ideals to religious criticism on the one hand, and does not, on the other, detect the moralistic effort of men to close the gap between individual sensitivity and social ambiguity on the other. That is why one type of liberal can lend himself to a religious support of the *status quo*, while another type can be uncritical toward Communism under the illusion that it establishes a community based upon the "service motive."

We must consider this "ideology of conscience" rather than of interest more carefully. If one form of ideology is meant to hide the force of self-interest in human life, the other form is meant to obscure the deep tension between the individual conscience and the moral realities of man's collective life with their bewildering confusion of coercion, conflict of self-interest, domination, and subordination. The one is meant to hide particular sins of particular groups. The other is meant to hide the moral precariousness of all human striving. For the collective life of man is a reminder to individual man of the moral ambiguity in all human virtue.

This second form of ideology is the most fruitful source of confusion in the relation of the Christian faith to the political order. Thus Augustine sees the realities of the political order very clearly and describes them accurately in defining the character of *civitas terrena*. But he wrongly assumes that the force of a self-love does not exist in the *civitas Dei*. The Church is for him a *societas perfecta*. Luther describes them with equal realism in his doctrine of the two realms; but he underestimates the residual capacity for justice among ordinary men, and the involvement of Christians in evil. Liberal Christianity thinks that collective self-seeking can be easily overcome by the spirit of love; and Calvinism falsely imagines that the "Rule of the Saints" can banish evil from the political order. This is another version of the Catholic error which imagines that the Church is a *societas perfecta* which can simply redeem the social order by claiming ultimate sovereignty over it.

It is instructive to note how the ideology which seeks to hide the moral ambiguity of the social order is almost as fruitful of evil as the ideology which hides the admixture of interest in particular ideals. Both forms of ideology are guilty of being so busy establishing human righteousness that no one submits human actions to the righteousness of God (Romans 10:2). The real problem of a Christian social ethic is to derive from the Gospel a clear view of the realities with which we must deal in our common or social life, and also to preserve a sense of responsibility for achieving the highest measure of order, freedom and justice despite the hazards of man's collective life.

If the Christian humility which has no illusions about our ideals and structures or about any of the realities of the community is the negative precondition of a Christian social ethic, the positive form of it is the application of the law of love to man's collective relations. The problem of the application of the law of love to the collective relationships of mankind contains within itself the whole question of the possibility of a Christian social ethic. When Catholic thought embodies the law of love into counsels of perfection and relegates these to the realm of ultimate possibilities of the "supernatural" life in the individual, and when it seeks to regulate the collective relations of mankind by the standards of "justice" which are given in the natural law, it is seeking to come to terms with the realities of the social order which seem to make the law of love inapplicable. This is also behind the logic of the thought of Protestant theologians who, following Luther, relegate love and forgiveness to the heavenly kingdom, as distinguished from the "earthly" one, where "the sword and the law" that is power and coercion prevail.

On the other hand, we have long since learned to recognize the sentimentality of Christian liberalism and other forms of liberalism which regard the establishment of "motives of service" in contrast to the "profit motive" as a simple possibility. The question is therefore how, if love is not a simple possibility, it may yet be relevant to our political decisions. This question really involves the relevance of our final Christian insights as individuals to our actions as members of a group. It is as individuals that we know about love as the final law of life, although in our political actions we act as members of the group. As individuals we know the law of love to be final, if we view life through the revelation of Christ. From the standpoint of that illumination we can see the self-destructive character of every form of self-seeking and the redemptive possibility of minding not our own things but those of another (I Corinthians 10:24). It is thus possible to condemn and to guard against national egotism and other forms of collective pride even though we know that they cannot be eradicated. It is equally possible to guard against the corruption of individual self-interest in establishing social institutions even though one does not expect it to be eliminated. The law of love is thus not something extra to be added to whatever morality we establish in our social relations. It is their guiding principle.

Thus, when the issue is raised whether one's own nation should adhere to an alliance of nations, one may well know that it is not possible for any nation to do this if it means sacrificing its own interest to the interests of the whole. In that sense the law of love is remote, if not irrelevant. But one also knows that it is wrong for a nation to prefer its own welfare to the welfare of a larger community. Therefore every form of political activity which exalts a class, nation, or group absolutely stands under condemnation. This is, of course, a fairly simple application of the law of love. It is more difficult when, as is usually the case, the conflict is between two groups, the family and the nation, or between two families or two nations or two classes.

The simplest application of the law of love is to ask the question: Are we doing this for ourselves? But this simple question does not always suffice, for it invariably gives the advantage to the other group, which may not deserve it. We cannot, for instance, solve the problem of our conflict with Communism by yielding to it as "the other," putting our civilization at a disadvantage because it is our own. We have to ask what universal values are embodied in our several collective efforts and then use the question to check the undue advantage which we give our own cause. We must try to do justice both to the general values which our cause embodies beyond our own interest and to our tendency to value these too highly because our cause embodies them. In very specific terms it would require that in the social struggle the business community should learn from the Gospel a certain uneasiness about its uncritical devotion to freedom, and that the industrial workers should learn to be less confident of the consequence of a policy of planning. It would not mean judging issues in terms of general principles but learning to understand the limit and ambiguity of every general principle and the taint of self-interest in every devotion to general principle. It would mean, in short, that insights into the mixture of motives in the espousal of ideals which can only be learned, as it were, in the final wrestling of the soul with God, should be incorporated into institutions which can know nothing of such wrestling.

In that sense the Christian faith must be a "leaven" which leavens the lump. It must derive, as the prophets did, insights for collective action which are drawn only from individual religious experience. They are applicable because the collective life of mankind conforms to the ultimate laws of God, as surely as does individual life. But they are not ascertained by the collective conscience, if indeed there is such an entity. They are mediated by the individual conscience to the collectivity.

In one sense, the applicability of the law of love to the complex problem of social ethics could be defined as the question how the heedlessness of perfect love can be related to the discriminate judgments which are required to weigh competing values and interests in the field of social relations. Perfect love is sacrificial love, making no careful calculations between the interests of the self and the other. Perfect justice is discriminate and calculating, carefully measuring the limits of interests and the relation between the interests of the self and the other. The spirit of justice is particularly well served if reason finds the points of coincidence between the interests of the self and those of the other and, if not, if it makes careful and discriminate judgments between them. What can this heedlessness of *agape* have to do with discrimination? It would have nothing at all to do with it, if there were such a thing as pure reason which could arbitrate between interests, and if there were recurring patterns of life so analogous as to reveal structures of justice which reason could discern.

Actually, the human situation lacks both of these elements upon which rationalistic ethical judgments depend so much. The reason with which we reason about each other's affairs and interests is not "pure" reason and it cannot be made "objective and impartial" by any rational discipline or scientific method. The self, whether individual or collective, is too deeply involved in its processes. Furthermore, the historic encounters between individuals and groups in which rights and interests must be adjudicated and arbitrated always contain so many novel and contingent elements that it is not wise to trust general rules and principles too much. There is, in short, no guarantee of justice in man's reason. There is a possibility of justice only in the self, provided it is not too sure of itself. The heedlessness of love, which sacrifices the interests of the self, enters into the calculations of justice by becoming the spirit of contrition which issues from the self's encounter with God. In that encounter it is made aware of the contingent character of all human claims and the tainted character of all human pretensions and ideals.

This contrition is the socially relevant counterpart of love. It breaks the pride of the implacable contestants and competitors in all human encounters and persuades them to be "kindly affectioned one with another, forgiving one another, even also as God in Christ has forgiven you" (Ephesians 4:32). This spirit lies at the foundation of what we define as democracy. For democracy cannot exist if there is no recognition of the fragmentary character of all systems of thought and value which are allowed to exist together within the democratic frame. Thus the *agape* of forgiveness as well as the *agape* of sacrificial love become a leaven in the lump of the spirit of justice. Or rather it would be better to use the other Gospel symbol and define them as the "salt" which arrests the decay in the spirit of justice.

The relevance of these forms of love, which transcend justice, to the spirit of justice will become apparent whenever communal life is analyzed—not as Aristotle and stoic rationalists analyzed it, as an order of vitalities which is prevented from falling into chaos by its conformity to particular structures which reason must ascertain—but rather as a vast series of encounters between human selves and their interests. The encounters are indeed regularized into patterns and stabilities, and the habit of conformity to these stabilities mitigate the encounters. But these social patterns are not "eternal laws" and they cannot hide the essential character of social life as an encounter between myself and another, whether individually or collectively. Whether the encounter is creative or destructive, cooperative or competitive, depends not so much upon the rule of justice which is finally found to compose an incipient conflict but upon the humility with which the pretensions of the self, particularly the collective self, are laid bare and the contrition with which its dishonesties in conflict are acknowledged. The law of love is, in short, always relevant to the field of social ethics whenever it is recognized that this field has to deal primarily with human selves and not with either mind, on the one hand, or subrational vitalities, on the other.

The relevance of the law of love to the field of social institutions and collective relations is established whenever the religious awareness of the individual, in conscious relation to the divine, is related to the intricacies and complexities of social relations. In that sense, a Christian social ethic requires competent technical judgments. But the relevance of the law of love rests upon a more basic religious consideration. It is established whenever religious experience bears testimony both to the law of love and to that

of self-love. For to understand the law of love as a final impera-
tive, but not to know about the persistence of the power of
self-love in all of life but particularly in the collective relations
of mankind, results in an idealistic ethic with no relevance to the
hard realities of life. To know about the power of self-love, but
not to know that its power does not make it normative, is to
dispense with ethical standards and fall into cynicism. But to
know both the law of love as the final standard and the law
of self-love as a persistent force is to enable Christians to have a
foundation for a pragmatic ethic in which power and self-interest
are used, beguiled, harnessed and deflected for the ultimate end
of establishing the highest and most inclusive possible community of justice and order. This is the very heart of the problem
of Christian politics: the readiness to use power and interest in
the service of an end dictated by love, and yet an absence of
complacency about the evil inherent in them. No definitions or
structures of justice can prevent these forces from getting out
of hand if they are not handled with a sense of their peril.

Naturally, the justice and harmony which is achieved in this
way is not the harmony of the kingdom of God, nor yet identical
with the highest possible harmony between individuals in their
personal evaluations. For this reason, there must always be a final
distinction between what the Gospel demands of us in our individual and spontaneous relations and what is demanded in the
institutions and structures of society. It is equally idle to expect
any system of law or any codified relationship to exhaust the possibilities of grace and freedom which can be expressed by individuals above and beyond the law, or to expect such spontaneous
and gracious relations to take the place of law. For on the one
hand Christians must seek to serve God, that is, consider the
ultimate purpose of their toil, no matter how inadequate may
be the structure of justice in which they are forced to toil. But
on the other hand they must always reconsider the organizations
and arrangements through which the toil of men is organized so
that impediments to life's more ultimate purposes may be removed.

Usually Christian sensitivity becomes becalmed and isolated in the realm of personal relations and sheds no light and offers no creative contribution to the political and economic problems of life. The liberal Christian form of sensitivity overestimates the moral possibilities of man's collective life while the more orthodox Protestant versions are usually overcome by a pessimistic over-emphasis on the evils in collective life, thus consigning it to the devil.

The task of any movement devoted to "social Christianity" must be, therefore, not so much to advocate a particular nostrum for the solution of various economic and social evils, but to bring a full testimony of a gospel of judgment and grace to bear upon all of human life, upon the individual in the final heights of individual self-consciousness, where it transcends all social institutions and historic situations, and upon human communities which do, on their own level, make contact with the kingdom of God, whenever individuals recognize that judgment and mercy of God are relevant to their collective as well as to their individual actions, and to the actions by which they order their common life as well as to actions in which they express themselves above and beyond every particular order or system.

[1953]

The Christian Faith
and the Economic Life of
Liberal Society (1953)

T HE "liberal" society which gradually emerged out of the disintegration of the medieval culture and the feudal-agrarian economy is generally characterized by democratic political institutions and by an organization of economic life which dispenses, as far as possible, with the political, and even the moral, control of economic activities.

It was the great achievement of classical economic liberalism to gain recognition of the doctrine that the vast system of mutual services which constitute the life of economic society could best be maintained by relying on the "self-interest" of men rather than their "benevolence" or on moral suasion, and by freeing economic activities from irrelevant and frequently undue restrictive political controls. It released the "initiative" of men to exploit every possible opportunity for gain and thus to increase the resources of the whole of society, at first through the exploitation of commercial opportunities and subsequently through the endless development of technical and industrial power. This new freedom was, in fact, so necessary for the growth of modern commercial-industrial society that it is difficult to determine whether modern commerce and industry developed because they were freed from traditional controls, or because their vitalities and complexities simply broke down moral and political controls which were no longer able to contain the vast flood of new energies or to preserve significant restraints amidst mounting complexities.

The doctrine of classical economic liberalism accompanied its emancipation of economic life with a theory calculated to set the mind and conscience of society at rest about the possible moral and political consequences of this new freedom. The theory was that justice would be the inevitable consequence of a free play of all competitive vitalities. The "free market" would automatically check disbalances of power and privilege. If it offered exorbitant profits provisionally, these would be dispelled in the end by attracting a larger number of competitors to rich pasture lands. In the same manner, meager returns, whether in wages or in profits, would be ultimately redressed by reducing the labor force and capital of the enterprise in a given field.

This assurance of the beneficent effect of a "hidden hand" which controlled the actions of men beyond their conscious contriving, of a "pre-established harmony of nature" which transmuted all competitive strivings into an ultimate harmony, was obviously a more dubious doctrine than the basic assurance that men must be engaged primarily through their self-interest to participate in the vast web of mutual services which has always characterized man's economic life and which increasing specialization of labor has made ever more intricate.

The perpetual debate among economists from the days of Adam Smith to our own may be said to center on the problem of how the indubitable benefits of freedom and initiative which flowed from the truth of the basic doctrine may be preserved, while the errors in the ancillary doctrine are corrected. In this debate it became more and more apparent that many cherished values of civilization are not protected by the operations of a "free market" and that there are conflicts in society which are not composed within the limits of a self-regulating competition. The errors and miscalculations which gave liberal society an undue confidence in the possibilities of an automatic harmony of economic and social interests may be finally reduced to two primary ones. (1) The liberal theory was strangely blind to the factor of power in man's social life and more particularly to the possibility that great disproportions of power would result in injustice. This error was the more fateful because it was introduced into Western social thought at the precise moment when a technical society began to develop. This society would quickly transmute the static inequalities of a feudal society into dynamic ones. (2) The liberal theory was informed by an economic rationalism which tended to equate every form of self-interest with economic interest. It believed men both capable of acting, and inclined to act, upon the basis of economic interest, and so obscured the motives of political and religious passion and interest, of ethnic and other loyalties, which impinged upon the economic sphere and were the very stuff of the sphere of politics.

There was consequently little in the liberal theory by which the great centralizations of power in modern economic society could be dealt with morally or politically. Modern society was actually subjected to more violent economic and other conflicts than more traditional and organic communities, thus offering ironic refutation of the liberal concept of social harmony and a self-regulating competitive struggle. The violence of the social conflict was accentuated by the fact that those classes of modern society (particularly in Europe) which suffered most from the periodic dislocations of a supposedly self-regulating economy, and from the poverty which follows inevitably upon powerlessness in competition, became informed by a social creed (Marxism) which contained even more miscalculations than the liberal creed which it challenged. In place of the concept of a natural social harmony it advanced the idea of an inevitable class conflict between propertied and propertyless classes. For the picture of a society in which prudence and competition seemed to have made power an irrelevance, it substituted the idea of a power conflict in which the powerful would become ever more so and the weak ever more exploited until, in a remarkable historical denouement, the powerless would become powerful by the force of their social resentments, the strength of their greater numbers, and the grace of a remarkable historical dialectic operating inexorably to redress the disbalances of history.

In place of the liberal fear of political power and obtuseness toward the realities of economic power, Marxism substituted a theory which assumed that all economic power would be destroyed through the abolition of the right of possession. Since the theory failed to take account of managerial power in the economic realm, the vaunted "socialization of property" actually permitted a concentration of both economic and political power in the hands of a single oligarchy. This oligarchy was allowed to assert its power without any significant restraints, for Marxism in its pure form had found the source of self-interest purely in the institution of property. Its oligarchs, being without property, were therefore supposed to be governed by interests identical with those of the "proletariat" in whose name they governed.

The miscalculations of pure Marxism have resulted in so odious a system of tyranny that the classes in Western society who benefit most from an unregulated economy are persuaded that the validity of their creed can be most simply established by pointing to the grievous errors in the Marxist dogma. But the whole social history of the Western world refutes this simple belief. For the healthiest democracies of the Western world have preserved or regained their social and economic health by using political power to redress the most obvious disbalances in economic society, to protect social values to which the market is indifferent, and to prevent or to mitigate the periodic crises to which a free economy seems subject. They have been prompted to these measures by political parties, primarily composed of workers, who were informed by modified and more democratic versions of the Marxist creed. And even when, as in America, the workers were not directly influenced by Marxist thought, they learned not only to set the organized economic power of the trade union against the organized power of finance and industry but also to organize politically. Through their political power they sought to enforce their demand that the community establish minimal social securities and that it intervene in the economic process whenever it seemed possible and desirable to do so in the interest of welfare.

The debate about the limits and possibilities of a free economy has, in short, not been an academic one. It constitutes the very stuff of political life and controversy in the Western world in the twentieth century. The debate has been inconclusive, and must continue to be so. It is inconclusive because only the most grievous extremes of the two warring creeds have been refuted by experience, while the wisest communities have mixed the two creeds in varying proportions. It is clear that absolute economic freedom fails to establish sufficient justice to make it morally viable. It is also clear that consistent socialization or even regulation of property unduly maximizes political power, replaces self-regulating tendencies in the market with bureaucratic decisions, and tends to destroy the initiative which helped to create modern technical efficiency.

Assuming that Western society will preserve sufficient economic and social health to ward off the virulent version of Marxism, which still takes root wherever there is great poverty or distress, it is probable that the healthier nations will, in varying ways, experiment with various combinations of "freedom" and "planning," but will also seek to avoid the perils of inordinate power, whether political or economic. Both justice and freedom may be secured if the mistake is not made of believing that the one flows inevitably from the other. The question how much liberty should be risked to establish justice, or justice sacrificed to preserve liberty, will be illumined by able social scientists.

But the question will also continue to be the subject of party conflict. In this conflict, one may expect that those classes in society which suffer most from dislocations in the economic process and benefit least from disproportions of power in economic society will espouse the cause of "control" and "planning." Those classes, on the other hand, which have most to gain from risk-taking and most to give through imaginative initiative will naturally be more zealous to preserve freedom in the economic process and most convinced that the whole structure of democratic freedom rests upon this one freedom. These ideological distortions are inevitable, as James Madison foresaw, and one may be grateful that in a healthy democracy it is not possible for either side to transmute the truth it holds into error by blindness to the truth cherished by the opposing side. For both sides in this ideological struggle obviously have hold of a truth which must be supplemented by the truth which the other side cherishes.

The ideological struggle is apparent internationally as well as nationally. The so-called "free" world, which is united in rejecting totalitarian collectivism, does not have absolutely common convictions on the relation of freedom to justice. A nation as wealthy as our own is more inclined than the poorer nations of Europe to prefer freedom to justice and to believe that justice can be achieved with only a minimal control of economic life.

The question is how the Christian faith enters this debate or makes significant contributions to its solution. Most thoughtful readers will observe that several authors, social scientists of great repute, have considered the ethical problems of our economic life without explicit recourse to uniquely Christian standards of judgment. Yet they are practically unanimous in finding no source for ethical standards in pure economic analyses and in recognizing that ethical norms are nevertheless either implicitly or explicitly involved in the judgments which economists and other social scientists make about our common life. All of these ethical judgments might, however, be reduced to varying interpretations of the concept of "justice." No doubt the Christian heritage of our civilization colors our ideas of justice, even when the civilization has become highly secularized. But no civilization can exist without some notion of justice, for it is not possible to form a real community if its several members do not have the desire to "give each man his due."

Does the Christian faith add anything significant to the concept of justice? The most immediate answer to this question is that it subordinates justice to an even higher standard, that of love. According to Christ, "all the law and the prophets" are summarized in the twofold love commandment, which enjoins both the love of God and the love of the neighbor. However, if it is assumed that the Christian contribution to economic and political life is simply contained in the purity of its ethical ideal of love (an assumption which some modern versions of the Christian faith have sought to inculcate), the relation of Christianity to man's economic and political life would seem to become even more problematic. For the question would then arise whether this ideal has any relevance to the organization of economic or political society. The most ideal social possibility for man may well be so perfect an accord of life with life that each member of a community is ready to sacrifice his interests for the sake of others. But, as David Hume observed, politics (and for that matter economics too) must assume the selfishness of men.

It is certainly significant that the highest religious visions of the good life always culminate in the concept of this perfect accord. The ideal of love is not superimposed upon human history by scriptural, or any other, authority. Human existence, when profoundly analyzed, yields the law of love as the final law of human freedom. Man's unique freedom, in which he rises indeterminately above his determinate existence, requires that his life be fulfilled not within himself but in others. It also requires that this realization of himself in others should not be pursued merely from his own standpoint. That is, he cannot regard others simply as tools and instruments of his self-realization.

Yet that is precisely what he is inclined to do. Any religious faith which merely discovers the law of love but does not also make men aware of the other law, that of self-love, is a sentimental perversion of Christianity. It is a perversion which lacks true inwardness of religious experience. For in such experience men become aware, as St. Paul testified, not only of the final law of life but of another law "which wars against the law that is in my mind."

It is from the standpoint of both of these laws, from the recognition of the validity of the one and the reality of the other, that Christianity must make its contribution to the organization of man's life, whether in economic or in political terms. From the standpoint of the law of love every scheme and structure of justice will be recognized to be tentative and provisional. Not merely the positive law of particular communities but also the notions of justice, from the standpoint of which positive law is criticized, are touched by interest and passion. They always contain an ideological element, for they tend to justify a given equilibrium of power in a given historical situation.

It was an achievement of Catholic moral theory that it recog-

nized the necessity of standards of justice for the institutional
life of mankind below the level of love. But it was a weakness in
the theory that love became a "counsel of perfection" and lost its
dialectical relation to the law of justice. Justice, meanwhile, was
conceived in terms of classic rationalism. It was assumed that
human history, like nature, had an inflexible structure to which
human actions must conform. The standards of human conduct
and of human association, ostensibly derived from an inflexible
"natural law," were, however, conditioned by the peculiar power
relations of the feudal-agrarian culture. Such standards could not
be applied adequately to the new economic vitalities and interests
developed by the rising middle-class civilization.

The consequence of this situation was the open rebellion of
middle-class life against traditional standards of justice. They had
become instruments of injustice precisely because they covered
particular historical social forms with the aura of the absolute.
In the relation of religion to culture it is important to distinguish
sharply between the absolute and the relative. If the authority of
religion is used primarily to give absolute validity to relative
values, the consequence is fanaticism. It is characteristic from the
standpoint of modern culture to ascribe fanaticism to religion,
and not without cause. It is, however, significant that modern
culture, which hoped to destroy religious fanaticism by the power
of reason, did not anticipate the even more grievous fanaticisms
of modern political religions which would express themselves in
the name of reason and of science. Modern culture did not, in
short, measure the depth of this problem, or rightly gauge the
persistence with which men will use standards of justice as instruments of their interest and use religion to obscure, and thus to
aggravate, the ideological taint in their reasoning about justice.

A modern Protestant analogue to Catholic conceptions of
"natural law" is the tendency of certain types of Protestant
pietistic individualism to endow "natural law," as eighteenth-century rationalism conceived it, with religious sanction. Thus the
characteristic prejudices of middle-class life, its tendency toward
extravagant individualism, its lack of a sense of community or

justice, its devotion to the principles of laissez faire, are falsely raised to religious absolutes; and confusion is worse confounded. Recently there has been a strong recrudescence of this type of thought in Protestant circles; and it has been so heavily financed by interested political and economic groups that its ideological corruption is even more evident than was the religious support of traditional "natural law" concepts at the rise of modern commercial society.

Standards of justice may be said to be (1) expressions of the law of love, insofar as the love of the neighbor requires a calculation of competitive claims when there is more than one neighbor and (2) a practical compromise between the law of love and the law of self-love. They are a compromise in the sense that norms of justice seek to arrive at an equitable adjustment of conflicting claims, assuming the selfish inclination of men to take advantage of each other. A Christian contribution to standards of justice in economic and political life must therefore not be found primarily in a precise formulation of the standard. It must be found rather in strengthening both the inclination to seek the neighbor's good and the contrite awareness that we are not inclined to do this. The inclination to seek the neighbor's good must be accompanied by an awareness that every norm of justice is but a very relative approximation of this goal. The awareness that even good men are not consistently inclined to do this will lay bare the ideological taint, the corruption of self-interest, in every historic standard.

Thus a genuine Christian contribution to the ideological conflict in democratic society must serve to mitigate, rather than aggravate, the severity of the conflict; for it will prevent men from heedlessly seeking their own interests in the name of justice and from recklessly denominating value preferences, other than their own, as evil. If Christian piety or any other kind of piety does not yield these fruits of humility and charity, it must be consistently rejected as the "salt that has lost its savor."

This interpretation of the contribution of Christian faith to a sane and viable organization of modern economic life would seem,

however, to be in conflict with what we have already defined as the
creative idea of classical economic theory: the idea of the necessity
and legitimacy of making use of self-interest for the purpose of
achieving a more flexible system of mutual services than the rigid
moral and political controls of traditional culture made possible.
It seems to be in conflict because the Christian analysis of human
motives arrives at a critical estimate of the force of the same
self-interest which economic life must harness. This supposed
conflict has, in fact, persuaded some economists to regard Christianity as a vast system of wishful thinking, which practical men
had better disregard. For Christianity seems to suggest that men
not only should, but also could, love their neighbors as themselves
if they tried hard enough. But practical men must assume the
persistence of self-interest in human affairs. This confusion has
been heightened by some modern highly moralistic versions of the
Christian faith. In those the solution of our economic problems
has been sought by suggesting that we need only to substitute the
"service" for the "profit" motive to cure the ills of our society.
This solution not only ignores the persistence and the power of
self-interest in human affairs, but it also obscures the fact that
most men seek whatever they seek not simply for themselves but
in the service of some community, more particularly the family.
The problem of the human community is not so much that of
egoism as that of alteregoism. It is the problem of finding an
equitable distribution of the values of life, not between individuals
but between various groups, most particularly between families.

If, then, the power of self-interest, whether egoistic or alterego-
istic, cannot be simply transmuted or suppressed and must therefore be used, what becomes of the Christian definition of this
power as "sin"? The correct answer to that question involves a
more rigorous distinction between the presuppositions of the Christian faith and those of modern culture than has thus far been
made. For the self-interest which was rightly harnessed in modern
economic theory and practice was wrongly defined by it as the
harmless survival impulse which man shares with all creatures.
From the eighteenth century to the present moment there has

been a tendency in modern culture, particularly in its naturalistic versions, to interpret human actions and motives in terms as analogous to nature as possible. When modern thought speaks of "laws of nature" which govern history and furnish the norms of human action, it means the concept to be taken literally. These modern "laws of nature" are not laws of reason intuitively known. They are even more dubious concepts. They are supposedly objective forms, analytically discerned. That is why historical evolution could be regarded as merely an extension of natural evolution. The numerous analogies between human history and natural history, made inevitable by man's affinities with other creatures, are usually emphasized unduly, and the uniqueness of man's freedom is not fully appreciated.

The consequence of this error is that the whole drama of human history is falsely interpreted. On the one hand it is regarded as subject to laws of natural development, as if the freedom of the human agent, who is both a creator and a creature of the historical process, did not introduce incalculable elements into the human drama. On the other hand this excessive determinism always finally gives way to an excessive voluntarism. At some point in the evolutionary process man is supposed to come into complete control of his own destiny. The reason this is regarded as possible is that the "mind" which is supposed to control the historical process is assumed to be akin to the disinterested mind of the natural scientist, even as the historical stuff to be mastered is assumed to be akin to the unconscious impulses of nature. Actually the stuff of history is much more recalcitrant to control than the stuff of nature. The simple will-to-live of nature has been transmuted by human freedom into the will-to-power, on the one hand, and into the desire-to-live-truly, that is, to fulfill the essential norms of human existence, on the other.

Furthermore, the "mind" which is supposed to bring historical destiny under control is a mind much more organically and deeply involved in the process to be controlled than the mind of the natural scientist is involved in the nature which he observes. There is, therefore, no simple "man" who can or cannot come into con-

trol of historical destiny. There are various men and groups of
men who have contradictory notions of what man's destiny is. At
the present moment, while the liberal world dreams of bringing
history under human control, its practical statesmen and its common people are preoccupied with a desperate struggle against a
horrible tyranny which is trying to do exactly what some dreamers
in the liberal world had hoped to do, that is, bring all of history
under the control of an elite of scientists, in this case of "Marxist-
Leninist" scientists.

The pretensions of complete disinterestedness by this elite are
of course bogus. But so are, in a greater or lesser degree, those of
any elite which pretends to speak for "man." Nor are the corruptions of their reason the inertia of "unintelligent and unconscious
processes." The corruptions are due to a curious compound of the
will-to-live-truly and the will-to-power. They are, in short, uniquely
human corruptions due, not to the inertia of natural impulse
operating against the more inclusive purposes of mind, but to the
pretensions of man as creature that he is not creature but creator
without qualification. If Communist pretensions have become
particularly noxious (as compared with the more innocent dreams
of the liberal world), that is due not so much to any particular
defect in the Marxist scheme of managing history (though there
are many obvious errors in it), but to the fact that the theory
actually provides for the investment of a specific group of elite
with actual power. The fury which they exhibit in its use may be
regarded as the inevitable consequence of the exercise of too
absolute power, on the one hand, and as the consequence of the
frustration when pretended omnipotence and omniscience meet
recalcitrant forces in history not obedient to their mind or will.

Human desires and ambitions are without natural limit. The
Christian's faith can make no greater contribution to the organization of man's common life than its interpretation of the root of
this inordinacy. For according to the Christian faith man is on the
one hand a free spirit "made in the image of God," who rises
indeterminately in his consciousness over nature, history, and self.
He cannot, therefore, be contained or explain the meaning of
his life within the limits of any system of nature. But he is on

the other hand a creature, driven by natural impulses and limited by conditions of time and place. These limitations reach into the very pinnacles of spirit, even as the freedom of spirit reaches down into every natural impulse and transmutes it into something less determinate than the impulses of other creatures. (One need only consider how the sex impulse, possessing a purely biological function in nature, is related to almost every creative and destructive force in the total human personality.) Thus from a genuinely Christian standpoint man can never be understood merely from the standpoint of his involvement in nature, on the one hand; nor can he, on the other, be regarded as a potentially discarnate spirit in whom historical development is progressively actualizing this potential. On the contrary, the evils to which human history is subject arise precisely from those forms of inordinacy which are rooted in man's vain effort to deny his creatureliness.

If we now return to the problem of the organization of economic life and to the necessity of harnessing self-interest, it will become apparent not only why it must be harnessed and not merely suppressed but also why the self-interest has a different dimension than was assumed in the theories of classical economics and in the whole of modern naturalistic thought. Self-interest must be harnessed for two reasons. It is too powerful and persistent to be simply suppressed or transmuted. Even if individual life could rise to pure disinterestedness so that no human mind would give the self, in which it is incarnate, an undue advantage, yet it would not be possible for collective man to rise to such a height. The institution of the family would alone prevent a simple substitution of "motives of service" for "motives of profit," as we have seen. For the self as "breadwinner" will seek to serve his family by seeking gain for his toil.

But self-interest must be allowed a certain free play for the additional reason that there is no one in society good or wise enough finally to determine how the individual's capacities had best be used for the common good, or his labor rewarded, or the possibilities of useful toil, to which he may be prompted by his own initiative, be anticipated.

Yet the self-interest which is thus engaged is not some harmless survival impulse as found in nature. It is not simply satisfied, as physiocratic theory assumed, when human toil yields returns adequate for man's primary needs. For human desires and needs rise indeterminately above the biological level. Self-interest expresses itself above all in what Bertrand Russell has defined as the "desire for power and glory." The two are so intermingled that we need not, for present purposes at least, distinguish them. Thomas Hobbes was able to describe this dimension of self-interest, which was obscured in the thought of his contemporaries, primarily in terms of desire for prestige. He spoke of the "constant competition for honor and prestige" among men. Yet his description yields a sense of the will-to-power lacking in the thought which lies at the foundation of liberal economics.

Because it did not recognize the unlimited nature of all human desires in general and of the desire for power and glory in particular, classical liberalism naturally underrated both the reality of the contest for power in man's social and economic life and the injustices which would result from great inequalities of power. In common with liberal thought, Marx obscured both the lust for power in the motives of men and the factor of power in social life. Self-interest is interpreted by Marxism, as by liberalism, primarily in terms of the economic motive, that is, as the desire for gain. The original state of man's innocency was, according to Engels, disturbed by "greed and covetousness." But since these inordinate desires were attributed to the corruption of the institution of property, it was possible for Marx to envisage an ideal state of society on the other side of the abolition of property. In this post-revolutionary society human needs and desires would be as limited and would achieve as simple a harmony as the liberal culture imagined possible on this side of a revolution.

Thus the foundation was laid for the tragic conflict in modern social history between two great political credos. In this conflict both creeds, in their purer form, generated monstrous contrasting evils from an essentially identical mistake. In the case of pure liberalism it was believed possible to abandon the whole economic life of man to a "natural system of liberty" because the forces in competition in the economic sphere were regarded as essentially determinate and of potentially equal strength. They were neither. Just as human freedom accentuates inequalities found in nature, so also a technical society accentuates the inequalities of more traditional societies. Marxism, on the other hand, allows the power impulses of an uncontrolled oligarchy to express themselves behind a façade of innocency, erected by the dogma that the possession of property is the only source of inordinate desire. In the one case the perils to justice arising from economic power, particularly from inequality of power, are not recognized. In the other case, the perils from the combination of economic and political power in the hands of a single oligarchy are obscured.

Thus the errors of both those who abjure every effort to control human enterprise and those who would bring it completely under a plan rest upon false estimates of the desires and ambitions of men which furnish the stuff of human history. The self-interest of men must be used, rather than merely controlled, not only because it is too variable and unpredictable to be simply controlled but also because the corruption of self-interest among the oligarchs, who would control it, is actuated by ambitions and power lusts, more dangerous than is dreamed of in either philosophy. On the other hand, the self-interest of men, when uncontrolled, does not simply create a nice harmony of competitive striving. That is why the healthier modern societies constantly experiment with social strategies in which neither creed is followed slavishly.

In arriving at this wisdom of "common sense," modern nations are revealing in the field of economics and politics insights into the character of human nature and history which belong to the Christian view of man and which both pure liberal and radical political theories have tended to obscure. This view of man recognizes that (in Pascal's phrase) the dignity and the misery of man are inextricably united. This is to say that both the creative and the destructive possibilities of man's actions in history are derived from the same uniquely human freedom. The misery (that is, man's capacity for evil) develops when he extends his power and wisdom beyond the limits of man as creature. The dignity of man implies his capacity to manage his own destiny and to create communities and social harmonies in which moral and political wisdom outwit the short-range desires and ends of man as creature. The evil in man implies the constant possibility of the corruption of this creative capacity. Therefore he is not to be trusted with too much power and his wisdom as manager of historical destiny is not to be relied on too unqualifiedly.

The Christian faith in its various historic forms has of course become involved in various errors which illustrate these corruptions. Sometimes it has championed concepts of justice or freedom which were ideologies of the strong. Sometimes it has exceeded secular culture in moralistic illusions based upon the idea of the dignity and goodness of man but lacking in understanding of man's capacity for evil. Sometimes it has fled from these errors into a quasi-Christian Marxism. In this view collectivistic economics is espoused in the name of brotherhood, but the perils of power in the collectivist organization of society are not seen.

A genuine Christian faith must always be ready to recognize the periodic involvement of its own historic forms in the various errors against which its true genius forces it to contend. It may be significant, however, that the healthiest national communities of our epoch are those in which the treasures of the Christian faith have never been completely dissipated and in which therefore the fratricidal conflict of modern technical society has been mitigated. For the cherished values of toleration, without which a democratic society would become impossible, are the fruit of a charitable understanding that all human wisdom is limited, that self-interest taints all human virtues, and that there is a similarity between our own evil and those against which we contend.

A viable democratic society cannot, of course, exist merely by tolerant understanding of the inevitability and the universality of the taint of self-interest in all the various positions taken by competing groups in the community. If each group were merely intent upon its own interests and if it used general concepts of justice merely as screens for these interests, the society would disintegrate into warring camps. Such cultures as the Confucian, for instance, have been unable to establish stable community on a wider level than that of the family because there was no moral impulse to affirm interests above those of the family. A healthy community requires that every family and every economic and social group should have, in addition to concern for its own welfare, some genuine devotion to the "general welfare." One must leave the concept of "general welfare" somewhat vague because it must include not only the welfare of the national community but that of the nascent world community.

The progressive development of ever wider communities in the history of mankind is accounted for by the fact that every individual has the ability to achieve some detachment from the communities to which he is bound by nature (the family) and by nature and history (ethnic and other communities), and that this ability is subject to historic growth. The wider the communities, whether national or international, the less they can count on organic, subrational, and submoral forces of cohesion and the more they must depend upon man's conscious sense of responsibility for the welfare of others than those who are peculiarly his own. In other words the law of love is the final law of human freedom; and the words of Christ, "If ye love them that love ye, what thanks have ye?" accurately state the indeterminate character of the love commandment, expressing the obligation of the individual to ever wider communities than those to which he is immediately bound.

While, as we have already observed, the love commandment is always partly contradicted in actual life by the immense force of self-love, particularly the self-love of groups and collectives, it remains nevertheless the law of life. Any theory of community, whether religious or secular, which presents the commandment to love the neighbor as the self as a simple moral possibility inevitably obscures the realities with which the political and economic order must deal. On the other hand, the "realistic" tradition in Western social thought has consistently committed the error of underestimating man's residual capacity for justice, which is to say, his genuine concern for his neighbor. This inclination to be concerned with life, beyond the immediate community in which the self lives, is strengthened by genuine religious piety. For in such piety the freedom of the self over its immediate necessities and ambitions is heightened and the self's profound and ultimate relation to all other selves is illumined.

When this religious impulse is deficient or lost, life sinks, not so much to an individualistic, but to a narrower and narrower level of alteregoism, that is, to a containment of life within some narrow community of family or clan. Then the immediate and limited communities of mankind exhaust the concern of the self for others, leaving the larger communities, whether national or international, in the anarchy of warring particular interests or a purely coerced unity. A creative relation of the Christian faith to the problems of society therefore requires that both the law of love be affirmed and the fact of the persistence of self-love be fully recognized. The Christian faith is most creative when this is done not formally by the mere preaching of precept but by the force of a genuine piety which emancipates the self from its narrower loyalties and at the same time makes it conscious of their persistence and force.

A Christian faith, informed by biblical norms, cannot issue either in an optimism which obscures the power of particular loyalties offering their resistance to the wider loyalties, or in the type of realism which denies man's capacity for the wider loyalties or even the binding force of such loyalties. For a truly Christian interpretation of the radical character of human freedom must illumine both the creative and the destructive possibilities of that freedom. A truly religious analysis of human experience must lead to a consciousness of both of these possibilities, not merely as social facts to be observed, but as intimate facts which the self may experience and know in his own life.

If such a relation between the Christian faith and the economic and political life of mankind is established, there will be little inclination to invest the whole capital of religious sanctity in particular norms of justice or specific technical structures of economic and political life. They will not be despised, because it will be recognized that the complexity of competing claims in the community requires that norms of justice be constantly defined and redefined, and that the power of particular interests in a community requires that balances and equilibria of power be constantly constructed and reconstructed. They must be reconstructed because new vitalities constantly enter into the field of concern, and old balances become unjust under new conditions.

But the whole capital of religious sanctity must not be invested in these norms. For these systems and structures of justice are not eternal norms to which life must perennially conform but rather *ad hoc* efforts to strike a balance between the final moral possibilities of life and the immediate and given realities. If certain moral, social, and economic traditions have become firmly established, they will not be lightly cast aside. The more it is recognized that there is not one single rational and just method of organizing the life of the community, the more will an established historic method be given due reverence, the more so if there is no illusion that some other method will overcome every past evil or be immune to opposite evils. A proper understanding of the historical and contingent nature of these various structures of justice will discourage both the revolutionary ardor which is always informed by some illusions and the conservatism which pretends that established norms are absolute.

The relation of the Christian faith to economic, as to political, life is not exhausted in its real or potential influence upon the moral and social norms of a community, nor in the insights which disclose the heights and depths of human conduct. All religion is an expression of the meaning of human existence. The Christian religion is unique in expressing the meaning of human existence in terms which partly involve and partly transcend man's historic existence.

The significance of man's life upon earth is affirmed, and all historic duties and tasks are taken seriously. But the Christian faith also insists that the final pinnacle of meaning transcends all possibilities of history. It is recognized that physical survival may be bought at too high a price. Thus Christ declares: "Fear not them which kill the body but are not able to kill the soul; but rather fear him which is able to destroy both soul and body in hell" (Matt. 10:28). This implies that the self in its integrity of spirit is not identical with the self as a physical organism, and it is recognized that there are situations in which men must choose to die rather than to buy their survival at the price of this integrity. In the same spirit Christ asks: "What shall it profit a man if he shall gain the whole world and lose his own soul?" (Mark 8:36). The question suggests that the physical advantages of life can be bought at too high a price. The warnings in the scripture against covetousness are frequent and explicit; and they are justified by the observation that "a man's life consisteth not in the abundance of the things which he possesseth" (Luke 12:15). In Christ's parable of the rich fool, the effort to protect the future against all contingencies by heaping up wealth is rebuked by a reminder of the brevity of the life of all men. "Thou fool, this night thy soul shall be required of thee" (Luke 12:20).

The final question about the relation of the Christian faith to the economic life of liberal society is concerned with the legitimacy of these warnings and their relevance to a society in which economic efficiency tends to become the final norm by which all things are judged.

The problem is whether what Professor Heimann defines as modern "economic rationalism" has not placed so much emphasis upon the tangible ends of life, in contrast to the more intangible values, that we have in effect created a culture in which all the biblical warnings are disregarded. This is a particularly serious problem for the United States because we are being criticized by both friends and foes in Asia and Europe for having become obsessed with the tools and gadgets of life. When we speak rather idolatrously of the "American way of life," our friends and critics profess not to be certain whether we are recommending certain standards of political freedom or are extolling our living standards. The latter have reached heights of opulence beyond the dreams of avarice for most of the inhabitants of the world.

Sometimes we seem to believe that these living standards are the fruit and the proof of our virtue; at other times we suggest that they are the necessary presuppositions for a virtuous democratic national life. In the one case we follow our Puritan tradition, which did not seek after prosperity in the first instance but was nevertheless certain that since "Godliness was profitable unto all things," prosperity was a mark of divine favor and a reward of virtue. In the other case we draw upon the Jeffersonian tradition in our national heritage. The Jeffersonians believed that the superior virtues of American democracy would be guaranteed primarily by the ampler economic opportunities of our virgin continent. These would avert for America the severity of the social struggle and the subordination of man to man in the overcrowded life of Europe. The Jeffersonian interpretation has one merit of recognizing that democracy is viable only in a society in which the economic margins are sufficient to prevent a desperate struggle for the economic resources of the community.

Whatever the merit of either interpretation, it is now apparent that there is no such simple coordination between economic welfare and the moral, spiritual, and cultural life of the community as we had supposed. The criticisms which European and Asian nations make of our cultural and spiritual life may not always be just. Frequently they are prompted by envy of our good fortune, and seem to rest upon the presupposition that virtue and good fortune are completely incompatible. An impoverished world is, indeed, involved in curious inconsistencies in its relation to a wealthy and powerful preponderant nation. For on the one hand the poorer nations insist that they require our help in establishing greater economic efficiency and productivity as a basis for a healthy democratic life. On the other hand they seem to believe that our wealth is proof of our vulgarity and possibly even of our unjust exploitation of others.

The widespread criticism of American prosperity and of American culture are usually not based upon distinctively Christian presuppositions. They therefore prove the more convincingly that the issue involved is not the mere rejection of an illegitimate Christian "otherwordliness" in favor of a more unequivocal affirmation of the meaning of man's historic existence. The issue is the relation between man's immediate and ultimate ends. The question to be resolved is whether the satisfaction of immediate ends will inevitably contribute to the achievement of the more ultimate ends.

In considering this question we must note that man's economic activities are devoted in the first instance to the satisfaction of his primary needs of food, shelter, and security. Ultimately, of course, men bring economic effort into the support of every end, spiritual, cultural, and communal. It cannot be denied, however, that economic activity is always devoted in the first instance to these primary needs and that modern economic "rationalism" gives these needs a preference because they are more "tangible." The proof is furnished by the fact that a nation which indubitably has the highest living standards cannot boast of the highest achievements in the moral and spiritual quality of its culture.

Naturally any community will devote economic productivity to other than primary needs as soon as these primary needs are tolerably met. Therefore economic efficiency and increased productivity will support all higher cultural activity. Human culture depends in fact upon the ability of an economy to establish margins of welfare beyond the satisfaction of primary needs.

There are, however, two reasons why the relation of economic efficiency to culture is subject to a law of diminishing returns. The first is that human needs and desires are, as previously observed, essentially indeterminate. There is therefore no natural limit for their satisfaction. The place of the automobile in the American economy is an effective symbol of this fact. The mobility which it provides is not exactly a "primary" need. But neither is it basically a cultural one. Yet the satisfaction of this need for mobility takes precedence over many needs, some of them cultural and others actually more primary. It is a question, for instance, whether the possession of a home has not been subordinated in the American economy to the possession of an automobile. Even if there had not been such an influence as "economic rationalism," which emphasized the more tangible values, human nature, under whatever culture, would have been inclined to exploit economic margins for immediate satisfactions in preference to more ultimate ones. There is therefore no "natural" system of preferences which will guarantee that economic means will not become ends in themselves and that tangible and immediate satisfactions will not usurp the devotion of men to the exclusion of more ultimate ones. One possible wrong preference involves the "dignity of man" as a producer being violated for the sake of achieving a high degree of productivity in favor of man as consumer. Furthermore, highly efficient economies may become involved in vulgarities to which more traditional cultures are immune. For in the more traditional cultures the imagination has not been prompted to seek and to desire the unlimited on every level of human satisfactions.

The second reason for the law of diminishing returns in the relation of efficiency to culture is the fact that technical efficiency is more effective in providing the basis for cultural and spiritual values than in contributing to its heights. The invention of writing, and subsequently of printing, were fateful chapters in the cultural history of mankind. Culture depends upon communication. And these arts of communication were creative instruments for all social, as well as for more purely spiritual, achievements of mankind. But the subsequent inventions which made "mass" communication possible and which culminated in the achievement of radio and television have had the general effect of vulgarizing culture. Some of this effect will be eliminated when the instruments are brought more effectively under the control of artistic and cultural purposes. But the degrading which is due to the necessity of reaching a total audience rather than selective groups with special interests will undoubtedly remain.

These diminishing returns in the realm of culture are symbolic of the general relation between quantitative and qualitative aspects of life. The quantitative increase of the comforts and securities of life, and of the technical efficiencies which furnish the foundation for every type of human achievement, does not lead to an indeterminate increase of the highest possibilities of life, measured culturally or spiritually. No degree of economic security can finally obviate the basic insecurity of human existence, finally symbolized in the fact of death. If preoccupation with these securities creates a culture in which human beings are incapable of coming to terms with life's basic insecurity through a serenity of faith, the culture stands under Christ's condemnation of the rich fool.

No technical efficiencies can guarantee the perfection of the poet's art, and no system of card indexing can assure that the historian will have an imaginative grasp of the drama of history which he seeks to portray. While a democratic society requires both a high degree of literacy among its citizens and enough economic margins to prevent the social struggle from becoming desperate, nevertheless the problems of social justice cannot be solved indeterminately by creating so much abundance that the question of justice is less desperately argued because the goods of life need not be divided too equitably.

There are certain problems of human togetherness which we assume to have solved in America because our expanding economy has postponed them. The original expansion of the economy through an advancing frontier and the subsequent expansion through ever new achievements of technical efficiency have created the illusion of life's unlimited possibilities. Actually human existence is definitely limited, despite its apparently unlimited possibilities. The serenity of man and the sanity of his life with others finally depend upon a wisdom which knows how to come to terms with these limits. This wisdom of humility and charity must be derived from a faith which measures the ends of life in a larger context than that which the immediate desires of man supply.

For this reason the Christian faith has a very special function and challenge in a culture in which a high degree of technical efficiency has been attained. If it becomes too defensive about its alleged "otherworldliness," if it fails to call attention to the limits of the "abundance of things a man possesseth" in achieving the serenity and charity without which life becomes intolerable, if it does not define the dimensions of life which create the possibility of contradiction between the desire to survive and the desire to live in integrity of spirit, if, in short, it capitulates uncritically to the cult of technical efficiency and the culture of abundance, it must lose its uniqueness as religious faith. Perhaps this is the issue on which the Christian faith must come most directly to grips with the prevailing mood of a technical culture. Such a culture is in mortal danger of "gaining the whole world" but "losing its own soul." Certainly its idolatrous devotion to technical efficiency has accentuated a peril which Jesus perceived, even in a culture in which the tendency to seek after treasures which "moths corrupt and thieves break through and steal" had not been accentuated by the modern preoccupation with material comfort and physical security.

It would, of course, be foolish to deny the moral and spiritual significance of the "conquest" of nature in our civilization or to yearn after the poverty-stricken conditions of nontechnical societies. Man has been given a rightful dominion over the forces of nature; and the whole history of human civilization is a history of his gradual extension of that dominion. But it is also true that this dominion cannot annul nature's final triumph over man; for even the most powerful and comfortable man must finally submit to the common fate of death. The only possible triumph over death for man is a triumph of faith, which is to say a conception of the meaning of life from the standpoint of which death is not the annulment of all meaning. In the Bible the effort of man to establish the meaning of his existence upon the basis of his own power and intelligence is consistently interpreted as the root of all evil. The rich fool who builds his barns for future security has not reckoned with the fact that he may die any moment. Those who build great houses are accused by the Psalmist, with subtle psychological insight, of having the "secret thought that they will continue forever."

The nonchalance of faith's triumph over life and death is

succinctly expressed in the Pauline word: "For whether we live, we live unto the Lord: and whether we die, we die unto the Lord; whether we live therefore or die, we are the Lord's" (Romans 14:8). In many ways the most basic distinction between secularism and a genuine Christian faith is at this precise point. From the standpoint of the Christian faith no achievements of culture and civilization can finally give man security. On the contrary most of the evils of life arise from the fact that man seeks frantically to establish absolute security by his power, wisdom, or virtue.

The preoccupation of a technical civilization with the external securities of life is due partly to a natural tendency of every culture to extol its unique achievements. Modern man has been remarkably successful in technics and is naturally prone to overestimate the significance of his success in this enterprise for the total problem of human existence. But there is also a deeper religious issue in this idolatry. The frantic pursuit of the immediate goals of life is partly occasioned by an uneasy awareness that this pursuit has not resulted in its promised happiness and by a consequent final and desperate effort to reach the illusive goal of happiness by a more consistent application of principles of efficiency.

If there is such motivation in the current preoccupations of a technical society, particularly in America, they may well be regarded as abortive, but also dangerous, efforts of the spirit of "secularism" in unconscious and therefore purer form to bring human destiny under the control of human power.

This problem is the most serious challenge to the Christian faith. It is the more serious because it cannot be solved by a simple denial of the significance of man's conquest of nature. It can be solved only by recognizing the moral and spiritual resources in the technical achievements on the one hand and by recognizing their limits on the other. The final limits remain the same for the most advanced as well as for the most primitive society.

[1953]

The Development of a
Social Ethic in the
Ecumenical Movement *(1963)*

I T IS one of Visser 't Hooft's many creative contributions to
the ecumenical movement, for which he has furnished such
brilliant leadership for almost half a century (if the prelude in
the Student Christian Movement is counted, as it must be) that
he has always insisted that a closer and more creative encounter
between the various non-Roman churches must be based upon,
and must result in, the renewal of the churches. Without this
presupposition and consequence the ecumenical movement will
merely result in added ecclesiastical machinery.

In no department of the World Council's activities is this
creative renewal of the churches more apparent than in the field
of gradually elaborating a Christian social ethic, which would
express the spirit of the Gospel on the one hand and be relevant
on the other hand to the ever increasing complexities of a technical civilization and a budding world community riven by a
"cold war" and living under the shadow of a nuclear catastrophe.

This task is, and was, an enormous one. It is so enormous
because the New Testament has only the barest suggestions of a
social ethic with its "nicely calculated less and more." The ethic
of the New Testament is eschatological and ultimate. The Sermon
on the Mount, which nineteenth-century liberalism regarded as
a fount of the "Social Gospel," represents ethics in the nth degree.
Professor Dodd rightly declares that it suggests the "quality and

the direction of our ethical motives" rather than detailed and
practical prescriptions for action in situations in which it is necessary to arbitrate between conflicting and competing claims. Jesus,
in answer to the man who implored him "Tell my brother to
divide his inheritance with me," replied rather gruffly "Who has
made me a divider between you?" The emphasis in the answer
deals with the attitudes which cause strife between the brothers
and not with the substantive problems of justice by which conflicting claims are adjudicated. This encounter presents in a nutshell the problem of relating a social ethic to, or deriving it from,
the spirit of the Gospel.

The ethic of the synoptic gospels is eschatological in its framework and in substance enjoins the purest love. The *agape* of the
New Testament is expressed in the Sermon on the Mount or in
St. Paul's hymn of love in I Corinthians 13, in which the apostle
goes so far as to distinguish *agape* from the most rigorous actions
of self-denial: "Though I give all my goods to feed the poor—
though I give my body to be burned, and have not love, it
profiteth me nothing." *Agape* represents a motive so pure that no
seemingly sacrificial action can guarantee its expression. We are
dealing, in short, with the pinnacles of the moral and spiritual
life in the pages of the New Testament and not with the stresses
and strains of a community of self-seeking men. The ideal community, the body of Christ, is compared with the body in which
the members are "fitly joined together," in which they are admon-
ished to "bear one another's burdens" and "If one member suffer
all members suffer with it" (I Cor. 12). In short, self-sacrificing
love is rightly regarded as the mainspring of mutual love. *Agape*
is transmuted into *philia*. But only in an ideal family or an ideal
Christian community is this mutuality attained. The real problem
of a social ethic is how to make justice, with its calculations of
rights, the instrument of love, that is of the primal love commandment which enjoins us to be responsible for our neighbor.

If an ethic were drawn merely from these eschatological heights
without any recognition that there is "a law in my members which
wars against the law that is in my mind," as Paul confesses

(Romans 7), Christianity would be no more than a system of rigorous moral idealism, prescribing responsibilities which are on the very edge of historical possibilities. It was the error of nineteenth-century liberalism to reduce Christianity to this dimension.

But the Christian faith is not simply a rigorous idealistic system after the manner of stoicism. It searches the heart and discovers the tragic antinomy between the law of love, which Paul calls the "law of God" and in which he delights "after the inward man," and the law in his members which is obviously the law of self-love. The whole New Testament *kerygma* presupposes a basic variance between human desires and ambitions and the divine will, for which the atoning death of Christ is the answer in terms of forgiveness and new life. Christ is not a noble martyr dying for his ideals but a revelation of the divine mercy: "God was in Christ reconciling the world unto himself." The New Testament *kerygma* is soteriological, dealing with the ultimate possibilities of human existence and with the tragic contradictions in the human heart. The problem of a Christian social ethic is how to profit from both the heights of its idealism and the depth of its realism in constructing systems of order and justice which provide for a tolerable harmony in communities of selfish men, who may or may not be touched by the divine law "written into their hearts."

We cannot come to terms with the problem of a non-Roman Christian social ethic if we do not take the comparative adequacy and final inadequacy of the whole system of social morality of the Catholic Church into consideration. Beginning with Origen, Catholicism borrowed, first from stoic and finally from Aristotelian, but always from classical, metaphysical sources, its elements of a social ethic. Classical metaphysical foundations were bound to betray it into the consideration of too-fixed norms of "natural law" in which the endless contingencies of history were obscured. Thus Catholicism, particularly through the Thomistic borrowings from Aristotle, was able to adjust the norms of the natural law to the ideologies of medieval feudalism and to obscure the rigors of the earlier stoicism, which had attracted Chrysostom and Augustine and made the Greek fathers so radical.

Roman Catholicism, by reason of equating the historically contingent standards of feudalism with the ultimate norms of the natural law, has proved itself incapable of giving radical criticism to the feudal structures or extricating itself from the medieval-feudal mold of community. But this great weakness, plus its incredible fixed position on birth control in a neo-Malthusian age, must not obscure its very considerable achievements in relating its life to, and guiding the conscience of, modern technical society, once the radical emancipation has been accomplished with the help of others. The obvious reason for this accomplishment is that it has never questioned the social substance of human existence. It always knew that a tolerable harmony in the community would have to avail itself of calculations of justice, though it may have underestimated the ideological distortions in its own conceptions of justice.

If anyone should question the reality of this achievement, one need only to cite the fact that the Catholic Church never lost the loyalty of the industrial workers in Western Europe to the same extent as Protestantism. The social and political realities in Belgium, Holland, Germany and America reveal the point.

The Reformation naturally had a greater emphasis on the realities of grace, and resisted the tendency to make love into a more rigorous law, which only the ascetic "first class" Christians could keep. It rightly regarded love as the fruit of grace, which was universally available. But we must not assume that the Reformation soteriology and doctrines of grace automatically made for an adequate social ethic, which must deal with that peculiar mixture of grace and sin embodied in any system of justice. A system of justice is a realm of sin because only a tolerable equilibrium of power will prevent sinful men from taking advantage of each other. It is a realm of common grace because only given and traditional modes of mutuality, beyond the moral capacities of any but the most virtuous individuals, can sustain a system of justice.

It is so important for non-Roman Christianity to build a real community in which the treasures of faith and life can be borrowed and exchanged for many reasons; but in the field of social ethics it is particularly important because the freedom which emerged from the disintegration of the medieval synthesis of biblical and classical modes of thought created so many complementary and contradictory emphases, that only a genuine sharing can bring together the achievements of various parts of the church and can garner the insights of the various postmedieval centuries.

Let us view the necessity of a new synthesis first in terms of the political and economic organization of the parochial, that is, national community. One of the hazards of the early Reformation, both Lutheran and Calvinistic, was that the new realism, derived from a Pauline and Augustine estimate of the sinfulness of all men and discarding the semi-Pelagianism which supported the medieval political ethic, naturally but dangerously assigned a purely negative function to the political order. It was an order of constraint designed to "keep sin in check." Luther's "earthly kingdom" was a realm of "chains, laws, courts and the sword." In short it was a restrictive order. The only norm of justice was Luther's *"Billigkeit"* or sense of equity. Since the papal authority over the civil state was naturally disavowed, the moral norms for criticizing positive law and contemporary institutions were obscured.

The excessive emphasis on Paul's admonition in Romans 13 to be "subject to the higher powers" because they are ordained of God and "a terror to the evil and not to the good," an admonition which had its own contemporary relevance in warning against eschatological irresponsibility with respect to civil authority, had the historical consequence of obscuring the moral ambiguity of political authority and of the political order in general.

The moral ambiguity of the political and economic order is in fact one of the perennial facts of man's collective existence which required ages of experience before the Christian conscience could be sufficiently at home in this milieu to act responsibly in it. The early church, with its eschatological perfectionism and political irresponsibility, could be negative toward and critical of the functions of government; and its radical stewardship doctrine or "distributive communism," derived from the time when members

"were of one heart and soul" and laid "all their possessions at
the apostles' feet," made the early church critical of property.
Government and property were in fact the two morally ambiguous
instruments for establishing a tolerable peace and order in a community of self-seeking men. The moral ambiguity of these instruments was due to the fact that they both established peace and
created injustice. The conservative impulses of Christianity, first
expressed in St. Paul, tended to be unduly appreciative of them
as instruments of order, while the more radical versions of the
faith were unduly critical of them because they imagined a more
perfect humanity which would obviate their necessity.

The Catholic tradition had its own way of dealing with this
paradox, which need not concern us, except provisionally. It expressed the radical criticism of the institution of property by the
voluntary poverty of the monastics; and the critical attitude toward
government by reverence for the Church as a "perfect society"
from the standpoint of which it was possible to be critical of all
secular government. Thus Gregory the Great could say, "The
kings have their dominion by perfidy and plunder" and Augustine,
whose *De Civitate Dei* laid the foundation for Christian political
realism, truly described the *civitas terrena* as an uneasy armistice
between competitive political forces and the dominance of one
force, which created order, as fleeting benefit. The governors of
the world will not have their authority long "for they used it not
well while they had it." Augustine was more critical of government than Luther. For him it was not an ordinance of God, but
the momentary results of the victory of one political faction over
another. This faction would inevitably offend the divine majesty
by ultimate pretensions unlawful for sinful men. Some of the
critical equalitarianism, borrowed from Chrysostom, and ultimately
derived from stoicism, is expressed in Augustine's sentiment,
"Hence the holy men of old were shepherds of cattle rather than
kings of men."

The Augustinian political realism was gradually eroded in the
medieval period after Gregory VII, when the Church established
dominion over the whole of Western Christendom as the senior

partner in a complicated arrangement in which the junior partner was the Western Empire constructed by the Pope with the crowning of Charlemagne as Emperor. Augustine's qualms about the identification of the Church with the *Civitas Dei*, were forgotten in Gregory VII's simple identification of the all-powerful Church with the city of God; and even the political realism, derived from Augustine's description of the uneasy balances of power in the political realm, was obscured in the complacent assumption that the dominance of the institution of grace over the political institution would cure the latter of its moral ambiguity.

The Protestant Reformation was primarily a religious protest against the conceptions of grace in the medieval Church. But in terms of our immediate interests in social ethics it was a protest against the political pretensions of an overarching sovereignty which had distilled political power from the prestige of sanctity and had used its alleged possession of the "keys of heaven" to unlock the doors of political dominion. The protest was well taken. But it is not usually observed that the Reformation, opening a new chapter in Christianity's approach to the moral ambiguities of the political order, frequently aggravated, rather than clarified the fact that there were in fact two almost distinct Protestant movements, the classical Reformation of Luther and Calvin, and the radical sectarian Protestantism of the Anabaptists of the sixteenth century and the Cromwellian sects of the seventeenth century in England.

The classical Reformation of Luther and Calvin was informed by a political conservatism, strongly influenced by Luther's emphasis on the Pauline doctrine of Romans 13. It gave extravagant reverence to political authority as ordained by God. It tended to assign political authority a purely negative function of restraining self-seeking men and maintaining order. There were differences, of course, between Luther's and Calvin's theories of sin and grace and providence and even in their view of the state. Calvin was more concerned to prevent tyranny by providing for a tension of power in the central power of government; while he also assigned the "lower magistrates" both the right and the duty to resist the tyrant. But both Reformers were inclined to ascribe injustice in the political order to a divine punishment for the sins of the victims of tyranny and to look for deliverance to providence.

The radical sects, on the other hand, approached the moral ambiguities of both the political and economic order from an opposite direction. They were inclined to emphasize the evils consequent on both the institutions of property and government. The Anabaptists were quasi-communist and utopian. The Cromwellian sects exhibited every type of social perfectionism, the communism of Gerard Winstanley and the libertarianism of Lilburne and the Levellers and Independents.

Actually all that is cherished in the standard of an "open society" in Western civilization had some roots in the curious blend of left-wing Calvinism and sectarian perfectionism of the seventeenth century. In addition it was necessary to garner those aspects of truth in the political policy of the English Reformation, particularly of the Elizabethan Settlement, so clearly elaborated in Hooker's *Laws of Ecclesiastical Polity* in which the conservative monarchism of Edmund Burke and the liberal theories of John Locke were both present in embryo.

Clearly an ecumenical movement was necessary to garner the diverse and often contradictory fruits of the Reformation ages and create a consistent Protestant attitude toward political reality. It was also necessary to keep the doctrine relevant to current experience as it was influenced by the world-shaking events which began with the first world war. Significantly the first conference on Life and Work was the conference at Stockholm after the first world war. This, with the other movement on Faith and Order, constituted the ecumenical movement, which in turn resulted in the organization of the World Council of Churches in the conference at Amsterdam. The conference did not fully mirror the crisis in our culture caused by the first world war. That crisis might be defined as caused by the shaking of the dogmas of the eighteenth and nineteenth centuries, affirming the perfectibility of man and the idea of progress.

These dogmas were as potent in religious communities as in secular ones. They had obscured much of the realism which Christianity had contributed to the analysis of the task of preserving a tolerable harmony and justice in a world of sin. Perhaps the triumph of the "democracies" in the bitter conflict gave the Wilsonian idealism, with its hope of "making the world safe for democracy," a special prestige. At any rate the conference breathed the spirit of liberal moralism. There was no evidence of the influence of the more conservative Reformation churches on social theory, perhaps because the defeat of Germany, the national center of Reformation thought, subdued this witness. Nor is there any evidence of the influence of the redoubtable neo-Reformation theologian, Karl Barth, who after Stockholm had increasing influence on ecumenical thought. In 1925, the year of Stockholm, his rebellion against liberal Protestantism, already expressed in his *Römerbrief*, was yet to be felt.

The economic theory of Stockholm, as given in the message, was simply expressed in the words:

We have declared that the soul is of supreme value and must not be subordinated to the rights of property or the mechanisms of industry and that it may claim as its first right, the right of salvation. Therefore we contend for the free and full development of the human personality. . . . Co-operation between capital and labour should take the place of conflict so that employers and employed alike may regard their part in industry as the fulfillment of their vocation.

This Christian individualism and moral idealism hardly came to grips with the problems of a growing industrial civilization. Stockholm could not of course foresee that the Marxist rebellion, initiated in Europe, should have found real lodgment in the defeated Russia after the first world war and that the class conflict in both domestic and international politics was to trouble the world in the next decades, and perhaps centuries.

In the vexing problems of a new international order, which the peacemakers at Versailles tried to solve by accepting Woodrow Wilson's League of Nations, the conference contented itself with the statement:

We have also set forth the guiding principles of Christian internationalism, equally opposed to national bigotry and weak cosmo-
politanism. We have affirmed the universal character of the church
and its duty to preach and practise the love of the brethren. . . . We
have . . . examined the constitution of an international order, which
would provide peaceable methods of removing the causes of war. . . .
We summon the churches to share our horror of war and of its futility
as a means of settling international disputes.

It is of course easy by the wisdom of hindsight, which incorporates the tragic experiences of a century which had not one,
but two, world wars and is now in the throes of a cold war and
a nuclear dilemma, to be critical of this vague moralism. But it
may not be inappropriate to make the judgment that Stockholm
did not exhaust the full dimensions of biblical faith in dealing
with the social problems of a tragic age. The encounter between
the churches had just begun.

In between the Stockholm and the Oxford conferences, many
smaller meetings did much spadework in working out a social
ethic. Thus in a conference of Christian social workers, held in
London in 1930, the statement of principles of Christian ethical
concern becomes much more specific. "In our opinion," declares
the statement,

the Christian virtues of love, service and brotherhood could be effectively implemented upon the basis of a theory of justice as treated
in natural law. We feel that, although capital is necessary in our
complex system of production, it fails to be held in constant reference to Christian principles in regard to production, distribution and
consumption.

This statement is not only more specific than that of Stockholm
but it profits by the Anglican witness in the ecumenical encounter,
revealed in the reference to "natural law." Protestantism, as a
whole, has a too-lively awareness of historical contingencies and
the unique occasion to accept natural law theories uncritically;
and the Reformation belief that reason is not exempt from the
fall, which is to say that reason may be the servant of the passion
and interests of the self, creates an awareness of the ideological

distortions which creep into even the most disinterested definitions of moral norms. Nevertheless the emphasis on natural law is creative in Protestant circles both because it typifies the quest for the most authoritative general norm; and because natural law conceptions invariably emphasize justice, rather than order, as the basic norm of political and economic life.

The Oxford conference on Church, Community, and State was convened in 1937, in an atmosphere of apprehension created by the rise of the Nazi movement in Germany. But it was not this worsening international situation, which was the primary cause of the greater degree of specificity and urbane Christian wisdom, which distinguished Oxford from Stockholm. Two decades of encounter between the churches and of course the encounter between the churches and the rapidly developing industrial and international crisis, helped the Oxford conference to make history in its comprehensive analyses of the complex problems of the political and economic order.

The Oxford report on "Church and State" reveals a truly ecumenical and balanced view of political authority in which the negative and positive approaches to the state, characteristic of the two types of Protestantism, both come into their own. "We recognize existing historical states as given historical realities," the report declares,

each of which is the highest political authority, but which stands itself under the authority and judgment of God. . . . At the same time we recognize that the state, as a specific form and the dominating expression of man's life in a world of sin, often becomes, by its very power and its monopoly of the means of coercion, an instrument of evil. Since we believe in the holy God as a source of justice, we do not consider the state as a source of law but as its guarantor. It is not the lord, but the servant, of justice.

There were, of course, some unresolved conflicting positions at Oxford, particularly in regard to the authority of the state to wage war. The conference recognized three historic positions on this question: (1) the position of the orthodox Reformation, which gave the state undisputed authority in the use of the sword;

(2) the majority position, that the state could wage war in self-defense and in the interests of justice (this position, championed, among others, by Archbishop Temple, perhaps the most influential Christian leader of the conference, was to play an important role in the subsequent "interventionist" debates which preceded the second world war); (3) the pacifist attitude toward war, which represented the viewpoint, not only of the historic "peace churches" but a considerable section of the other churches, was recognized as a legitimate Christian witness. Dr. Temple's immense authority did not succeed in persuading the conference to define pacifism as a "Christian heresy." Since Oxford the second position has become regnant. The first position was refuted not only by the ecumenical consensus but by the encounter of the Church with Nazism. The pacifist witness has remained, as is proper, a recognized minority witness in the Church.

In dealing with the relation of the love commandment to political and economic structures, Oxford was wise and circumspect. It warned against two errors:

The one is to regard the realities of justice, incorporated in given systems of order, as so inferior to the law of love, that the latter cannot be a principle of discriminate judgment between them but only a principle of indiscriminate judgment upon them all. . . . The other error is to equate a particular system with the kingdom of God.

The report wisely suggests that this error leads conservatives to give religious sanction to the status quo, and the critics of the status quo to give religious sanction to a new system, which, when its defects are revealed, leads to disillusion. The report indicts the prevailing capitalistic system of the Western world for aggravating acquisitiveness and for not correcting flagrant inequalities. It thus points to what has since been achieved in Western democracies in the form of the minimal securities of the welfare state, and the combination of social planning and free initiative of a mixed economy.

The report makes a necessary distinction between the duty to create more perfect structures of justice on the one hand and the responsibility of love which transcends any given structure and comprehends the dignity of the person in the most perfect and imperfect of social and economic structures. Finally the report calls for self-criticism of both the groups which are tempted to complacency by their ideological commitment to an established order and the rebellious group who invest an alternative with an ultimate sanction which it cannot deserve.

The conference encouraged Christians to be responsible in a wide variety of social reform efforts but warned that no program could claim the right to be called "Christian." Long before Russian Communism revealed the evils of an omnicompetent state, Oxford warned against simple alternatives of socialization of property to the present system. It declared: "Recent Russian history warns us of the danger of irresponsible political power supplanting irresponsible economic power, if the democratic control of power is destroyed."

In short the Oxford conference laid the foundation for what has developed into an impressive system of Christian pragmatism. It is Christian in the sense that the law of love on the one hand and the Christian awareness of the law of self-love as a ubiquitous and persistent force describes the upper and the lower limits of a social order in a sinful world. Love describes the upper limits in two ways. It is a constant principle of discriminate, rather than indiscriminate, judgment upon various structures of justice; and it makes demands upon the individual which transcend every system of justice. The persistence of self-love in any system warns against all utopian illusions, particularly those which derive social evil from a specific source or institution, whether in the economic or political order. The approach is pragmatic in the sense that it becomes increasingly aware of the contingent circumstances of history which determine how much or how little it is necessary to emphasize the various regulative principles of justice, equality and liberty, security of the community or the freedom of the individual, the order of the integral community and, as is now increasingly the case, the peace of the world community.

The first Assembly of the newly organized "World Council of Churches" embodying both the "Life and Work" and "Faith and

Amsterdam, 1948

Order" movements, met in the summer of 1948 at Amsterdam, Holland. The tragic second world war had ended but a few years and the Communist movement had grown to world-wide proportions. The pressures of current experience and the additional encounter between churches of various viewpoints served to accentuate the note of sober realism in the social doctrines of the ecumenical movement of the non-Roman churches.

The emphasis on "Middle Axioms," initiated by Archbishop Temple, embodied the truth in the natural law theories, namely the perennial principles of social policy stemming from perennially operative forces in the human community and from the intuitions of justice or the rational calculations and discriminations which seek to make justice into an instrument of the love commandment.

The political dogmas of both right and left, of both "free enterprise" and "socialization" are increasingly dissolved by history and common experience. The report on political and economic organization declared:

The Church cannot resolve the debate between those who feel that the primary solution (of the social problem) is the socialization of the means of production and those who fear that such a course will merely lead to new and inordinate combinations of political and economic power [but it is prepared to say] to the advocates of the socialization of property that the institution is not the root of the corruption of human nature. We must equally say to the defenders of existing property relations that ownership is not an unconditioned right. It must be preserved, curtailed and distributed according to the requirements of justice.

The report observes that:

the revolt of the multitudes against injustice gives communism much of its strength. . . . Christians who are the beneficiaries of capitalism should try to see the world from the perspective of those who are excluded from its benefits and who see in Communism a means of deliverance from poverty and insecurity.

The Amsterdam report nevertheless goes on:

The churches should reject the ideologies of both Communism and *laissez-faire* capitalism and should draw men from the false assumption that these extremes are the only alternatives. Each has made promises that it could not fulfil.

This well-balanced statement, which current history has validated, seemed to many in the West as merely an effort to preserve a balance in the first signs of the "cold war." On the other hand there were critics of capitalism who challenged the term "laissez-faire capitalism" (incidentally suggested by the distinguished American layman Charles P. Taft) as a way of breaking the impact of the judgment upon Western institutions. It was in fact a recognition of the obvious fact that Western democracies had slowly corrected the injustices of early industrialism by bringing the freedom in the economic order under progressive moral and political control. The subsequent consistent development of the welfare state and of a mixed economy proved the correctness of a definition of Western institutions which condemned the original dogma but not the present mixed realities. The first Assembly of the World Council expressed in every domain of life and analysis a note of sober realism, a circumspect distinction between the soteriological and ethical dimensions of human existence, of the realms of grace and of law; and a freedom from the political dogmas of the past, which potentially put the ecumenical movement in a reconciling position in the political dogmatic debates which would erupt in the next decades.

The second Assembly of the World Council, held in 1954 in Evanston, Illinois, built its social doctrine on the foundations laid in Oxford and Amsterdam. The rapidly developing world situation naturally prompted attention to new areas of concern. In international problems Evanston particularly commended the United Nations for its declaration of human rights and for its technical assistance program. It failed, at one point, to anticipate the actual course of international events. It rightly warned against the efforts of the great powers to dominate the organization, despite the constant reiteration of the principle of the "equal sovereignty" of all states great and small. But it did not prepare the conscience of the churches for the dread realities of the present in which two great powers competitively share responsibility, both for the development of technically backward nations and for the prevention of a dread nuclear holocaust. In one respect the United Nations has, however, fulfilled the hopes of the Evanston Assembly. It has become a forum in which the small nations can fashion world opinion which may ultimately place a check upon the great powers and can furnish the tissue of world community.

The two problems, one age-old and the other new, which engaged Evanston with a new sense of urgency were racial tensions and the desire of the technically undeveloped nations for both political independence and technical competence. Its plea for racial and ethnic brotherhood was uncompromising but, fortunately, not uniquely Protestant. The recent Papal Encyclical *Mater et Magistra* gives witness to the concern of the Catholic Church for the universality of the responsibility of brotherhood, inside and outside the Church. And the secular community has frequently contributed to the cause of racial understanding in ways which might shame complacent churches. In this realm it is not necessary for the churches, Roman and non-Roman, to develop a unique social ethic, but merely to make an honest application of the universalistic elements in the Christian ethic.

In the realm of assistance to what became known as "areas of rapid social change," the World Council since Evanston has broken new ground by establishing a special commission to study and explicate the responsibilities of the churches in those areas of the world in which political independence and the impingement of technical and industrial forms of community upon old, organic forms of community create many new problems while solving the age-old problem and burden of penury. The most recent study by the secretary of the commission, Dr. Paul Abrecht, entitled, *The Churches and Rapid Social Change*, is an excellent example of the increasing detail with which the ecumenical movement explicates its essential position. The splendid work of this commission is the last fruit of the growing tendency toward empirical and pragmatic approaches to specific moral and social problems, which is held within the general framework of the love commandment, the law which fulfills and dissolves all specific laws, fashioned for particular occasions, but soon dated and outmoded by new occasions.

The Protestant and Greek churches cannot claim to have any monopoly of wisdom available to a harassed humanity, living amidst the revolutions of race and nations, and standing under the impending judgment of a nuclear catastrophe, which, in prospect at least, will be of eschatological proportions. They may, however, modestly claim that their experience of brotherly encounter with each other has enriched the common heritage, overcome the fractional character of various traditions, and adjusted and applied the whole to the rapidly changing world situation.

[1963]

PART THREE

Liberty and Equality *(1957)*

Yale Review

INSOFAR as the debate between conservatism and liberalism is a contest between the beneficiaries and the victims of any given status quo, it may be politically potent but it is philosophically uninteresting. It merely reveals the ideological taint in our political preferences. But the debate may mean more than that. It may involve the significance of the two principles of liberty and equality as principles of justice. Traditional conservatism and liberalism have contrasting attitudes toward those principles, conservatism being usually indifferent to them, while liberalism appreciates them as regulative principles and sometimes erroneously regards them as simple historical possibilities.

But even a debate on this level tends to become otiose because the history of the great democratic nations tends to separate truth from falsehood in each political philosophy and to create a legitimate conservatism and a legitimate liberalism, which are nearer to each other than either is to a cynical conservatism or to an abstract liberalism. We must try to find the reasons for this development in political thought. They are related on the one hand to the inevitability and on the other hand to the corruption of the social gradations and the nonvoluntary forces of social cohesion which enter into every form of stable community.

Every community is organized through a hierarchy of authority and function, and its forces of cohesion contain such nonvoluntary and subrational forces as kinship feeling, geographic contiguity, common memories and common fears, and ultimately the police power of the state, the community's chief organ of unity and will. The principle of "equality" is a relevant criterion of criticism for the social hierarchy, and the principle of "liberty" serves the same purpose for the community's unity. But neither principle could be wholly or absolutely applied without destroying the community.

To validate this thesis it will be necessary to analyze in turn the relation of equality to the realities of the social or political hierarchy and the principle of liberty to the realities of communal cohesion and stability. The necessity of a gradation of authority and function in any community or common enterprise must be obvious to even the most casual observer. Every school with more than one room is coordinated under the authority of a "principal"; and every school system with more than one school has a superintendent. Most churches have a hierarchy of superintendents, deacons, or bishops. Communities of common work reveal the same gradations of function and authority. A specialized production operation is governed by a foreman, and the total production is governed and coordinated by a "production manager." The other specialized functions of sales, promotion, and finance each have their managers or, in this latter day, "vice-presidents." The whole enterprise is governed by a president or general manager, who is usually under the authority of a board of trustees, representing the owners, in the modern case usually multiple owners. The managerial oligarchy has proved more important than the original theories of ownership anticipated, but that is another story. The political order is integrated by the same sort of hierarchical structure.

Political communities of early days grew gradually from tribe to city-state and from city-state to empire. The instrument of cohesion in an early empire was usually some dominant city-state, even as the instrument of unity in the city-state was a king, originally a tribal chieftain, or perhaps, as in Greece, the authority was wielded by a whole aristocratic class. The national community was a fairly late development in Western history; its unity was usually the result of ethnic kinship, a common language, and the dominance of the king over the nobles. Democratic institutions were the final but not the first instruments of national unity. Democracy has brought arbitrary power under check and made it responsible, but it has not seriously altered the hierarchical structure of the community. Even democratic communities are integrated by military and civil bureaucracies and by local legislative assemblies and governors. The military order depends upon a rigorous adhesion to the "chain of command."

The distinctions in function invariably involve a distinction of authority for the higher functions, and greater authority means greater power. Prestige or "majesty" is the inevitable concomitant of power, and it in turn becomes the very source of power, insofar as power is usually the ability to win uncoerced consent. Special privilege flows inevitably from the exercise of power. The distinctions of power and prestige are very great in traditional communities because they are necessary to achieve the unity of the community. The majesty of the king is, in fact, usually the symbol and instrument of the majesty of the community. Its inordinate degree is intended to discourage dissent, for traditional communities have not yet found a way of allowing dissent within the framework of unity. But besides this functional necessity of excessive distinctions in prestige there was always the ideological factor that the greater the authority and power of a leader, the more he himself determined the degree of power and prestige he was to enjoy. One must regard it as axiomatic, therefore, that gradations of power and prestige were never exactly proportioned to the social function which furnished their basic justification.

Inequalities of privilege were of course always partly proportioned to prestige and function. But they never corresponded exactly to these inequalities of function. They exceed the requirements of social function ever more obviously as one ascends the social hierarchy. We thus confront the two basic realities of the community's social hierarchy. The one is that such a hierarchy is necessary, and the other is that the prestige, power, and privilege, particularly privilege, of its upper levels tend to be inordinate. That is why there can be no simple solution for the problem of social gradation. That is why equality must remain a regulative principle of justice and why equalitarianism is the ideology of the poor. They resent the inequalities, rightly because of their inordinate character; but they wrongly imagine that all inequalities could be abolished. Inequalities are no doubt more excessive in traditional communities than they are in modern "liberal" states. They are unduly so partly because the traditional communities, whether in the medieval West or in modern Asia and Africa, needed to pay the price of inordinate gradation of prestige and power for the boon of communal unity, and partly because the communities lacked sufficient equilibria of power to establish equality.

Modern business and industrial civilization was regarded by the strict equalitarians, the Marxists, as tending to accentuate the inequalities of traditional societies; and there were indeed early indications that this would be the case. The business community, on the other hand, whether honestly or ideologically, expressed the hope that political liberty would gradually lead to general equality, in the economic and in the political sphere. This hope was mistaken in the short run but not in the long run. Political liberty did not yield relative equality until the poorer classes achieved both political and trade-union organizations by which they could set organized power against organized power.

This equilibrium of organized power has refuted the catastrophic predictions of Marxism and rendered the Western world safe against revolutionary resentment. But it has not eliminated the necessity of the gradation of function and authority, as presupposed by an abstract equalitarianism. The social hierarchy is as omnipresent in a "liberal" community as in a traditional one, and for that matter in a Communist one. Nor has it eliminated excessive privilege for the higher degrees of authority and competence. In fact, a commercial and competitive society adds competition for the highest positions as a further reason for excessive privilege. That is the reason that the great business executives draw salaries greater than the salary of the President of the nation. The corruption of a necessary gradation of authority is as inevitable as the gradation itself, and justifies the criterion of equality as a permanent challenge to the real and potential injustices in the community, and as a way of reducing the excesses by scrutinizing every privilege in relation to the function to which it is attached.

The principle of liberty is related to the unity of a society as the principle of equality is related to the hierarchical structure of the community. It is a twin regulative principle, and it is in the same danger of being regarded as a simple historical possibility. The unity and stability of traditional communities, from primitive days to the end of the medieval period in the West, and to the present day in Asia and Africa, were achieved by permitting as little dissent as possible and by enforcing conformity, not chiefly by force and terror, as in the modern totalitarian state, but by a culture-and-custom-enforced idolatrous devotion to the community as the final end of human existence. Every community seeks unity and stability as the price of existence itself, for chaos means nonexistence. The long popularity of the dynastic monarchy in the history of nations was due to the efficacy of this institution in assuring a single unchallenged organ of unity to the state and in assuring a method of transmitting authority from generation to generation without exposing the community to the chaos of conflicting choices of authority. The unity of the community seemed to eliminate liberty as a possibility as rigorously as the hierarchical structure seemed to eliminate equality. The unity and stability of the community makes liberty even today less than an absolute right. Nevertheless the tendency of the community to claim the individual's devotion too absolutely, and to disregard his hopes, fears, and ambitions which are in conflict with, or irrelevant to, the communal end, makes it necessary to challenge the community in the name of liberty. Liberty is just as unrealizable in the absolute sense and just as relevant as the principle of equality.

According to democratic mythology, particularly in France and America, it was the French Revolution which first introduced these twin principles of liberty and equality to history (together with the ideal of "fraternity" which was at once more relevant and more irrelevant to practical politics). It was certainly the French Enlightenment which nourished the illusion of the historical realizability of the two principles. But they originated in the previous century among the Christian radicals on the left wing of Cromwell's army. The Enlightenment merely provided a secular version of the apocalyptic visions of these Christian sectaries. But one of the two principles had a much longer history than that: "equality." It was first introduced by Greek stoicism as a principle of justice, and strangely enough was popularized by the Roman stoics, who were politicians and lawyers rather than philosophers, and who insisted on the relevance of the principle despite the hierarchical structure of the Roman imperial state.

Aristotle defined justice as the disposition "to give each man his due" and was careful to apportion the "due" of the superior and the inferior man. His political philosophy was influential in sanctifying not only the classical but the medieval aristocratic structure. In contrast, Seneca, who with Cicero may be deemed the father of all modern political sentimentality, thought that free man and slave "were but names springing from ambition and injury." Stoic equalitarianism did not seriously affect the class structure of the Roman state. In fact the stoic idealists were more realistic than their French inheritors because they relegated the principle of equality to a mythical "golden age," in which the *Jus Naturale* was absolutely applied. In actual history the institutions of slavery, government, and property were observed to be universal restraints enjoined or allowed by the *Jus Genitum*, the law of nations. Thus stoicism expressed, if not consistently, the idea that equality was a regulative principle of justice but not directly applicable to the life of the community. That insight was superior to the simple equalitarianism of the French Enlightenment.

The classical age did not put the principle of liberty in conjunction with the principle of equality, but neither was it discovered by the French Enlightenment. The English sectaries were the first to join liberty with equality as one of the two principles of justice. The idea of the freedom of the individual did not emerge until it had the support first of the Christian faith, with its high value for the uniqueness of the individual and with its belief that the individual had a source of authority and an ultimate fulfillment transcending the community. But this alone did not establish individual liberty as a principle of justice. If the religious foundation had been all that was necessary to grant the individual freedom from the communal whole, liberty would have been propounded and achieved in the Christian ages of Europe. But Catholic Christianity had its own interpretation of liberty. For it liberty meant the right of the individual to seek his "eternal" rather than his temporal end, and this end could be guaranteed by the Church rather than the political community.

Even the Protestant Reformation, which rebelled against the authoritarian Church, did little to vindicate the right of the individual against the state. Luther's ideal of "evangelical" liberty was religiously potent but politically irrelevant because it did not challenge the authority of the state over the conscience of the individual. It wasn't until Milton interpreted the well-known words of scripture "Give unto Caesar the things that are Caesar's and to God the things that are God's" to mean "My conscience I have from God and I can therefore not give it to Caesar" that the religious ideal became relevant to political and civil liberty.

But the rise of the commercial middle class, with its more mobile forms of property and with its desire for individual initiative, was required to break the mold of a purely organic and traditional society and to insist on liberty as a regulative principle of justice. Ever since the seventeenth century, libertarian principles have been motivated by both ultimate and economic motives; and middle-class libertarianism was expressed both in John Stuart Mill's "Essay on Liberty" and Adam Smith's "Wealth of Nations." In the one case the individual was vindicated against the community, and in the other a philosophical basis for "free enterprise" was laid down and the hope was held out for the achievement of justice through the automatic balances of a market economy.

There were both libertarians and equalitarians in the radical forces of seventeenth-century England and eighteenth-century France. In Cromwell's army the Levellers tended to be libertarians and the "Diggers" equalitarians, and the ideological difference between the preference for liberty and the preference for equality between the middle classes and the poorer classes has been apparent from the Cromwellian to this day. Neither the libertarians nor the equalitarians realized that equality and liberty are in paradoxical relation to each other and that it is possible to purchase the one only at the price of the other. This paradox was obscured by the hope of the libertarians that political liberty would ultimately bring the fruit of equality and by the hope of the equalitarians that the abolition of property would ultimately result in the "withering away of the state."

The libertarians proved more right in the long run than the equalitarians. They had illusions about the immediate efficacy of liberty in creating equal justice, but these illusions were harmless so long as a free society made it possible to create balances of power in both the political and economic sphere which would make for justice. The equalitarians proved themselves wholly wrong because their theories made it possible for a group of elite to establish a monopoly of power in the name of utopia. But the superiority of libertarian over equalitarian liberalism is not as interesting in this context as the fact that both forms of liberalism were abstract and unrealistic in coming to terms with the perennial factors of social hierarchy and social unity and stability, which made liberty and equality the regulative principles but not the realizable goals of the community.

It is rather significant that both the Christian radicals of seventeenth-century England and the secularist radicals of eighteenth-century France were utopian. Perhaps it was not possible to challenge the organic unities and social hierarchies of traditional society without a measure of illusion. Illusion may have been the necessary motive force of social protest. Subsequent history tended to develop a viable form of liberalism which was conscious of both the dangers of an organic unity and an excessive social hierarchy, and of the perennial character of these two phenomena in any community. It also developed a viable conservatism, which was distinguished from a viable liberalism only by an ideologically conditioned emphasis on either the necessity, or the corruption, of these two phenomena.

But in order to analyze these forms of liberalism and conservatism more exactly we must consider the history of liberal and conservative thought in the three great nations—France, Britain, and America—which have given us the most characteristic embodiments of a democratic society. In the American imagination France was the first nation to shatter the mold of an organic aristocratic civilization. It was in fact, however, the second and not the first, the Cromwellian Revolution in England having preceded the French Revolution by more than a century. But meanwhile the Restoration had again put a king on the throne in England. Since monarchy was the symbol of malignant power for both French and American equalitarians and libertarians, the Cromwellian Revolution was forgotten and France became the symbol of the new day of liberty and fraternity both in her own esteem and in ours. This was a pity, for as a matter of fact France also became the embodiment of all abstract liberalism. The first danger of such abstract idealism is that the ideals are not in sufficient contact with reality to engage the stuff of history, and abstract liberalism becomes irrelevant liberalism. The second danger is that an heroic effort will be made to apply the ideal to the social stuff without any recognition of its paradoxical character. French liberalism became involved in both errors.

The first danger came from the attempt to apply the ideals rigorously. Though the revolutionary ferment of the Enlightenment favored libertarianism more than equalitarianism, the actual course of the revolution led to the annulment of liberty and the effort to establish equality by methods which Edmund Burke described as "leveling everything which had raised up its head." The annulment of liberty in the Jacobin fanaticism was the fruit of a simple rationalism, which agreed with the Catholic position that "error" does not have the same right as "truth" and could not imagine any truth contradicting the truth it had perceived. Thus the foundations were laid for what Talmon calls "Totalitarian Democracy." The presuppositions of this kind of democracy naturally led to Bonapartist absolutism. There was no recognition in it of the fragmentary character of all human knowledge and virtue, nor of the necessity of guarding against all centers of power, even if, and particularly when, power pretends to speak in the name of the "people." The Communists' version of "peoples' democracy" reveals that they are quite conscious of the deep affinity and historical connection between the first and the second version of totalitarian democracy.

Idealistic fanaticism, which does not recognize the uses to which ideals may be put, is dangerous. But it is equally dangerous to cover the perennial realities of man's social life with an idealistic slogan. Thus France never "restored" the traditional order as in Britain. But in another sense the revolution had never abolished it. Parliament was governed by revolutionary slogans but the bureaucracy which really governed France frantically preserved the ancient distinctions and inequalities. The rising middle class thought it sufficient to liquidate the aristocracy in order to achieve "equality," but it proved itself desperately anxious to maintain its privileged position against the rising industrial classes.

Despite the fact that the freedom of economic enterprise had its inception in the French physiocratic theory, the French business classes were singularly lacking in "enterprise," so that a moribund capitalism, together with the frantic class consciousness of the middle classes, succeeded in driving the industrial workers to revolutionary desperation in a nation which had presumably established liberty and equality. The imperial relations of a technical to a nontechnical nation, more specifically the relation of France to North Africa, were also approached in terms of an abstract universalism. Algeria was simply incorporated into metropolitan France, and this was supposed to satisfy Algerian aspirations. Tragic events of recent history prove that the organic and historic forms of human togetherness cannot be so easily dissolved by abstract individualism and universalism. France as a nation must finally come to terms with the budding nation of Algeria and with the fact that the Algerians cannot be made into Frenchmen by an act of parliament.

Whether it be fair to make France the symbol of an abstract liberalism, it has certainly proved that such liberalism is dangerous, whether it believes in the possibility of realizing simply the principles of liberty or of equality, or does not really believe in either but merely obscures the actual realities without being critical of them.

England has obviously had some historic advantages over France in coming to terms with the moral realities of an open society. It is not quite clear whether these advantages alone will account for the superior wisdom of English culture in welding the virtues of a traditional civilization with those of a technical one. Some of the advantages derive from the character of the forces operative in the Cromwellian Revolution. They contained not only utopian equalitarians (such as Winstanley) and utopian libertarians such as the Levellers, but independents who genuinely believed in liberty as such and not merely in liberty for themselves. Some of them understood too that liberty can be sustained only by a spirit of tolerance which understands the fragmentary character of all human knowledge, and confesses with John Saltmarsh that "my truth is as dark to thee as thy truth is dark to me until the Lord enlighten all our seeing."

Some of the superior wisdom undoubtedly derives from the remnants of traditional virtues which were represented in the forces of Cromwell's army. There was, for instance, Ireton's shrewd observation that he preferred "the rights of Englishmen to the rights of man," meaning that a mutually acknowledged right and responsibility was a more reliable guarantee of justice than abstractly conceived "inalienable rights." All the superiority of a common law tradition, of an unwritten constitution, and a history in which "liberty broadens down from precedent to precedent" is expressed in this preference.

Some of the superior wisdom may have derived from a man like Richard Hooker, who combined the sense of historical reali-

ties with the Thomistic concepts of "natural law," and who thus
became the father of the theories both of John Locke, the philosopher of the English Revolution, and of Edmund Burke, the
critic of the French Revolution. At any rate there was enough
virtue in the thought and the achievements of a traditional society
to permit a "restoration" when the revolutionary fever had spent
itself and Cromwell could not maintain himself without annulling
democracy. The Restoration did not, however, restore the traditional society without embodying the truths and justices of the
revolution. It finally led to the constitution of 1688 which not
only established William and Mary on the throne but also added
the idea of the peoples' sovereignty to the idea of monarchy as
a symbol of the continuing will of a people distinct from the
momentary will by which governments were made and unmade.
A more pluralistic society was established in this way than by the
way of pure revolution, and guards were set up against monopolies
of power.

Above all, the traditional and inevitable social hierarchies and
communal stabilities were protected against too simple applica-
tions of the criteria of liberty and equality, while the hierarchies
were subjected to the judgment of these criteria of justice and
placed under the check of universal suffrage. Thus a community
was created which could absorb, and profit from, both the middle
class and the workers' rebellion without rending the wholeness
of a traditional culture and community. This community was in
time to confront the world with the spectacle of an aristocratic
society quickened, after a terrible war, by the socialist slogan of
"fair shares for all." In obedience to that slogan it could set up
a welfare state under the aegis of a constitutional monarchy. It
could even liquidate an empire and transmute it into a commonwealth of nations. Both a nation and an empire were remolded
gradually and therefore more wisely than by revolutionary fanaticism. The organic aspects of community were protected, but their
excesses were corrected by the new balances of power made possible in a commercial civilization.

American thought and practice can be understood only as the

unique experience of a democracy created on virgin soil and without an aristocratic historical background. But it is also helpful to realize that we have drawn our theories mostly from France and our practice from Britain. The effort to build a balance of power into the very heart of government by the "separation of powers" was a novel invention, drawn from Calvinistic sources. *— p. 202* On the whole the founding fathers had a less roseate view of the perfectibility of man than the French philosophers. They therefore wisely took precautions against any monopoly of power establishing itself, including monopolies which tried to speak in the name of the people.

America developed a plutocracy rather than an aristocracy. Although such a society of money power does not have the security of an hereditary aristocracy, we nevertheless had a common-sense appreciation of the requirements of national unity and gradation of authority which went beyond the wisdom of traditional liberalism. Yet we were able to build a remarkably "open" society, partly by grace of an advancing frontier and a continually expanding economy. These favorable circumstances, rather than French prestige, are probably responsible for the note of sentimentality in our political thought. We have regarded both liberty and equality as more easily realizable than they are. But we have realized them beyond the dreams of any European nation.

We failed catastrophically only on one point—in our relation to the Negro race. This "American dilemma" is on the way to being resolved, and one of the instruments of its resolution has proved to be the constitutional insistence on equality as a criterion of justice. This insistence the Supreme Court has recently implemented after generations of hesitation in regard to the application of the principle to our relation with a minority group, which has the disadvantage of diverging obviously from the dominant type in our nation and which still bears the onus of former subjugation in slavery.

At last the seeming sentimentality of the preamble of our Declaration of Independence—the declaration that "all men are created equal"—has assumed political reality and relevance. It is not true that all men are created equal, but the statement is a symbol of the fact that all men are to be treated equally within the terms of the gradations of function which every healthy society uses for its organization. We have, in other words, done tolerably well in transmuting sentimentalities into relevant criteria of justice. But we have done it partly by grace of a virgin continent, an advancing frontier, and an expanding economy. Hence our political thought always lags behind our practice. Our performance is wiser than our theory; and we are more virtuous than we claim to be.

We still present ourselves to the world in terms of pure libertarian slogans. Either the world misunderstands us because of these slogans, or it knows us well enough to realize that our achievement has been not so much the attainment of pure liberty as the attainment of equal justice and social stability within the framework of a free society. But such an appreciation must be gained against the influence of caricatures of ourselves which both we and our Communist detractors insist on making.

Both a purely libertarian appreciation and a purely equalitarian criticism of our political realities distort the true picture of American democracy.

[1957]

Power and Ideology in National and International Affairs (1959)

E VERY student of politics knows that political communities
and relations must deal with "power" rather than pure
persuasion on the one hand or merely with "force" on the other
hand. Force may be defined as the physical power to coerce the
will against the inclination. It is always an alloy in the structure
of power, whether in internal or in external affairs; but power is
something much more complex than force.

Power is, in fact, composed of the authority and prestige which
gains the implicit or explicit consent of the subject or the ally
with a minimal use of coercive force. Pure force may be necessary in conflict situations in which it is impossible to influence
the foe; and force, therefore, becomes the *ultima ratio* of conflict.
In domestic situations, where the sovereignty of a government
rests upon the ability to wield police power alone, sovereignty and
tyranny become identical.

Ferrero, in his *Principles of Power,* has taught us to distinguish
between legitimate and illegitimate government in terms of the
authority of the one to gain either implicit or explicit consent,
and the inability of the other to establish authority except by
"force and fraud." The significance of this distinction is that it
places both democratic and traditional governments in the category of "legitimate" governments. The former relies upon explicit
consent for the authority of a particular government, but must

also rely on implicit consent for the authority of the system of government which permits the alternation of particular governments by popular will. The latter is more legitimate than pure democrats are inclined to believe because it has enough implicit consent to dispense with fraud and to rely on only a minimum of force. In short, the source of power is the authority of a government to gain consent without force. In international relations, this authority is transmuted into prestige, which is able to win allies and gain cooperation without coercion.

If power is identical with authority, it follows that the climate of a culture or its "ideology," which sanctions a particular type of authority, is really the ultimate source of power. The implicit consent for the system of government which allows alternations of government by explicit consent was established in Western society only through four centuries of tortuous history in which it was proved that such freedom and flexibility was not incompatible with, but actually a resource for, stability and justice. The Western world was rather tardy in proving that justice and freedom were compatible. The fact that the case was not proved in the period of early industrialization in nineteenth-century Europe was responsible for the rise of the competitive ideology of Communism.

Before the rise of democracy, legitimate governments drew their authority from various ideological systems which were identical in their emphasis upon justifying the authority of government chiefly by its ability to maintain order, if the order was not bought at too great a price of justice. That is to say that it was taken for granted that the concentration of power in government was a necessary evil, which would result in some injustice. But if the injustice became intolerable, as it did in the later stages of absolute monarchy, the authority of government broke down. In other words, justice is always a secondary, though not a primary, source of authority and prestige. The primary source is the capacity to maintain order because order is tantamount to existence in a community, and chaos means nonexistence.

The ability to maintain order in traditional governments since the rise of the first empires in Egypt and Babylon rested on the authority derived on the one hand from the prestige of continued rule and on the other hand from the prestige gained from the claim that the political order was an extension and an application of the cosmic order. In the one case the "legitimacy" of dynastic inheritance guaranteed the transmission of authority from generation to generation. In the other case idolatrous claims were made for the priest-kings and god-kings of Egypt and Babylon in order that both legitimacy in the narrow sense and in the sense of the ultimacy of the order would guarantee the "majesty" necessary to prevent chaos. In both cases, reverence for an order which a generation could not create but from which it could benefit was involved. This is the religious element in the majesty of government. The priests did not create this reverence for providence but they could manipulate it. They were, therefore, the chief agents of the "organization of consent" in the ancient empires.

While the rise of Christianity eliminated the explicitly idolatrous element in the majesty of government, it is interesting that political authority in the West, since Emperor Constantine, made religious claims for the source of its authority, and that with the Hildebrandine papacy the Pope sought to overtop these claims by asserting the supremacy of the sacerdotal. The Protestant Reformation was, at first, so intent on challenging the claims of the Pope in the name of the king, and it was so afraid of chaos if the latter's claims were not religiously supported, that the post-Reformation era gave little support for the rise of a democratic ideology. In short, the ideological support for political power, whether of Pharaoh, Emperor, Pope or King, whether in pagan or in Christian cultures, was contained in the twin emphases upon providence: the stability of a dynastic house, transmitting authority through the generations, and its relation to cosmic or divine order and intention.

Through all these millennia it was order, and not justice or freedom, which was the primary concern of the architects of the political community. Nevertheless, the modern free society slowly came into being in which the prestige of justice was added to the source of authority, and freedom was made a prerequisite of justice. How did this ideological shift occur? One answer is that the monopoly of power in absolute monarchy or in the papacy became so vexatious that the injustice which was the by-product of monarchial order destroyed the implicit consent by which dynasts ruled. The breakdown of dynastic rule made room for the ideology of an open society in which the "consent of the governed" was made into the ultimate source of authority. Stated in absolutely consistent terms this principle made for either anarchy or tyranny, as it did in the French Revolution, for it is not in the power of each generation to engineer the consent for a system of government but only for a particular government.

A free society must have a proper reverence for the principle of government as a source of order and a proper insistence that the power of government must be brought under control of the people, and that the majesty of government must be partly derived from its capacity for justice. This proper balance was first achieved in the political theories of the later Calvinists and since has been elaborated by both sectarian and secular political theorists, so that modern political authority is derived from the capacity of the ruler to maintain both order and justice. It must be observed that these ideological changes in the approach to the political order were not purely rational or religious. A certain shift in the power relations of the classes was instrumental. The middle or commercial classes, kept politically impotent in the communities in which priests and soldiers shared dominion from the rise of Egypt to the decline of the Middle Ages, became the real protagonists of the theory of the consent of the "governed" by claiming political power and authority. Commensurate with their growing economic power, they formed a society in which a monopoly of power was not easy for any portion of society, and which gradually proved by tortuous history that this freedom and flexibility could be made the servant, rather than the nemesis, of order. For these commercial classes had created a commercial civilization. In the flexibilities of that new civilization a more flexible instrument of political authority was necessary.

Thus through four centuries of Western Christian history, political authority was gradually elaborated which could grant freedom and which needed the prestige of justice as the source of its authority as well as the prestige of being the instrument of order. The culture and climate, the "ideology" which supports democratic authority in the Western world is thus drawn partly from the peculiar flexibilities and necessities of a technical society, partly from the Christian tradition, which valued the individual as transcending any social process and political community, and partly from modern secularism and empiricism which generated the temper of criticism and punctured the religious pretensions which were the source of so much political authority in the past.

The ideological resources of a democratic political authority are, in fact, so various that one is tempted to be skeptical about the capacity of any culture to create this kind of power or authority if it does not possess both the flexibilities and mobilities of a technical society and the ultimate religious presuppositions of the Judaeo-Christian culture. These presuppositions are important because, in contrast to the mystic religions of the Orient, they emphasize the dignity of the individual and his responsibility transcending all political processes and cohesions. The democratic "way of life" faces an original embarrassment in seeking prestige beyond the confines of the West by the fact that it seems a luxury which only our kind of civilization can achieve. The embarrassment increases as we find ourselves in competition and conflict with the Communist power precisely on the two continents of Asia and Africa on which the achievements of democracy in making freedom compatible with both justice and stability seem unattainable, at least in the short run, and in which our prestige derived from justice is defective when applied to foreign, rather than domestic, relations.

It would be simple to solve the problem by defining the Communist competitor as a power system based upon "force and fraud." It does generate terrible injustices by its monopoly of power, and its claims of justice are on the whole fraudulent. But such a solution of the problem is too simple because the Communist competitor derives both its political authority at home and its prestige abroad from an ideological system, which, however mistaken, has sufficient plausibility to impress the colored continents. Let us, therefore, consider the ideological presuppositions from which the authority of Communist governments derive.

The ideological system which makes Communism something more dangerous than a system of power based upon "force and fraud" is drawn partly from the sectarian apocalyptic visions of a kingdom of perfect justice and partly from the materialistic but ethically idealistic concepts of "totalitarian democracy" which had their rise in the French Revolution. It gained lodgment in the West precisely because a democratic society had not, in the early period of industrialization, perfected its equilibria of power sufficiently to guarantee justice. The authority of democratic governments was challenged on the ground that government was an engine of injustice rather than an instrument of justice. The primary dogma of Communism was that government played this sad role because it was an instrument of an outmoded property system which could be abolished only by a revolution. Communism had a secondary dogma according to which the dominant classes of a capitalistic society exploited not only the internal proletariat but the "colonial" nations, that is, the nations of the nontechnical world. It is the secondary dogma which concerns us particularly in our ideological conflict with Communism on the colored continents. We must recognize that this is primarily an ideological conflict. It cannot be solved by appeals to arms even though arms must be held in readiness for the possibility of various conflicts of pure military force.

The ideological situation in Europe is most briefly described by recognizing that the original injustices of a free society have been so far corrected as to give the free governments of the Western world sufficient prestige of both justice and stability to make the whole technical civilization practically immune to Communism. Significantly, the Communist creed is a live option only in the moribund capitalism of France and the semifeudal culture of Italy. It has, until recently, triumphed in Eastern Europe, partly by sheer force of arms and geographic propinquity, and partly by ethnic "Slavic" sense of kinship, and partly because the economy of Eastern Europe was sufficiently feudal and agrarian to give the Communist dogma a certain plausibility. One of the ironic facts of history is that Communist dogma hopes for a climax of revolution out of the mounting injustices of capitalism, but actually achieves the greatest plausibility in decaying feudal societies, which have exactly the imbalances of power and resulting injustices which first gave rise to the middle-class revolt against the feudal order. In the context of European civilization the very historical complexities which validated the democratic authority served to refute the ideological illusions upon which the Communist authority rested.

Developments in the Communist empire since the death of Stalin reveal that we are not dealing merely with a system of power but with an ideological system in which the peculiar authority of the Communist priest-kings found support and then declined. It could, of course, be defined as a system of "force and fraud," for Stalinism certainly made many fraudulent claims. But it would be more accurate to define it as a power system in which force and ideological illusion supported each other. The illusion was derived from the Marxist apocalypse, according to which governments are merely the agents of property holders, and will wither away when property is abolished. This illusion was very real in the early days of Marxism. The facts of history tended to refute the illusions; and Stalinism may be defined as the system of force and fraud designed to prevent the refutations from becoming known. The intolerable monopoly of power became so vexatious, even to the oligarchies which shared the rule of the tyrant, that they ventured the bold step of discrediting the dead tyrant and admitting the grave injustice which flowed from the monopoly of power. It is clear that though Stalinism was primarily a system of terror, it was still supported by many ideological illusions. That is proved by the decay of authority with the destruction of the Stalin myth.

Naturally the decay of authority was most telling in the satellite nations, where a great deal of force, compounded with Marxist ideological illusions, was used to keep the central authority un-challenged. The refutation of the universalistic illusions of the original myth by Russian national interests served to hasten the process of disillusionment. In Poland, the fear of Germany and other factors made it possible to reconstruct the authority on a nationalist-Communist or Titoist basis. But in Hungary, where ethnic kinship did not support the Russian authority and where the fear of Germany did not serve to keep the nation loyal to a hated tyranny, the revolution quickly broke beyond the limits of Titoist nationalism and has been cruelly repressed by military force. The catastrophic effect of this development on the Commu-nist parties of the West proves that the ideological illusion in the Communist dogma was still a considerable source of prestige, even after all the disillusionments of the past decades. The events in Hungary have reduced the political prestige of Communism in the West and completely destroyed any remnant of prestige in Hungary so that authority rests purely upon bayonets and machine guns, the ultimate in tyranny.

But it would be foolish to suppose that the refutation of the primary dogma of Communism in the context of a technical society has guaranteed a democratic alliance a simple victory in the ideological struggle on the two colored continents, where the secondary dogma of Communism has never lost a certain measure of plausibility and where colonial and ex-colonial peoples either dreamed of liberty and equality or celebrated their emancipation by residual resentments against a previous domination. For it is a fact that the nineteenth-century impingement of the technical West upon the nontechnical world was "imperialistic" in the way that power always impinges upon weakness. The prestige derived from domestic justice was not sufficient to obscure the loss of prestige due to imperial dominion, even though that dominion was never as purely exploitative as the Communist dogma assumed. The creative elements in the imperialism of the West were, more-over, obscured by the racial arrogance of the white man in his relations to the colored continents.

The brutal suppression of Hungarian liberty by the Communist power which finally discredited Communism in Europe was synchronous with the Anglo-French attack upon Egypt which symbolized the evils of "colonialism" to the colored continents, even though the operation of the Suez Canal by an international authority was hardly as flagrant an expression of exploitation as the Egyptians and Russians pretended to believe. But the British and the French attack upon Egypt gave a new ideological plausibility to the Communist dogma.

We thus have an ironic historical coincidence. The final refutation of the Communist ideology in Europe was synchronous with a very telling seeming proof of the ideology on the colored continents. These events in Europe and in Egypt prove that the West cannot be too complacent about the refutation of the Communist ideology in Europe when it is still such a vital force on the colored continents by the power of its secondary dogma about imperialism.

While the West rather too complacently sought to alleviate, by technical assistance to backward nations, the poverty in which Communism ostensibly breeds, the Communists entered into competition with us in offering technical assistance, thus revealing that they no longer relied on revolutionary discontent of the "masses" but upon the residual or real resentments of colonial or ex-colonial governments. Thus Communism had found allies among hitherto subject peoples and these peoples found a protagonist in the Communist power which had learned to master the crafts of a technical society without going through the tortuous self-denying experiences which made a technical civilization in the West the generator of a democratic political order. The old organic forms of collectivism could exchange their organic forms for the more dangerous forms of technical collectivism, and the technically proficient Russian tyranny could threaten the democratic and technical Western world with isolation on the colored continents.

It could even prove more flexible in interpreting its own dogmas than the West, which offered technical assistance to prevent revolutions in Asia and Africa, while the Communists offered it to enable dictatorial governments to embrace Western technology

without embracing the democratic creed of the West. As a source
of internal authority, the creed of democracy was too complex and
too varied in its sources to be obviously available to the recently
emancipated feudal or pastoral cultures of Asia and Africa. The
delicate balances of power which made freedom compatible with
justice seemed out of reach to the newly-born nations. At the
same time, the ideological support of Western democracy was
defective as a source of prestige in external affairs because it was
tainted by the memories of the previous impingement of technical
power upon nontechnical nations, which according to the Communist creed could be made to appear as the inevitable consequence of "capitalism."

Domestically, democracy was too difficult and in foreign affairs
its ideology was too tainted to have the obvious advantages which
the West fondly assumed its creed to possess. In the ideological
conflict for prestige between the Western nations and Russia the
disadvantages from which the West suffers are more desperate
than we have ever admitted to ourselves. In fact, there is a danger
that we will be driven into a new fit of hysteria once we recognize the true state of affairs. Since the struggle is not purely
ideological we can feel secure for some time under the umbrella
of an atomic stalemate. Both sides have admitted that neither
side would explicitly risk a global nuclear war.

But these military factors also aggravate our problem. They
have tempted us, since the aggression in Korea, to think too much
in terms of containing the Communist power by military defense
pacts. These pacts have cost us the friendship of India and
Afghanistan.

While military power is the *ultima ratio* of conflict with a
foe, it is clearly not a source of prestige, either for the internal
authority of a government or for its relations with other nations.
The Communist empire has discovered to its cost that the
exertion of military power in relation to "allies" is subject to a
law of diminishing returns.

In fact the constitution of modern society in a technical age
has invalidated most of the sources of authority which governed

the authority and prestige of traditional societies. Force has remained as an alloy but not as a basic metal of authority; and its limits as a source of authority are almost as clearly defined in an age which has experienced tyranny as in the age of the dynasts. The prestige of uninterrupted rule has disappeared as a source of authority and the pretension that the political order is intimately related to the cosmic order (the core of the religious element in authority) has evaporated in an age which is acutely aware of historical contingency. There remains only the achievement or the hope of justice as the source of authority and prestige. The hope of justice, or the pretension of having achieved it, is almost as potent as the actual achievement. That is why the Communist totalitarianism, with its ideological remnants of utopian hopes, is so rigorous a competitor with democracy for the favor of peoples, particularly on the colored continents.

While prudence dictates that we begin our estimate of the ideological struggle between democracy and tyranny on the colored continents with an objective consideration of the disadvantages under which the West labors in this competition, we must not adopt a defeatist view from a consideration of these disadvantages. We must be realistic enough to know that the initial advantages are on the other side, despite the recent self-discrediting of the Communist empire. But the ideological struggle may nevertheless be won if we are patient enough to allow historical experience to refute the illusions of the Communist dogma and to correct the errors in the approach of technically competent civilizations to technically backward ones.

We must also be resolute enough to protect the free world when it is threatened as it has been in the Middle East by a combination of military power and political chicane. If we do not understand the power-political realities sufficiently to know that whoever controls the Middle East also controls Europe, all ideological considerations will become irrelevant through forces which act more quickly than the slow movements of shifting prestige and the ideological systems which support that prestige.

On the level of ideological conflict we must free ourselves of

the burden of the charge of "colonialism" on the colored continents. This cannot be done simply by calling attention to our
own anti-colonial past and by inference fastening the charge
more securely on our Western allies. Secretary Dulles attempted
this gambit in the Suez crisis, with catastrophic results, for it
helped Russia and Nasser to defeat our allies in the Middle East,
a defeat they aggravated by military action which failed to unhorse
Nasser, precisely because Russia and Nasser could count on us to
support them for "moral" reasons. Europe is consequently
threatened from the Middle East and we are in danger both of
being isolated and of adopting a new policy of pacifist isolationism.
We are inextricably bound up with the fate of Europe and we
cannot avert this fate by calling attention to the ideological
differences between us on the matter of colonialism. We would
have a much better chance of winning both the ideological and
the power struggle if we discriminated more carefully between
those European powers which have creatively extricated themselves
from previous colonialism and have tutored hitherto subject nations in good faith for eventual independence and those nations
which are hopelessly bogged down in colonialism. Broadly speaking, that means the distinction between Britain and France.

Every indiscriminate designation of the European powers as
"colonial" by us is bound to support the Communist ideological
claims and to obscure the great achievement of Britain in liqui-
dating an empire and creating a commonwealth of nations in
which Asian nations have equal rights with European ones, and
in which even the backward cultures of Africa are being trained
in the arts of democracy. This achievement is somewhat clouded
by the desperate policies of Britain in the Mediterranean, particularly on Cyprus and the Suez, policies which were, however,
dictated by the consciousness of the strategic value of the Mediterranean lifeline and its importance for the whole European
economy. We contributed to the desperation by pressing the
British to leave Egypt in order to avoid the charge of colonialism.
The consequent success of Russia in winning essential control of
the Middle East proves that the power struggle must not be too
rigorously subordinated to the ideological struggle.

The case of French colonialism is quite different. France was unable to maintain her empire in Indo-China because she could not offer sufficient independence to Indo-China to give moral dignity to the fight against the Communists, posing as nationalists. She is now bogged down in a similar stalemate in Africa, trying vainly by force of arms to prove that an Islamic African dependency is really a part of metropolitan France. There is no hope of winning the ideological struggle with the handicap of French failures upon our cause. Since the end of the Fourth Republic and the quasi-dictatorship of de Gaulle it is rather unclear what the French policy is, or will be. De Gaulle evidently wants to change the French Union into a kind of Commonwealth, but it is not clear that Algeria will have sufficient freedom from metropolitan France to be a part of this commonwealth.

A wise course for us would be not to wage ideological warfare against our two strong European allies in the name of our "anticolonialism," but to establish a more intimate alliance with Britain so that the two nations which are freer of the ideological handicap than any other may form the core of the alliance of free nations and may gain sufficient prestige to dissuade France from her present course, which has such catastrophic consequences in the ideological struggle. Meanwhile, we can confidently expect that the stresses to which the Communist empire is exposed in Europe will generate policies of desperation, as in Hungary, and that lingering illusions will more and more be replaced by recognition of obvious fraud. Furthermore, the forum of the United Nations fortunately insures that the force and fraud which Communism practices in Europe, because of its low moral and political prestige, will become better known in Asia and destroy its prestige on the colored continents where it has long posed as the emancipator from colonialism. Our cause is by no means hopeless, though it is more serious than a comfortable nation is inclined to admit. The safety of the free world requires a much shrewder calculation of both the ideological and power factors than we are accustomed to give them.

It must be emphasized in conclusion that we cannot win the ideological struggle on the continents where technical civilization is in its infancy, if we equate democracy with extravagant forms of individualism, which may be regarded as a luxury only the richest of all nations, our own, can afford. The rest of mankind must try to develop equilibria of power and a tolerable justice within the framework of freedom and to extend freedom on the base of domestic stability and foreign prestige.

[1959]

American Hegemony and

the Prospects for Peace *(1962)*

(Annals of AAPSS)

IT IS difficult to define the framework of the world situation, in which the character of the hegemony of our nation in the so-called "free world" must be considered, without, in Santayana's phrase, "holding the candlelight of the obvious to the daylight of common experience."

On the one hand, the precarious peace of the world is threatened by the possibility of a nuclear catastrophe, which may always occur by technical or political miscalculation or misadventure. On the other hand, the peace is preserved because, for the first time in history, both contestants possess nuclear destructive power of such magnitude that the party which initiates the ultimate conflict is bound to be met with a retaliatory strike which may well be more destructive than the sum-total of all the wars of history. The peace secured by this "balance of terror" is obviously dependent upon a fairly stable balance, despite the fact that each side is bound to increase its advantages in this or that category of nuclear weapons or means of delivery or to redress any real or imagined disadvantage in each category. This "arms race" is pregnant with its own dangers, which ought to be and will be discussed by competent authorities. It will not be discussed within the limits of this chapter, both because of the author's lack of technical competence and because of the conviction that the balance of terror gives us, ironically enough, a precarious peace, which is bound to shift the problem of the prospects of peace to the political sphere.

The real problems of a tolerable and enduring peace under this strange umbrella of a tentative peace through a balance of terror are in the political sphere, for a catastrophic defeat of one side or the other might well tempt the imperiled side to grasp after the ultimate weapon in a mood of desperation. The political sphere presents us with as strange and novel a situation as the nuclear umbrella itself. For it exhibits a contest of power between two blocs of nations under two hegemonic nations, each with an imperial dimension of power, dwarfing the power of all the storied empires of history, whether the Roman Empire of antiquity or the British Empire of the nineteenth century. Each hegemonic nation possesses this power by reason of presiding over a continental economy which dwarfs that of all the nations, including the complex of European nations now increasingly pooling their economic resources in the economic mutualities of the Common Market. Each of the hegemonic nations, chiefly by reason of its economic strength, also has a practical monopoly of the dread nuclear weapons. This military might is not used to cow its lesser allies into submission but is the ultimate security of the bloc in the ultimate conflict. Nuclear power, in short, serves the same function, and generates the same prestige, which the castles of the Middle Ages served and generated in the feudal period of political organization. Lesser sovereignties huddle under this security.

Here the similarities between the two imperial or hegemonic powers end. The blocs are different, and they are as different as their respective blocs. Russia is the holy land of a new secular religion, designed for the last stages of European capitalism, irrelevant in a European culture, but strangely plausible to the emerging nations of Asia and Africa whose traditional feudal culture and primitive economy create conditions which are roughly similar, particularly when modern techniques impinge on ancient cultures and dissolve their organic forms, to the social situation of early-nineteenth-century Europe.

The Communist political religion, with its utopian dreams of world redemption not only from political evils but from all evils to which the human flesh is heir, was able to devise a political movement relevant to the revolutionary situation, created by the decay of the whole Russian social structure after the defeat in the first world war. It substituted an elite of dedicated revolutionists for Marx's vague "dictatorship of the proletariat," which gave this elite a monopoly of power and which transformed the utopian universalism of Marx into an effective instrument of Russian imperialism. Thus an empire was created whose ideological prestige was derived from the pretensions of anti-imperialism. This implausible utopian dream was able not only to generate a world-wide imperial structure, with pretensions of universality to hide its imperial realities, but also to devise the indirect instrument for lifting a "backward" feudal social structure into a technically competent modern society equipped with all the instruments of technical power, including the dread nuclear weapons. Thus was added, to the original ideological prestige, the prestige that a technically competent nation has among the poorer nations panting after the abundance which mastery of nature promises and sometimes realizes.

The prospects for peace are intimately related to, and derived from, the ability of the non-Communist world under the hegemony of our nation to meet the challenge of so strange and formidable an adversary. World peace requires that the dynamic of this strange political movement be contained, its ambition to control the world be frustrated, and its revolutionary ardors be tamed by firm and patient resistance. Any lack of firmness on our part, and, on the other hand, any lack of soberness, any lapse into hysteria, might well prove fatal to the uneasy peace which stands between us and disaster.

The task confronting us is sometimes defined journalistically as "winning the cold war," but that is defining it rather too simply and optimistically. For the hazards we face are tremendous. Not all of them have to do with the capacities of the hegemonic nation, vaulted so suddenly into the position of leadership of the non-Communist world. The most formidable obstacle is that the system of self-government which prevails in Western Europe is not immediately relevant to the budding nations of Africa and Asia. Democracy may be a necessity of justice. Any monopoly of power, such as the Soviet oligarchy possesses, generates injustices which persuade us of the virtues of a government which checks every center of power with countervailing power and destroys immunity from criticism for every center of authority.

But the democracy of Western Europe made itself compatible with the necessities of an industrial civilization by tortuous process and required the full nineteenth century to refute the original Marxist indictment that government was merely the "executive committee" of the "propertied classes." Moreover, the free governments of Europe could avail themselves of linguistic, ethnic, and cultural forms of cohesion, which were developed with the rise of the new nations, roughly two centuries before the rise of democracy. The new nations must wrestle with various forms of pluralism, and they do not have the time to make democracy compatible with the technical civilization impinging upon them and offering them both abundance and the corrosion of their organic or traditional social patterns.

These hazards do not and must not spell the doom of democracy in its contest with Communism across the vast expanses of Asia and Africa. They do indicate that self-government is no simple alternative to Communism and that the Western powers, and particularly the hegemonic power, must exercise discrimination in their marshaling of the disparate forces of the non-Communist world. This means that we must be prepared to encounter defeat in Laos, for instance, where the social patterns make Western democracy irrelevant but dare not be complacent about any policy which threatens the democratic "heartland" of free governments in Europe. It also means that we require discriminate judgment in dealing with the various compounds of democracy and dictatorship which the cultural and economic variables across the world make inevitable. We will regard one-party systems, whether in Tunisia or Mexico, with certain sympathy and will be concerned but not desperate when a new nation, such as Ghana, develops the tyrannical and dangerous potentialities of the one-party system. We should know the difference between reversible nondemocratic regimes and those which are irreversible because their power is informed by the fanatic dogma of Communism.

We have assumed the importance of the adequacy of the political sagacity of our hegemonic nation, vaulted so suddenly into a position of leadership in the "free world." We must now analyze its capacities and its inevitable weaknesses more fully. The most obvious weakness stems from the fact that our hegemony is derived from our undoubted economic power and from the military—chiefly nuclear—power for which economic power is the obvious basis. We have had no apprenticeship in dealing with the endless imponderables of the political realm and are, therefore, inclined to alternate betwen belligerency and defeatism in meeting the endless exigencies of the contest with Communism. We lack, after all, the experience of Britain, for instance, in meeting the hazards of the Napoleonic revolution in the nineteenth century and the Nazi upsurge in the twentieth century.

The task of exercising our hegemony in the non-Communist world without alternate moods of belligerency and defeatism is complicated by the fact that, in our sudden rise to power we have gone through the ironic experience of knowing less frustration in the period of our weakness and continental security than in the era of our seeming omnipotence and insecurity in the hazards of the global dimensions of the cold war and the nuclear dilemma. We must live through decades, and perhaps centuries in which no clear-cut victory can be recorded and in which there can be neither relief for the burdens we bear nor promise of an obvious reward for bearing them.

It is an important but not obvious fact that these burdens are the means of disciplining the richest nation of the world in such civic virtues as are relevant to our health and the welfare of the democratic peoples. Foreign aid is not a popular enterprise in any democratic assembly, where the representatives of the people are bound to be more conscious of the fears of taxpayers than of the needs of poor nations trying to gain both technical competence and capital funds for industrial equipment. Our ability to render such aid in competition with the Communist oligarchy is, therefore, the litmus test of the capacity of a democracy to survive in the contest.

Perhaps the chief moral and political problem with which we have to contend is derived from the fact that we have a strong anti-imperialist tradition and yet are an imperial power, or are a hegemonic power possessing resources of imperial dimensions. Our anti-imperialism is drawn, on the one hand, from our former colonial past, and, on the other, from the presuppositions of the liberal-democratic creed, which ran through our life from Thomas Jefferson to Woodrow Wilson and which attributed imperialism to the institution of monarchy in somewhat the same fashion as Communism attributed imperialism to the institution of capitalism. Both creeds tend to be blind to the perennial pattern of the impingement of strength upon weakness in the international realm and to the possible creative, as well as exploitative, consequences of this impingement. Our anti-imperialistic tradition has the virtue of making us sensitive to the possibilities of injustice arising from the dominance of strong nations in the community of nations, particularly when their strength is not disciplined by a constitutional framework.

But it does make for a certain hesitancy in exercising the responsibilities of our imperial power, since we fear that we may violate the cardinal principle of liberalism, the "self-determination of nations." We cannot afford such hesitancy, even in a world in which the weak nations are as preoccupied with anti-imperialistic slogans as we are. If the social conditions of our client nations— whether in South Vietnam, South Korea, or, possibly, Saudi Arabia—are the kind which invite Communist infiltration, we must exercise the responsibilities of our power to correct them, even if such a policy can be effective only if the power is exercised with a minimal affront to the dignity of sovereign nations. The Alliance for Progress, recently devised for our relations with

Latin American nations and designed to use our economic power in order to encourage needed land reform and educational progress, is perhaps the best illustration of the capacity of the hegemonic nation to use its power creatively through the modern adaptation of the old policy of "indirect rule."

A less creative aspect of our anti-imperialistic tradition is that it tempts us to ambivalence in dealing with our European allies, who were undoubtedly involved in imperial ventures in the nine-tenth century. These ventures were not as creative as their champions asserted, and only their weakness after the second world war prompted their withdrawal from their imperial ventures. Significantly, the greatest statesman of our age, Winston Churchill, was so reluctant to relinquish the British hold on India that only his fortunate defeat by the Labor party after the war made it possible to liquidate the empire in India without a struggle.

Yet the creative aspects of the imperial connections were not appreciated either by the Communist critics—who, after Lenin, made the charge of "imperialism" the chief weapon of their global polemic against Western democracy—or by the Americans. Even the intimate partnership of two world wars did not dissolve the prejudice of Americans against British "imperialism" or open our minds to the creative aspects of the imperial connection with its tutelage of the new nations in Asia and Africa. Perhaps the French mission in black Africa should be included in the evidence of the creative aspects of imperialism with the obviously successful British midwifery of democratic nations in Asia and Africa. The result has been confusion both with respect to our friends, whose virtue we suspected, and to our adversary, whose pretensions we accepted. Thus, General Eisenhower could say after the second world war: "The past relations between Russia and America were no cause to regard the future with pessimism. Historically the two nations had preserved an unbroken friendship. . . . Both were free of the stigma of empire building by force."[1] The barb against our British ally in this curious ascription of democratic innocency to both the old and the new Russia

[1] Dwight D. Eisenhower, *Crusade in Europe* (New York: Doubleday and Co., Inc., 1948), p. 457.

was unmistakable. Eisenhower's views were not unique but the staple of British-American relations throughout the war, despite the intimacy between Roosevelt and Churchill.

Our confusion about imperialism was a source of confusion between us and our European allies as late as the Suez crisis, when Britain and France—unwisely, as it turned out—took the law into their own hands to protect the Suez life line of the European economy against Nasser's ambitions because they had become impatient with our complacency induced by our desire to be untainted with all semblances of "colonialism."

Mr. Robert Good enumerates the instances when this strain in our tradition prompted ambivalence toward our European allies. Some of the ambivalence was no doubt due not to confusion but to the embarrassments of an imperial power trying to satisfy both its European allies, tainted with the charge of imperialism, and the new nations, filled with resentments against their former masters for good and inevitable, though not adequate, reasons.

Fortunately, our growing maturity and discrimination was recently revealed when we consistently supported the United Nations in its opposition to the secession of the copper-rich Katanga Province from the new Congo nation after it became obvious that the Belgian copper interests had initiated and supported the rebellion. In this case, the anti-Communism of a genuinely imperial venture, which elicited the support of conservative business interests in the West, did not deflect us from a policy of guarding the unity of a new nation against divisive colonial influences. This form of discriminate judgment did much to atone for the mistakes which we had made in the confusion resulting from the anti-imperialistic illusions of a nation with imperial responsibilities. An independent African nation, supported in its secession by Western mining interests, would be a symbol of the caricature of Western democracy which Communism would be glad to exploit.

Fortunately, the prospects for peace do not all depend upon the adequacy of the policy of our own hegemonic nation in preserving the unity, enhancing the health, and supporting the morale of the non-Communist alliance. Historical forces are also affecting the posture of the adversary. Some of them may rob the Russian center of Communist power of the demonic dynamic which a revolutionary movement always generates. The very success in technical advance which gave it so much prestige in the "backward" nations now seems to rob its post-revolutionary generation of oligarchs and technicians of any stomach for policy hazards which might lead to war.

If some of the journalists in Russia are right, it was the reluctance of these new "bourgeoisie" which prompted Khrushchev to moderate his policies in regard to the Berlin crisis. Russia's new wealth has certainly given the nation a stake in the status quo, which the poorer and more revolutionary China does not have. Nor does China share the Russian and American proleptic responsibility for avoiding a nuclear catastrophe. This common responsibility may be the one tissue of community across the deep chasm of the cold war.

Whether the emergence of another Communist center of authority, that of China, more revolutionary and irresponsible than the old Russian holy land of the Communist faith, will increase or decrease the prospects for peace can be answered only by Sino-Soviet experts, if at all. The lay observer can only speculate that the emergence of a "pure" revolutionary power will tend to place Russia in a triangle with China and the United States. It will probably increase the Russian tendency to bourgeois caution, but who can say whether it may not also increase the violence of the Russian propaganda designed to prove that it has not departed from Leninist orthodoxy.

Some of the lines of destiny are not within the power or decision of the most powerful hegemonic nations. A vivid case of an issue which affects the prospects for peace, in which American policy has only a very indirect influence, is the problem of France and Algeria. France has involved itself in the unhappy situation of living by the fiction that the budding nation of Algeria was really an integral part of metropolitan France. Eight years of war have refuted the fiction. Yet Algeria separated from France would lead to catastrophic results for both France and Algeria. Unfortunately, this seemingly insoluble problem can be solved only by one man, the President of the Fifth Republic, Charles de Gaulle. But de Gaulle's capacity to solve it has seriously eroded. Before these lines reach the reader the issue may be joined and we will know whether or not France will continue with the Fifth Republic under de Gaulle or whether the rightist conspiracies against de Gaulle will succeed. If they do succeed, the capacity of both France and North Africa to withstand Communist infiltration will be seriously impaired.

The inability of this great nation to digest the revolution in almost two centuries—two constitutional monarchies, two Bonapartist empires, and five republics having added to the instability of the nation in their various abortive efforts to sluice the new wine of revolution into the old bottles of tradition—this checkered history is itself a vivid witness to the fact that the paths of democracy are indeed thorny.

Fortunately, the other path, the alternative of authoritarian oligarchy, is equally thorny. The problems of communism are bound to increase as the hiatus between the original dream of utopia and the realities of empire and despotism widens. In this situation, it is idle to affirm that time is either on our side or on theirs. It is possible, however, to draw hope from the fact that history continues to reveal unpredicted and unpredictable emergencies, and that ultimately the principle of democratic government can prevail over all the hazards which tend to make what is essentially a necessity of justice into a luxury available only to the few nations that have the capacity to manipulate the delicate balances of justice in a free society.

It would certainly be hazardous to make any predictions about the possibility of peace in the fateful contest between the two systems. Too many contingencies obscure the picture of the future. All one can affirm, which ought to be sufficient to affirm, is that the defense of an open society is not morally or historically futile and that we will ennoble, rather than corrupt, the quality of our culture by undertaking the burdens of defense.

[1962]

The Social Myths in
the Cold War *(1967)*

Journal of International affairs

EVERY class and nation defends itself and justifies its interests by a social myth. The myth also is used to detract from the moral prestige of adversaries. Social myths are constructed by imaginative elaborations of actual history. They are hardly ever made out of whole cloth. They arise because reason is more ambiguous in relation to the individual or social self than some rationalists assume. Reason is never the sole master of the acquisitive and anxious self. It is always part master and part servant of that self, particularly the collective self of the nation.

Naturally a social myth must be protected against the criticism of a general community and against competitive myths of competitive collectives in a community. In modern life, the integral national community has the sovereign power and necessary communal consensus to challenge, criticize, and transmute all social myths on the subnational level. But it has neither the inclination nor the power to challenge the mythical content of its own pretensions to virtue that it presents to the larger world, in which neither sovereign power nor consensus exists as a moderating factor upon the self-esteem of nations.

One must analyze this universal character of the mythical nature of all collective self-images and views of the adversary before pointing to the inevitability, but also the error, of the

presuppositions of the so-called "free world." There is supposed
to be a radical difference between the—supposedly—rational and
true approach of the free world to reality, and the noxious myths
of the Communist adversary. This adversary gained its political
prestige and subsequent economic power on the basis of a most
comprehensive myth, rooted in an apocalyptic, semi-religious, and
pseudoscientific program of revolutionary social redemption from
all social injustice. Their social presuppositions obviously have a
more vivid mythical content than those of the Western democracies. In addition, the Marxist vision of a just society turned
out to be a mythical support for a political party that claimed
and achieved a monopoly of power, a monopoly necessary to guard
the myth from the corroding influence of a free society.

Western democracies assume that the contest between the
U.S.S.R.—nation and superpower—and the political forces based
on the principle of freedom is indeed an ultimate conflict, probably as ultimate as the Communists, from the viewpoint of their
comprehensive myth, declare it to be. Their definition of this
conflict, however, contradicts our own definition: It is not a
conflict between "freedom" and "tyranny" but between "imperialism" and "democracy."

Before we accept this version of the conflict between free institutions and "tyranny," we must take another precautionary view
of the relation of myth to reality. Our review is prompted by a
certain apprehension that the advantages of political freedom in
discounting myths may have been ignored by the free societies.
For the history of their social, political, and economic development does not correspond to either the bourgeois or the proletarian myth. In the modern democratic nation-state the sovereign
power was secure enough to allow—through the process of
pressure and counter-pressure—the industrial workers to organize,
so that the collective power of the trade unions was set against
the collective power of management. Thus, the whole development shows that more than pure reason or conscience was
necessary to correct injustices rooted in the mythically pure
individualism of the original bourgeois democracy. In other words,

it was a tolerable equilibrium of power that produced the free societies.

But is this principle of democratic freedom—so important as a presupposition and indeed as an ingredient in the development of the modern democratic nation-state—applicable or even relevant in the larger arena of international relations? Also, can we expect democratic nations, which have challenged the myth of the messianic class in their own history, to recognize their own mythical pretensions in relation to other nations? The conflict of the cold war between the Communist world and the free world is described conventionally as the struggle between good and evil, freedom and tyranny, and even as between truth and myth. Yet such distinctions, especially and ironically the last one, themselves partake of the nature of myth. As we have seen, myths are essentially distortions of complex historical events. Undue simplifications of such complexities therefore may be regarded as mythical.

At this juncture in the world-wide struggle involving men and nations, the two "superpowers," the U.S.S.R. and the U.S., have imperial dimensions and also wield imperial power—economic, political, and military; they surpass, in their impingement upon weaker and client nations, the empires of ancient and medieval eras, as well as the nineteenth-century empires of Europe. Each exercises hegemony in its respective bloc of nations: the U.S. in the non-Communist bloc, and the U.S.S.R. in the more highly integrated Communist empire, consisting of nations that have either opted for the Communist creed or were compelled to accept it by the force of the Russian army.

Although we present ourselves as the leader of the democratic bloc of nations, democracy is only rarely the achievement of the non-Communist nations. More frequently it is either the aspiration or the pretension of the non-Communist nations in our bloc. Naturally our principles prevent us from incorporating the democratic ideal into an explicit imperial structure. The Russians have no such inhibitions; hence we speak polemically, but also accurately, about "Communist imperialism."

It is one of the most vivid ironies of modern history that both these superpowers express ideals of anti-imperialism. The Russians derive their anti-imperialistic idealism and pretension from Marxist dogma and from Lenin's belated amendment to it. According to this dogma, imperialism is the fruit of capitalism, the external expression of the acquisitive impulse that capitalism exhibits in domestic relations. Lenin's amendment to this indictment was borrowed from the English liberal and anti-imperialist J. A. Hobson, whose thesis was simply that the capitalistic quest for markets, raw materials, and investments was accentuated when the capitalist system was in crisis, as it allegedly was.

The Marxist indictment of capitalism was a mythical distortion of an historical fact. All modern European nations used their technical, commercial, and political superiority over the nontechnical nations in various expansive, imperialistic movements to extend their dominion. But the motives behind this expansion were complex. They included the pride of power, the exploitative motive of economic profit, and the missionary motive of universalizing moral, political, or technical ideas and values beyond the boundaries of the nation-state. The mythical distortion of the adversary's expansiveness consists simply in singling out the most unacceptable motive, such as the exploitative. A mythical distortion of one's own expansiveness, on the other hand, consists in singling out the missionary motive, rather than the exploitative or power motives. This self-serving shifting of emphasis accounts for that curious phenomenon of an anti-imperialistic Communist imperialism.

Naturally an imperialism rooted in a utopian apocalypse would emphasize its missionary motive. Theoretically, therefore, it desires power for the sake of strategic advantage for the whole "socialist camp." Theoretically, again, it opposes non-Communist nations not because they have free societies, but because they are tainted with "imperialism." Most of the European democratic nations did in fact extend their dominions in Asia and Africa, and their motives were mixed in various proportions. They were usually not as "missionary" as they claimed, whether in behalf of democracy, technical efficiency, or culture. But the relation of Europe to the undeveloped nations was, in fact, not as exploitative as the Communists have claimed. Great Britain, for instance, has been the midwife of autonomous and democratic nations in Asia and Africa, though it must be conceded that the British imperial power bestowed the final grant of freedom because of its own weakness rather than its sense of mission.

We must analyze the imperial impulse and the anti-imperialist pretensions of the Soviet Union in the light of the peculiar history of the Communist apocalypse of social redemption. Designed by Marx for the hoped-for crisis in advanced industrial nations, it instead inspired the revolutionary seizure of power in a traditional, monarchic, and feudal civilization that had collapsed after its defeat in the first world war.

The Russian Revolution, informed by this utopian apocalyptic vision, introduced an economic system that embodied all the Marxist miscalculations. It was ruled by a party that substituted trained revolutionists for Marx's vaguely conceived "dictatorship of the proletariat." The proletariat, marked as the messianic redeemer of all mankind in the original apocalypse, was in fact such a negligible force in the nontechnical Russian economy that it could not be a real power in the revolutionary government. But the party, surrogate for the working class in whose name it spoke, turned the tables on the original apocalypse by guiding a nontechnical nation to greater technical efficiency.

Two errors contributed to a monopoly of power in the revolutionary consummation. Marx had assumed the supremacy of economic over political power. He also equated the ownership of property with economic power. Thus when the original dream turned into actual history both errors were refuted by this ironic monopoly of economic and political power in the hands of a political party that could dominate the state and also control state-owned property. The party bosses proved the supremacy of political over economic power. Their management of state-owned socialized property proved that ownership of property was not as important as the power of the manager, a fact that has likewise been demonstrated in free societies.

The combination of omnicompetent political bosses and their

subordinate managerial oligarchy was ideal for forcing a peasant economy to become technically competent. The government's power over the peasants, once Stalin had collectivized their holdings, enabled it to squeeze capital for industrial investment from this impotent class. Thus Communism, designed to redeem the poor, became in fact an efficient instrument for rapid industrialization at the expense of the poor.

When China, also having a traditional peasant economy with only a nascent industrial sector, copied the Russian revolutionary model, it became quite clear that a nation of politically and economically impotent peasants could not challenge the monopoly of party power, and that the nation actually would profit from such a monopoly.

The contradiction between the apocalyptic dreams and myths and the post-revolutionary power realities was thus not a hindrance, but an aid, to the expansion of Communist power in the nontechnical world. In contrast, the workers in Western democracies had the freedom to challenge the contradiction between myths and post-revolutionary reality. They also had the means, within the shifting equilibria of a fluid economy, to set collective power against the collective power of management. The Western industrial workers therefore never were as desperate as the Marxist myth assumed. Even though bourgeois democracy was slow to discount and correct the original bourgeois individualistic myths, Western democracies proved themselves immune to the Communist virus. The Communist myth evidently was plausible in the nontechnical world but irrelevant in the advanced nations of the West, where political freedom had been established before the development of modern industry.

This contrast between the Communism of the nontechnical cultures and the capitalism and democracy of the West throws light on our subordinate thesis that the sovereign power of free nations is able to refute the myths of its subnational groups and classes, not only because a free society gives all classes the opportunity to criticize and challenge the claims and pretensions of its competitors and allies, but also because the sovereign authority of a relatively neutral state, whose authority transcends the prestige of all classes, is able to change an equilibrium of power for the sake of tolerable justice and in favor of a comparatively powerless class.

It was this achievement of free societies in Western Europe that refuted the Marxist apocalypse of doom. For the individually impotent workers, who were robbed both of their skills and of their tools by the modern power machines, were given the right to organize and bargain collectively, and thus to construct a new equilibrium of power that has established a situation of tolerable economic justice in all Western industrial, democratic states. Thus the old, irrelevant individualistic competition, which exposed the workers to the competitions of a market economy in the realm of labor, was gradually transmuted into the modern "welfare state."

It would be idle and dangerous to obscure the great contrast between domestic economies and cultures, between free societies and those governed by political oligarchies inspired by the Marxist myth, a myth shielded from scrutiny by the oligarchies' monopoly of power. But it would be foolish to assume that this contrast between the two systems would be pertinent to an analysis of the mythical statements of foreign policy by which both systems present their pretensions to the outside world.

The U.S. and the U.S.S.R., which exercise hegemony over the so-called "free world" and "socialist camp" respectively, accuse each other of imperialism. We speak of "Communist imperialism" for the simple reason that the Communist myth sanctions a supranational imperial structure. The Communists accuse us of imperialism simply because their myth defines imperialism as the ultimate fruit of capitalism. Are we not, therefore, imperialists, despite our avowal of innocence?

There are, of course, differences in the myths by which each nation avows its innocence. We have previously defined the apocalyptic myth of Communism. Our myth of innocence may be described as "nostalgic." John Locke, rather than Marx, was the source of a liberal democratic universalism and anti-imperialism. Locke wrote:

The end of government is the good of mankind, and which is best
for mankind: that the people should be always exposed to the bound-
less will of tyranny, or that the rulers should be sometimes liable to be
opposed when they grow exorbitant in the use of their power. . . ?[1]

Our founding fathers regarded our nation as innocent because
of our war of independence against an imperial power. This
sense of innocence was preserved in spite of our development and
growth to mature strength, for the simple reason that our
hemispheric economic expanse made classical imperialism unnecessary.

Thomas Jefferson was probably the first of a long line of
American liberal democratic anti-imperialists to equate democracy
with an ideal of universalism. He wrote in 1820:

We exist and are quoted as standing proof, that a government so
modelled as to rest continually on the whole of society, is a practical
government. . . . As members therefore of the universal society of
mankind, and as standing in a high and responsible relation to them,
it is our sacred duty not to blast the confidence we have inspired of
proof that a government based on reason is better than one based
on force.[2]

The most explicit expression of America's sense of messianic
mission was Woodrow Wilson's address in 1916 before we entered
the first world war. Wilson said then:

We are holding off, not because we do not feel concerned, but because when we exert the force of this nation we want to know what
we are exerting it for. We ought to have a touchstone . . . that it is
truly American, that the States of America are set up to vindicate the
rights of man against the rights of property, or the rights of self-
aggrandizement and aggression. . . . When you are asked, "Aren't
you willing to fight?" answer yes, you are waiting for something worth
fighting for.[3]

[1] John Locke, *Two Treatises of Government* (Oxford: Basil Blackwell,
1946), *Second Treatise*, Chap. XIX, par. 229.

[2] *The Writings of Thomas Jefferson*, Andrew A. Lipscomb and Albert E.
Bergh, eds. (Washington, D.C.: Thomas Jefferson Memorial Assn., 1904),
Vol. XV, p. 285.

[3] Quoted in Edward Buehrig, *Woodrow Wilson and the Balance of Power*
(Bloomington: Indiana University Press, 1956).

When our nation became darkly conscious of the fact that our peace and security were dependent upon the British navy and that a German victory would imperil British control of the sea, unrestricted submarine warfare gave us a moral excuse for entering a conflict that an idealistic nation, unconscious of its normal impulses of survival, was hesitant to enter. Wilson was again in perfect accord with the American sense of messianic mission when he projected a moral goal for the conflict we had entered. It was a "war to make the world safe for democracy."

The Wilsonian doctrine was an ideal moral fig leaf for a messianic nation in its first encounter with the problems of a nascent imperial dimension of power. He gave an additional buttress to our self-image as a pure nation by projecting the "League of Nations" as the ultimate end of the conflict. This goal would substantiate our moral reasons for engaging in the conflict and refute criticism that we were motivated by self-aggrandizement. Needless to say, the League was rejected by the nation that proposed it, partly because the draconic peace of Versailles offended our perfectionists, and partly because our self-regarding patriots thought the League provided inadequate security for our national interests. The moral of the Wilsonian adventure in world politics might be that it is as difficult for a messianic democratic nation as it is for a Communist one to veil the hiatus between myth and reality in international relations.

If there is any consistent line between Jefferson's and Wilson's mythical images of the purity of American international goals, it may be significant that many aspects of our foreign policy between Jefferson and Wilson were conveniently forgotten in our search for a plausible myth of national purity. Two intervening chapters of our national history must be recalled to measure the capacity for self-deception, even on the part of democratic nations, in projecting mythical self-images to the world.

One chapter consists of our expansion in this hemisphere immediately after our birth as a sovereign nation. That expansion challenged all other sovereignties in the hemisphere with the threat of war, or with war itself (as in our acquisition of Texas from

Mexico). This imperial or expansive movement was undertaken under the slogan of "Manifest Destiny." In short, it vividly revealed the inclination to express expansive policies in the name of an ideal that explicitly denied the legitimacy of expansion. "Manifest Destiny" merely affirmed that a democratic nation was "destined" to occupy a hemisphere because the purity of its democratic ideals would justify this expansion. Yet this very expansion was obviously in conflict with the ideal used to justify this inevitable imperial impulse of a growing nation. The expansiveness of "Manifest Destiny" was thus a vivid revelation of the fact that nations, as individuals, tend to deceive themselves when they project a self-image to the world that obscures the dominant motives of foreign policy. Thus, the less acceptable expansive impulse of the nation is given the cover of professed moral or "democratic" purpose.

Wilson's conviction that our nation was "the most unselfish nation in history" evidently was informed by a mythical sense of virtue, which must have ignored a second chapter of our national history. This chapter is the record of our venture in overt, rather than covert, imperialism. Because it was prompted by Spain's attempt to enforce her imperial sovereignty over a rebellious Cuban colony, there was some substance to our moral pretext for challenging Spain in a war that gave us the booty of the entire Spanish imperial domain in the Caribbean and Pacific.

Naturally our traditional anti-imperialism made it difficult for us to swallow the colonial morsels suddenly placed before us. The anti-imperialist conscience of a nation that had never before embarked on an overtly imperialist venture was eloquently expressed by Senator Hoar of Massachusetts. Our founding fathers, said the Senator, ". . . would have never betrayed these sacred and awful verities, that they might strut about in the castoff clothing of pinchbeck emperors and pewter kings."[1]

President McKinley—a Republican whose Vice-President was none other than "Rough Rider" Theodore Roosevelt, one of the

---

[1] Quoted in George Kennan, *American Diplomacy, 1900–1950* (Chicago: Chicago University Press, 1952), p. 16.

many heroes of our new imperialism—was sufficiently under the influence of our anti-imperialistic myth of national innocence to have qualms of conscience about our acquisition of the Philippines. He reported that these qualms were eased by a dream in which he received the inspiration that "We keep the Philippines, evangelize, Christianize and educate them."[1] Significantly, the dream contained the myth of national purity in a nutshell.

But these moral qualms also resulted in an ambivalence, of which the Platt Amendment to the treaty with Spain was a significant, though dubious, fruit. The Platt Amendment disavowed any territorial ambitions in regard to Cuba, though it reserved our right to maintain a naval base there. This abnegation of overt imperialism in regard to Cuba might be considered dubious because it was irresponsible. In this respect, it was in marked contrast to our policy in the Philippines. While we were gradually creating the resources of autonomous nationhood and democracy in the Philippines, Cuba, though politically free, was being exploited by economic imperialists and ruled by one corrupt dictatorship after another, until it finally fell prey to the revolutionary movement led by Fidel Castro.

The difference between the destiny of Cuba and that of the Philippines might instruct us about the virtues of a responsible imperial sense of mission, and the weaknesses of an irresponsible, covert, usually economic imperialism that is devoid of any sense of obligation for guiding new nations to a viable national independence and democratic government.

The myth of our innocence, that we were untainted by imperial expansiveness, was maintained despite our growth in economic power, because of our continental economy. Thus, despite our power, size, and wealth, we continued to be anti-imperialistic. Accordingly, we were able to criticize the empires even of our democratic allies in Europe.

The embarrassment to our allies over our self-righteousness must have been particularly acute in the case of Britain. The intimate friendship between President Roosevelt and Winston

[1] *Ibid.*, p. 18.

Churchill, and the effective alliance between the two Anglo-Saxon democracies could not overcome our sense of superior virtue, even when the anti-Nazi alliance of Britain, America, and Russia yielded so much evidence that our affinities with Britain were stronger than those with Communist Russia. Although President Roosevelt regarded his occasional siding with Stalin as an important strategem of peace, it may have been partly prompted by the feeling that the British, tainted as they were by imperialism, were unworthy of our wholehearted cooperation.

In the days before the "cold war," it was taken for granted that the U.S. and U.S.S.R. shared a common tradition of anti-imperialism. Thus General Eisenhower could write in 1948:

The past relations between America and Russia were no cause to regard the future with pessimism. Historically the two nations had preserved an unbroken friendship, dating back to the birth of the United States as an independent Republic. . . . Both were free of the stigma of empire-building by force.[1]

Though the General was not an historian, he could not possibly have intended to absolve the old Russian empire of the guilt of "empire-building by force." One can only view this remarkable statement of Russo-American affinity as indicating the author's sense of the similarity between the Communists' and our own pretensions to anti-imperial virtue. Even so, the statement is rather startling in the light of subsequent history. Mr. Eisenhower could not foresee that the Communist ideology would become the cement holding together a multinational empire; that it would overcome the anti-Russian resentments of the subordinate nations, such as the Ukraine; and that it would provide the sense of a common cause, superior to the ideology of the Orthodox Church, by which the Islamic Asiatic republics could be integrated into an imperial nation. Even the conquest of the Eastern European satellite nations ultimately would be defended by an appeal to the validity of the Communist mythical universalism.

It is somewhat ironic now to recall this American recognition

[1] Dwight D. Eisenhower, *Crusade in Europe* (New York: Doubleday and Co., Inc., 1948), p. 457.

of a shared anti-imperialism, for the cold war meanwhile has seen each nation intensify its criticism of the other's myths. Russia, in the context of its own myth, was the holy land of the new religion of Communism, destined to redeem mankind from all capitalistic and imperialistic injustices. But she is regarded by all the nations of the "free world" as the hegemonial power of a new imperialism; and not without reason, for the Communist myth ordained the supranational economic integration of all Communist nations.

The Communists saw this supranational integration as nothing but a "fraternal" relationship between the holy land of the new religion and all the smaller, often nontechnical, nations. According to the Communist myth, there are no power rivalries in the "socialist camp." They were all eliminated by the elimination of the source of all evil, property. With the socialization of property, the world obviously must experience a new reality in which power rivalries would no longer figure in the relationship of strong and weak nations.

Naturally that part of the world not influenced by Communist mythology saw the imperial realities rather than the Communist rationalization of them. But the Communist indictment of all imperialism except its own had a particular effect upon the United States. We were, according to the Communist myth, the leader of the imperialistic nations, because we were the most powerful of the "capitalistic" nations. Naturally we were outraged; for was there not, at least among our utopians, an original conviction that both the U.S. and the U.S.S.R. were innocent of the charge of "empire-building by force"?

Perhaps the fervor of our anti-Communism was partly prompted by the divergence and contradiction between these two myths of world redemption. Ironies were compounded when historical providence made our innocent American democracy into one of the two imperial nations. Common sense certainly suggests that there were similar imperialistic impulses in both these powerful nations. But since both were by definition innocent of these impulses according to their own myths, both continued to proclaim their respective innocence. At the same time, the differences in their myths prompted them to cast each other in the role of the devil. We, as well as the Russians, are incapable of correcting or modifying our own national myths. Thus modern history is fated to be governed by two contrasting myths of the two superpowers, one of which uses the injustices of early-nineteenth-century European industrialism to prove its indictment of capitalism, long after these injustices have been corrected by the new equilibria of power perfected by the free nations.

But even our own imperial nation, though democratic, finds it hard to revise the charge against "Communist tyranny," even though a decade has elapsed since the Twentieth Party Congress, under Khrushchev's leadership, revealed the capacity of the oligarchies of a managerial society to take steps to protect themselves from the cruel despotism of a Stalin. This new development did not herald, as some optimists hoped, the gradual emergence of democratic institutions. Russia remained a managerial political society. But the "free world" did not adjust the language of its popular indictments of "Communist despotism" in accordance with these developments, though our experts and learned men discussed them in detail.

In analyzing the capacity of the two superpowers to become hegemonial in their respective alliance systems, it becomes apparent that each nation tends to universalize its own domestic achievement. Democracy, for example, is regarded by many as universally desirable and applicable. But since democracy is an achievement that requires cultural, technical, and other capacities on the part of a population, it may be a political myth to regard the democratic achievement as a possibility for all cultures and economies. Historical evidence shows that only a few nations of Western Europe had the necessary homogeneity, educational level, and political skill to make the democratic principles of "authority by consent of the governed" workable.

Our own superpower is inclined to regard democracy as a universal option for all nations. We are inclined toward this democratic utopianism because of our unique history. We built our nation on a virgin continent that lacked all the problems which European nations had to surmount before free governments became viable. Although we did not have the ethnic and religious homogeneity that proved so important a precondition of free governments in Europe, we did have one language; and our hemispheric expanse made it possible for us to scatter our immigrant population so that no one language or race was localized. Great Britain, in contrast, did not absorb its Gaelic minorities in Wales and Scotland in one step. First Henry VII brought England and Wales under a single sovereignty. Then, when James VI of Scotland became the legitimate heir of Queen Elizabeth, he became James I of England and Scotland. Naturally the unification under royal auspices was solidified by centuries of cultural integration and the remarkable political and religious accommodation of the Elizabethan Settlement. The sovereign being the Defender of the Faith and head of the Church, this meant that the monarch was Anglican in England and Presbyterian in Scotland.

This shrewd contrivance shows how ethnic diversity was compounded when identical with religious diversity; for religious loyalties tend to give a more ultimate dimension to other ethnic or linguistic loyalties and diversities. The nations of Europe suffered from religious wars for centuries after the Reformation. Our own nation, religiously the most pluralistic of any Western nation, found the secret of making this religious pluralism a resource, rather than an obstacle, for the unity of the nation. The secret was a rigorous separation of church and state, which helped to secure the loyalty of the most diverse groups to the national community. But our nation alone possessed the prerequisite for the rigorous separation of church and state: the absence of any religious group so dominant that it would oppose this religious neutrality.

Most of the democratic nations of the West could not validate their free societies until they had come to terms with the problems of modern industrialism, and proved that it was possible for a free society to grant political and economic power to the industrial workers. Though our nation had the usual maladjustments, social protests, and ferments—showing that even liberal democracies required a century to come to terms with the social and economic problems of modern industry—we were fortunate, being a purely bourgeois culture without a feudal background, that modern injustices were not superimposed on feudal class resentments. The Marxist rebellion did not appeal to our workers, despite their early resentments as powerless individuals in a collectivist economy. We were therefore unconscious of the many stages of social adjustment that a free society must undergo before it can validate itself. In the economic realm, as well as in problems of ethnic or religious diversity, our own superpower was therefore tempted to regard free institutions as more easily achieved than Western history has proved them to be. Hence our tendency to project our free institutions as world-wide options.

There is much evidence, however, that our failure to consider the obstacles posed by ethnic, linguistic, and cultural diversity to the establishment of free societies makes our projection of democracy as viable for all nations somewhat of a utopian myth. India, for example, is troubled by many economic problems in negotiating an entrance into modern industrial civilization. But her linguistic and cultural diversity, as revealed by her recent language riots, also threatens her democratic order. India availed herself of the English language of her former masters; but the universal use of English is strictly provisional. Once the educational process of a new generation, lacking competence in English, has run its course, the unity of India under free institutions may well be imperiled.

The new nations of Africa all have problems of linguistic and tribal diversity, stemming from their primitive past. The difficulties in establishing either unity or democracy in the Congo are well known. But the Congo was notoriously unprepared for either independence or democracy; therefore the tribal chaos, from which even a United Nations intervention failed to rescue her, cannot be regarded as typical.

Nigeria, on the other hand, was scrupulously prepared by her colonial masters for both autonomy and democracy. But she lacked political parties that transcended the confines of her three regions.

The Islamic northern region was politically integrated compared with the other two regions of the Yorubas and the Ebos. Her first federal Prime Minister, Balewa, was a symbol of the political power of the Islamic northern region. A bloody military revolt, initiated by the two southern regions, resulted in the death of Balewa and the abolition of the democratic institutions so carefully nurtured by the British. The situation, which is still in flux, may well illustrate the problem of building democratic institutions when confronted with tribal, regional, and religious diversity.

Clearly the problem of diversity, which we in this country were able to solve because of very favorable circumstances, is a tremendous hindrance to the growth of free institutions in Africa. We often seem to forget that the democracies of Europe evolved free institutions during centuries of pre-democratic triumphs over the diversities of language, religion, and race, usually under the auspices of royal sovereignty. Therefore, we must not regard free institutions as viable instruments of national unity in Africa in the immediate future. Presented to the new nations as a universally applicable alternative, democracy takes on the qualities of a utopian myth.

Fortunately, the Communist myth of redemption has even less credibility than our utopian democratic myth, since the African nations lacked the feudal background that made the Communist myth credible in European or Asiatic economic conditions. Conditions in Africa are more favorable for a socialist economy, which would bring all economic processes under political authority.

We have been comparing the myths and realities in the contest between the Soviet Union and the United States, both of whom have power of imperial dimensions and foreign policies informed by myths. This comparison must conclude with an analysis of the advantages and disadvantages that these two hegemonial nations derive in their contest from the fact that the Communist myth sanctions an imperial structure, whereas our democratic ideology does not sanction any policy that challenges the sovereignty or pride of any independent nation.

In an era in which pride of national autonomy is the main

concern of both old and new nations, the Communist myth is an embarrassment to the Soviets. It obviously offends the national pride of the old nations of Eastern Europe. Since the Hungarian uprising in 1956, the European satellites have been increasingly restive under the yoke of Soviet imperialism. China, whose size alone would cause her to resent Soviet hegemony, has in fact invented a new Communist myth that challenges Moscow's imperial authority, particularly its claim to be the authoritative interpreter of the Communist dogma. The inclination and capacity for inventing a new myth, which makes the Russian version guilty of "revisionist" heresy and China the real authority on revolutionary orthodoxy, is in fact a clear indication that powerful nations can and do revise their imperial myths when the original myth is in contradiction with the national interest.

Russia is both white and technically competent, and therefore affluent. China is both colored and poor. It was almost inevitable that she would be tempted to revise the myth in terms that would suit her national interests, rather than those of Russia. Russia has no national interest in exporting revolution, though there must be many Russian devotees of the original Marxist myth. In any case, there must be many more who know that Russia's national interests will not be enhanced by risking her new affluence in courting a nuclear war. With China, on the other hand, there is a perfect conjunction between national pride and the prospective world-wide revolution of the poor and colored nations. Thus, there are two Communist imperial nations competing with each other for prestige among the Communist parties of Asia and Africa. It must be very disconcerting to the old believers in the original Marxist dogma.

Our concern for the independent nation, on the other hand, gives us a tremendous advantage in a day in which budding nations in Asia and Africa are jealous of their freedom and suspicious of any imperial pretensions. Military revolts against Ben Bella in Algeria, Nkrumah in Ghana, and Sukarno in Indonesia were all prompted by the armies' patriotic concern that these revolutionary political dictators were too subservient to the imperial interests of Communist imperial nations.

But our satisfaction over this advantage must not obscure the tremendous political problem of honesty that a nation like ours faces when it is challenged to use its military force in pursuing its hegemonial responsibilities. The average voter knows little and cares less about these imperial responsibilities, such as assuring the safety of the non-Communist nations on the fringes of Asia, but is moved only by appeals to our common democratic idealism, which usually is informed by a static anti-Communism. Our engagement in Vietnam has consequently forced the Administration to create a series of obvious fictions or myths calculated to obscure the hiatus between our idealism and our hegemonial responsibilities.

The hiatus is obscured by resorting to the previously analyzed myth of projecting national self-determination as a universal possibility for all cultures. Our military presence is needed to guarantee the security of the non-Communist nations on the fringe of Asia. Our air bases in Thailand ensure the presence of our military power. But we also need a harbor for our ships. That indicates Vietnam as the locus for our presence. Very well, we will invite ourselves to defend the "right of self-determination" for the southern half of the partitioned nation. President Johnson and Secretary Rusk are very Wilsonian in their idealism, and, accordingly, we are told that we are only protecting a small nation from the "aggression" of its neighbors.

Unfortunately, these myths and pretensions of our foreign policy are not sufficiently credible to obscure our real hegemonial purposes. None of the three small nations of Indochina seems capable either of integral nationhood or of self-government. Their peasant cultures lack both the technical and cultural prerequisites for Western-style democracy. When the Geneva Conference picked up the pieces of the fallen French empire in Indochina, only Vietnam was partitioned. The other two nations, Laos and Cambodia, were neutralized. Vietnam was partitioned because it contained a group of Catholic anti-Communists, who moved to the non-Communist South.

We were originally sucked into this vacuum in Indochina by the offer of financial help and "military advisers." Our aid has since grown to astronomical proportions, including billions of dollars and thousands of American lives. Our original fictional justification was that we were defending a democracy. But when the Diem regime was toppled by a bloody army revolt, this fiction was exposed by the obvious realities. The American expenditure of money and blood has increased, though South Vietnam is now obviously governed by a series of army juntas who have difficulty acquiring not only the fig leaf of constitutional government, but also the control of many of the villages over which they claim to exercise sovereignty.

One of the many reasons why this large commitment of an affluent nation has not been more successful is that the leader of North Vietnam is the legendary Communist boss and national patriot, Ho Chi Minh, who is regarded by the peasants as the father of his country, that is, the whole of Vietnam. He has the aura of a national patriot because he led the successful revolt against the French colonial masters. Ironically, in his estimation we are merely the successors of the French imperialists, whereas according to our own democratic myth, we are the big brother of all weak nations.

The public reaction to this essentially unpopular war is compounded of various motives. The idealistic democratic myth is important for many voters. On the other hand, the fear that our prestige as an imperial nation may suffer if the Communists make our position untenable influences many members of Congress. Despite the negative attitude of most of our university scholars and experts, an attitude supported by many church leaders and journalists, a shifting proportion of the public, and probably most of the military, support the war effort because they fear an ultimate military conflict with Red China for which our foothold on the peninsula is alleged to be a strategic advantage. Thus the confusion of myths—involving problems of prestige and power—and the fears of a conflict with a dominant power in Asia hold a great democratic nation in the grip of a pitiless commitment.

Whether it is feasible, necessary, or even possible to challenge a great Asian power by military force remains an unexplored question. Undoubtedly we have given additional evidence for the old saying that foreign affairs are the Achilles' heel of democracy. The myths underlying our foreign policy seem to lead an open society into confusion.

The Secretary General of the United Nations, U Thant, gave the verdict of an uncommitted observer on this strange and awful mythical struggle in the little nation of Vietnam: "I see nothing but danger in the idea, so assiduously cultivated outside Vietnam, that this conflict is a kind of holy war between two powerful political ideologies."

[1967]

Johnson and the
Myths of Democracy

New Leader 1964

MOST knowledgeable observers seem to agree that no Republican candidate has a chance of defeating President Johnson in the next election. Johnson's ascendancy has many causes. He is the legatee of the late President's rather impressive domestic and foreign programs, and the beneficiary of the aura of martyrdom which invested those programs with a new dimension of sanctity. He has added to this legacy his own considerable skill as a political manipulator; indeed, he may just succeed where it is quite possible that John F. Kennedy might have failed, in the crucial civil rights struggle.

This last reason for President Johnson's ascendancy, his great skill in manipulating the political myths of the American democratic tradition, is worthy of special attention. Democracies are in need of myths as are, more obviously, monarchies and countries with utopian programs. Myths have the function of sanctifying historically contingent value with absolute worth, and of simplifying the complex realities of political life. Monarchies exist by the patent notion of the "sacred" ruler, which enables them o avoid confusion in the crisis of succession by the absurd myth of dynastic legitimacy. Utopian revolutionary governments utilize the myth of the innocent bearers of political power (the "proletariat"), and the devilish opponents of virtue (the "bourgeoisie," the "imperialists," the "ruling circles") whom they are destined to defeat.

Democratic myths usually also give an extravagant account of
their opponents—the monarchists for our founding fathers, the
"atheistic Communists" for the present generation of bellicose
idealists. But democratic myths are more concerned with the
sanctity of their own cause than with the demonic character of
their opponents. Modern democracies are of course "open societies"
with no absolute coercive power in any organ of government. In
this sense, democracy means "freedom." Actually, a healthy democracy must always measure freedom in the context of the community's need for order and justice, which makes freedom a regulative
rather than an absolute value. In an era of extremely rapid technical progress, Jefferson and Locke's rather too simplistic veneration of liberty comes in conflict with the endless bureaucratic
instruments of order and justice. But this is to put the matter
analytically. The myth of democracy is "freedom." We are defending "the free world," even though it includes the police state
of Chiang in Taiwan.

Since we in the U.S. had a bourgeois beginning, and since the
tortuous process of emancipating ourselves from an overly consistent bourgeois individualistic outlook throughout the nineteenth
century is not as lively in our imagination as the era of our birth,
we prefer to speak of democracy as the twin of "free enterprise."
In this way we give a mythical account of the actual realities of
a mixed economy and the complicated balance of planning and
initiative which actually saved Western democracies from the
Communist rebellion. Only Barry Goldwater nostalgically believes
in the old free enterprise system. But even Nelson Rockefeller,
conducting his increasingly desperate candidacy, accuses the Democrats of not understanding the "free enterprise system."

In the process of our adjusting to the social realities of modern
technology, our bourgeois civilization reluctantly—and belatedly
—allowed industrial workers to organize and bargain collectively.
This resulted in the emergence of an equilibrium of power manipulated by two quasi-sovereignties, management and labor. The
move was a creative one and it redeemed Western democracy
from circumstances which seemed to give plausibility to the

Marxist indictment of bourgeois democracy as nothing but a coercive instrument in the hands of the "capitalists." But the realities it created seemed contrary to the original myths of our democracy. So we solved the problem by employing the mythical term "free collective bargaining." Thus the concept of freedom obscured the fact that this bargaining was futile except as a contest of power, and that the right to strike was part of the new instrument of justice. It is to our credit that "free collective bargaining" became almost as sacred as the right of suffrage— the old, but not completely adequate, instrument of equal power in a democracy without which justice in a technological age is impossible.

All the realities of power and interest are obscured in our idealistic eyes by the myth of "freedom." Not that actual freedom is a myth. What is mythical is our venerating it apart from the context of social processes involving interest and power. Open societies are not merely political devices for choosing rulers by the "free consent of the governed." They are fluid communities in which interests and powers can compete with each other and displace one another as dominant or cooperative forces in society.

The rise of free governments, propelled by the bourgeoisie against the static structures of feudalism and monarchism, is a matter of ancient history—that is, of the seventeenth and eighteenth centuries. The accommodation of these democratic societies to modern industrial civilization, and the acceptance of the industrial workers as competitive partners in the achievement of industrial justice, is a matter of recent history—that is, of the nineteenth century and, in America's case, of the New Deal. This latter step really justified and saved the democracies, though it involved shaping new realities and complexities to the older, simpler bourgeois myths of "freedom."

But now let us return to current history and President Johnson as the manipulator of political myths. Current history means that remarkable technical progress sometimes defined as "automation." It means, *inter alia*, that diesel engines on the railroads have displaced firemen, and thus aggravated the problem of unemployment in a day of prosperity. The firemen, availing themselves of the right of collective bargaining granted only three decades ago in the Wagner Act, threatened a nationwide strike.

We have entered a new era, though. The unhappy railroad workers could only bargain for the dubious right of "featherbedding," i.e., preserving useless jobs. Moreover, a strike on a nationwide public utility meant striking against the economy, the "common welfare" of the whole nation. Confronted with this emergency, President Johnson sought and was granted a postponement of the strike for fifteen days. He hovered over the bargainers like a fond uncle. The dispute seemed insoluble, for the railroads had much to gain and the workers much to lose. The final settlement proved the disparity of prizes; the roads saved 350 million in abolishing useless jobs and granted only 50 million in various fringe benefits.

The disparity of prizes and the virtual certainty that an act of Congress would prevent the right to strike upset the careful equilibrium of power gradually erected over a century. All things indicated a radical change in a new era. The President kept the whip—Congressionally imposed compulsory arbitration—carefully out of sight, but not out of mind, of course, or the bargaining could not have succeeded. When it did succeed, two days before the deadline, Johnson called in the television cameras, and flanked by both the union chiefs and the company representatives, announced: "This is a great day for free enterprise and free collective bargaining." It was as simple as that.

Johnson's was the strategy of our new era, and the jolt of entering this new era was cushioned by his shrewd appeal to the slogans and myths of past eras. Incidentally, the ailing railroads were promised some tax concessions by the government to prompt acceptance of the settlement; "free enterprise," the myth of bourgeois democracy, was scarcely relevant.

"Free collective bargaining" symbolized the achievements of the era of industrial democracy into which bourgeois democracy had been painfully transmuted in the social and political struggles of the nineteenth and early twentieth century. This concept was mythical only in the sense that it partially obscured the element of power—the right to strike—without which the allegedly rational bargaining process would have been futile. President Johnson's strategy as a manipulator of political myths consisted of his stretching the myths of two eras to cover the realities of a radically new period. The ironic aspect of this strategy turned on the fact that the right to strike, previously subsumed in the symbol of "free collective bargaining," has now been stretched to cover an entirely new reality, the prospective denial of the right to strike, at least in those jobs made obsolete by technological advances.

No one can foresee all the realities of power—the negotiating procedures, the role of government and the outlook for justice and order in this new technocratic age. All one can say is that a shrewd politician has, in an election year, veiled the perils of a new age by appealing to the partly mythical symbols of two bygone eras. Poor Governor Rockefeller will talk eloquently of the "mainstream of American politics" which Senator Goldwater has defied, but his eloquence will be futile. Johnson has already occupied the mainstream and, in addition, has commanded the ferries which ply from shore to shore.

International politics is understood even more than domestic politics in terms of symbols and myths because the realities which underlie foreign policy are complex and not directly experienced. Democracies are particularly dependent upon symbols to make complex facts of international relations simple enough for a general electorate. In this sphere President Johnson is less the shrewd manipulator than the inheritor of persistent myths in his task of guiding a once isolationist nation to its world-wide responsibilities. One remembers F.D.R.'s "Four Freedoms" address in which he promised that we would universalize "freedom from want" and "freedom from fear." It was a utopian promise from a very non-utopian pragmatic politician.

Strangely enough, both the U.S. and Russia—the two imperial powers of current history—are similarly compelled to find mythical justifications to legitimize their power under the guise of their common "anti-imperialism." The Russians are "anti-imperialistic" by definition, because imperialism is, in their ideological lexicon, the vice of capitalism. Accordingly the myth that currently presides over their foreign policy suggests that they simply want to "liberate" colonial peoples from the domination of the "imperialists" of the West.

We, on the other hand, are "anti-imperialists" because our history shows that we, too, fought a revolutionary war to free ourselves from imperial domination. The illusion that we are more innocent than our European allies, all of them touched with imperialist sin, worked havoc in the Suez crisis some years ago. When France and Britain mounted their abortive attack on Egypt, they did not trust us enough to disclose the nature of their project to us. They were mistaken, however, in not anticipating that the U.S. would respond both as an imperial and an anti-imperialist power, ordering them out of Suez in the famous "forthwith" United Nations resolution, which incidentally rescued Nasser's prestige. The idea that this move represented a victory for the "majesty of international law" proved illusory, because the United Nations was not, as President Eisenhower believed, a world government in embryo.

Our present involvement in the struggle between Communism and the "free world" in Vietnam is a baffling situation in which the U.S. is using the myth of "freedom" to cover not only its interests as an imperial power but its responsibilities within the whole non-Communist alliance. President Johnson blandly explains that "Any nation which wants to preserve its freedom to live its own life can count on our help," but we now know that the Diem regime, an oppressive police state, was not exactly an exemplar of democracy.

Two revolutions have failed to rally the peasants of South Vietnam to the cause of rigorous anti-Communism. They are probably indifferent to the issues of democracy and Communism. Meanwhile the North Vietnamese regime, guided by the tough old Communist, Ho Chi Minh, supports the Communist cause under an aura of nationalism. The facts are so complex that it would be foolish for an amateur to attempt to elucidate them. Let us simply say that we are caught in the power vacuum created in remote Indochina by the collapse of the French empire in that region.

Indeed, the three nations wrought out by the 1954 Geneva agreements, Laos, Cambodia, and Vietnam, are subject to Communist pressure and are scarcely able to achieve valid democratic governments. The neutralist compromise in Laos has not worked; and its failure indicates that de Gaulle's proposal for a neutralist Indochinese region would be tantamount to capitulation to Communism. Undoubtedly we must continue our support of South Vietnam indefinitely, though there is no indication that more technical support will hasten victory in a vicious guerrilla jungle war. Nor is Richard Nixon's proposal for carrying the war to the North very plausible as an alternative. The U.S. is simply caught in one of the most complex struggles between two imperial nations, and on terrain not very favorable to democracy.

Mounting deaths of American soldiers, coming especially in an election year, is obviously forcing the Administration to prove that Vietnam is not turning into another Korea. Still, the abandonment of the whole peninsula (including not only Indochina but Thailand) to Communism, would mean a tremendous loss in prestige. Would it also mean more specific and definable strategic losses? We might debate that point, since the European hard core of our open society is not involved. But it has so far proved to be more plausible to cover over the whole desperate problem with the President's bland assertion that "If any nation wants to fight for its freedom, we will help them." That declaration brings the whole problem into the framework of the symbolic image of America as the big brother of all the oppressed.

Ultimately, of course, the substitution of mythical images for the complex realities which confront imperial power will not solve our problems. In the end, we must debate and decide about the conflicting demands of prestige and strategy in a part of the world in which our form of government is not immediately viable and also not obviously imperiled. But the complexity of such issues may be beyond the interest and competence of the general electorate. After all, the "mother of parliaments" in Britain, with its longer experience in managing imperial power, reserved foreign policy for the cabinet and the foreign office.

[1964]

Foreign Policy in
a New Context *(1967)*
(New Leader)

T HE mills of historical experience grind small and usually chew up the ideological pretensions and preconceptions of power politics. Frequently they recast them into ironic shapes. Thus historical vicissitudes have made the Soviet Union and the United States the arbiters of the world's fate. Both preside over a continental economy, and both possess an arsenal of dread nuclear weapons with terribly destructive power. What peace we enjoy rests upon a "balance of terror," upon their equal ability to destroy each other and the world. Since signing the Limited Test-Ban Treaty, they even have a nascent partnership for avoiding a nuclear catastrophe. (Incidentally, that treaty was probably the greatest achievement of President Kennedy's all too brief Administration.)

In short, the U.S. and the U.S.S.R. possess not merely massive economic and military strength but a capacity to determine human destiny beyond their own national boundaries, dwarfing that of the ancient and the nineteenth-century European empires. Yet both of these imperial nations govern their international relations by the light of dogmatic presuppositions which their own power, and sense of power, have clearly refuted.

According to their respective political doctrines, they are actually anti-imperialist. The U.S.S.R. is an anti-imperialist empire because Marxist dogma defines "imperialism" as the unique sin of capital-

ism; consequently, nations such as Russia, having nationalized
industry, are by definition free of this taint.

Our own anti-imperialistic pretension has more diverse sources.
It springs partly from the fact that we were the first nation to
gain freedom from an imperial power in our war of independence.
(Not long ago, at the time of the initial Bandung Conference,
there were some among us who believed that the new nations
collected there would surely recognize their affinity with us.) In
part, too, our anti-imperialism is due to our natural wealth, making
overseas expansion unnecessary. And in part it has been drawn
from an idealistic innocence, expressed from the days of Thomas
Jefferson to those of Woodrow Wilson. This nostalgic myth was
possible because our liberal democratic idealism attributed imperialism to either monarchism or militarism. We were obviously
a republic and so could not be guilty of royalism. We did have a
military establishment, but until recently military leaders were
not distinguished in class terms. Jefferson could therefore assume
that our foreign relations were conducted "by reason, rather than
force."

Since it is dangerous for modern imperial nations to base their
foreign policies on dogmas and illusions disproved by historical
experience, it becomes important for us, as an imperial nation,
to re-examine the virtues and vices of imperial power. An analysis
of the complexities of imperialism will yield the conclusion that
traditionally there have been three motives for the exercise of
imperial power, and that they were present in varying proportions
in ancient as well as nineteenth-century empires.

1. The most obvious motive of nineteenth-century European
empires was economic exploitation of subject nations for the
sake of furnishing the imperial master with raw materials and
markets. The Communist indictment of imperialism made this
economic motive the dominant or even the sole purpose of empire
building.

2. The second motive was political, the impulse to enhance
the power, prestige, or "glory" of the imperial nation.

3. The third motive was "missionary," that is, the desire to

confer some high value on the colonial nations, whether that high value was conceived as religious zeal, technical competence or political democracy.

The Communists usually obscured the second and third motive in their indictment of the first motive; while the imperial nations emphasized the missionary motive. Both positions reflected the hypocrisy which characterizes all collective attitudes. True, it would be cynical not to appreciate the genuine character of the missionary motive, manifested in the universalization of moral, technical and cultural values from their original homes to the benefit of more primitive, i.e. technically backward, nations. France regarded itself as the bearer of "civilization," and Britain saw itself as the midwife of democracy among peoples of backward cultures. But these moral claims were generally as extravagant as the Communists' charges of economic exploitation as the sole motive of empire.

It is certainly significant that the two modern empires, the U.S.S.R. and the U.S., are comparatively free of the economic motive. In the case of the Soviets, this has been true since the second stage of their development when they ceased to use the satellite European nations as sources of raw material for industry. The United States foreign aid program, of course, has run into the billions. The motives of today's two great imperial nations are, in fact, a unique compound of lust for power and prestige, and missionary devotion to their overarching value systems.

The Soviet Union is the holy land of the Communist scheme of social redemption. Thus many of its current policies can be understood only in terms of the conflict of interest caused, on the one hand, by its being a pillar of order as the partner of the U.S. in the effort to prevent a nuclear catastrophe, and on the other hand, by the need to guard its ideological prestige—particularly in Asia, where China sneers at Russia's pretensions of orthodoxy and accuses this now technically competent nation of "bourgeois revisionism." The Russian embarrassment has been heightened by the war in Vietnam. President Johnson's assurances that our objectives there are limited do not impress the Russians.

They are bound by their ideology to support the Communist cause,
especially when political adversaries within their own camp seek
to rob them of ideological prestige because they have become, in
effect, the allies of the hated "capitalist imperialists." The dogmas
of the past always have an ironic effect on the sober realities of
the present.

But the Soviet embarrassment is minute compared with American ideological confusions in Indochina. We are the hegemonic
nation in the presumably democratic non-Communist bloc. Our
democratic ideals properly prevent us from transmuting our hegemony into an imperial structure of power. So we find ourselves
championing anti-Communist nations even though their politics
are bereft of democratic substance, or trying to create democracies
in peasant cultures lacking all the technical and cultural prerequisites of self-government.

When the French empire in Indochina collapsed, the Geneva
Conference neutralized the two small countries of Laos and
Cambodia and partitioned Vietnam. Our military presence was
considered necessary to protect the non-Chinese nations, chiefly
Malaysian, against China. We might have made Thailand our
base. We might have made this choice without blood, despite
Thailand's rule by a hereditary monarchy and a military junta.
We chose instead a more dubious alternative, or were inadver-
tently drawn into it.

We adopted the southern sliver of divided Vietnam and pro-
ceeded under President Eisenhower to support it economically
and through the presence of "advisers." Our imperial prestige was
more heavily invested during the Kennedy Administration, when
our democratic presuppositions and illusions about Indochina
prompted us to create the Ngo Dinh Diem regime and proclaim
to the world that we were supporting a "democratic nation." Our
popular press hailed poor Diem as "the Churchill of Asia." In
fact, he was an oppressive Catholic Mandarin ruler, whom the
nonpolitical Buddhist peasants feared probably more than they
feared Ho Chi Minh.

As is now all too well remembered, the regime was overthrown in a bloody army revolt. Both Diem and his brother Nhu were murdered. There were reports that President Kennedy, appalled by their suppression of the Buddhists, indirectly brought on the revolt by ordering the C.I.A. to cease furnishing Nhu's Special Forces with secret funds. The day of Diem's overthrow is now annually remembered in a special South Vietnamese holiday; and the ferocious Vietcong represent the Communist portion of the electorate.

Since Diem's downfall, the South has been governed by a series of military juntas. All of them have not only had trouble with the Buddhist monks and peasants, but have found it difficult to preserve harmony among the civilian and military factions representing different regions, conflicting religions, Northern emigrés and the indigenous Southerners. There have been many indications, in other words, that the South is not ready to organize an integral nation, no less a democratic government.

Yet these difficulties did not prevent Washington from defending its venture to preserve our imperial prestige in strictly Wilsonian terms. We were defending "the right of self-determination." We were "resisting aggression." The President even insisted that if we did not make our stand in Vietnam we would have to defend ourselves in either Honolulu or Seattle. This astounding justification surely implied that we were resisting aggression not from North Vietnam but from China. It also implied that the Chinese would not hesitate to cross the Pacific and challenge us on our own soil. We were subject to political confusions derived from the attempt to hide our concern for imperial prestige behind the idealistic terms of Wilsonian libertarianism. This was a new version of "making the world safe for democracy."

We reiterated our desire for a peace conference. But both Ho Chi Minh and Mao Tse-tung were so confident of the effectiveness of guerrilla warfare that neither bombing nor a pause in bombing could bring them to the negotiating table. China and America's prestige were at stake; only a face-saving device for both imperial powers would suffice.

Meanwhile, the phenomenal expansion of the Vietnam venture

from a few "military advisers" to a still growing army of over 400,000 U.S. soldiers, the mounting American casualties that equal or exceed local casualties in a bloody civil war, and the ever-mounting costs running into billions create the suspicion that our loyalty to Wilsonian international ideals (or in the President's phrase, "our determination not to desert our principles or our friends") was not powerful enough to motivate this tremendous expenditure of blood and treasure. Some unconscious and uncon-fessed motives must have been behind this vast undertaking.

The most obvious motivating forces must have been the un-conscious concern of the people for the pride and prestige of their imperial nation, and the unconfessed identical concern of our political leaders. To these one has to add some vague residual fear of Communism which ignores the recent developments that have disintegrated the Communist monolith, the so-called "inter-national Communist conspiracy," and have made China and Russia political adversaries. This places our foreign policy in a new context.

In our ventures in a little nation so close to China, we must be wary of disturbing the nascent nuclear partnership with Russia on which peace in a nuclear age depends. The President's assur-ances of our "limited objectives" have not relieved the Russians of their embarrassment vis-à-vis China. The British Foreign Min-ister, George Brown, on a peace mission to Moscow, was told pointedly that he would do better to address his appeal to Wash-ington. Prime Minister Harold Wilson, despite strenuous efforts during Premier Kosygin's visit to London, in the end could not do much better either.

The attempts to meet the responsibilities and hazards of our world-embracing power by following the concepts Woodrow Wil-son used in his futile effort to beguile an isolated nation into world responsibilities after World War I are bound to distort present power realities. That is why cynical journalists in Wash-ington speak of a "credibility gap." The magic of even the most ingenious politician will never transform the southern portion of Vietnam into an integral democratic nation; nor will it transform the motives of a world power concerned about its prestige into Don Quixote's desire to help the helpless.

If a less ingenious and shrewd statesman than Lyndon Johnson were President, this foreign undertaking would have been abandoned. Increasing casualties and costs may yet prompt the nation and the President to sober second thoughts. Johnson's immense prestige was won by his rigorous domestic policies, by his extending the welfare state and offering the Negro minority our belated justice in equal civil rights. The cost of the war, with its attending perils of weakening the Great Society program, inflation, tight money and probably higher taxes, could erode this prestige.

If the Republicans were shrewder they would mount a viable alternative. But they are more "patriotic" than the President in supporting the war. They foolishly suggest greater cuts in our welfare and antipoverty programs. And they have no popular war hero to win an election by promising to end the war in Vietnam, as Eisenhower did in Korea.

The Republicans may of course reduce the Democratic majority for the President and in Congress, sparking Congressional rebellions which Johnson's immense prestige and ingenuity have so far succeeded in suppressing. But ultimately our great democracy must find ways of extricating its peace and the security of civilization from the hazards of guiding a mature world power by ideas inherited from our Wilsonian adolescent engagement with world problems.

[1967]

A Question of Priorities *(1968)*

M EN generally regard themselves as rational creatures, though individuals have been known in whom reason is the servant rather than master of passion or ambition. In the case of collective or national behavior, however, this conception is usually refuted; the moral prejudices, commitments and notions at this level are so obviously formed by capricious juxtapositions of men, forces, and events.

Consider our morality as a nation in this era when the age-old debt we owe our Negro minority must be measured against the debt we owe to nascent democracy in an obscure Asian nation. The scales weigh strikingly in favor of our domestic disadvantaged. Still, we argue that we have a greater commitment to defend democracy against Communism, contracted in the last quarter century as a result of becoming a hegemonic nation. So we spend billions of dollars and thousands of precious young lives in fulfilling this debt, while we spend only a fraction of that on the civil rights and antipoverty programs. To comprehend fully the irrationality of preferring an obligation incurred yesterday to an obligation incurred at the very moment of our birth as a nation, we must analyze and compare our responsibilities in each of these unsolved problems.

The practical necessity of creating a national union, including both slave and free colonies, prompted us to accept a built-in moral contradiction in our national life. Human bondage was obviously at variance with the ideals professed in our Declaration of Independence, yet its author, Thomas Jefferson, was himself a slaveholder. Abraham Lincoln movingly expressed this idealism in his Gettysburg Address: "Our fathers brought forth on this continent a new nation, conceived in Liberty, and dedicated to the proposition that all men are created equal." But even a "dedicated nation" can be suspended in the hiatus between the principles men profess and the customs or prejudices upon which they act.

And if the white majority quickly forgot, the Negro minority had to remember that some of the founding fathers who subscribed to the Declaration of Independence were not above haggling with the slave states about the number of representatives in Congress. They agreed that this should be determined by the number of voters; but also that the slave states could have representatives for three-fifths of their voteless chattel. Our founding fathers were not Machiavellians or hypocrites. They merely bowed to the need for establishing national unity among all the colonies, slave and free.

Our founding fathers did not share the utopianism that characterized the almost simultaneous French Revolution. They probably regarded liberty and equality as regulative principles of justice, rather than simple historical possibilities. They were therefore more sober builders of a national community than were the French revolutionaries. They must have known that modern nations are communities where a common race and common language ultimately contribute more to cohesion than social idealism.

One offers these excuses for the builders of our nation to stress that they were virtuous and honorable men, and certainly no villains. All of these excuses, however, cannot obscure the fact that our free society and democratic system incorporated human bondage into the community. We have thus had to spend centuries eliminating this contradiction to our ideals of justice from our basic scheme of order and law. Perhaps it is overly generous to say we have devoted centuries to the task, for despite our sense of political virtue, we were not as a nation too intent on putting an end to slavery. Fortunately, though, the abolitionist minority at least tried, not very successfully, to arouse the national conscience against the awful degradation involved in permitting the existence of an institution that allows some men to regard their fellow human beings as property.

The Civil War brought the emancipation of the slaves, and this ought to have wiped out the evils of human bondage. But an honest patriot can ease his conscience little with that war. As Lincoln wrote quite honestly to Horace Greeley, "My primary purpose is to save the Union." The emancipation was merely a tool in the hands of the Federal forces, and Richard Hofstadter has rightly described the proclamation as "having the eloquence of a bill of lading." What is more important, it did not conclude the long history of injustice to our Negro minority. After Lincoln's death, in the days of Reconstruction, ex-slaves were not given land to earn their livelihood; they were simply turned into debt-ridden tenant farmers. The craft unions first accepted them as apprentices a century after the Civil War. The Negro, in short, was destined to live in poverty.

There were, of course, the post-Civil War constitutional amendments. One was designed to give Negroes the vote without regard to "race, color, or previous condition of servitude." But the white racists negated that guarantee of universal suffrage by refusing to register Negro voters, intimidating them with threats of violence or economic pressure. The power of universal suffrage was thus denied to the Negro minority until a belated national consensus resulted in the Civil Rights Act of 1964, providing for Federal control of voter registration. The "equal protection of the law" amendment was consistently defied by the South's segregated school system and *de facto* segregation in the North's ghettos until the Supreme Court's historic 1954 school decision. Yet more than a decade after this decision, we still confront merely token compliance with the law.

All these dismal facts reveal that neither the power of the law nor the conscience of the individual can bring rapid change in social attitudes and customs. They reveal, too, that our Negro minority has been confronted with unkept promises and disappointed hopes throughout the long years since the Civil War, the war that we are taught freed them from the injustices and evils of slavery.

But what of the period after the Court decision and the Civil Rights Act? Does it not refute the pessimist and support the view of the optimist?

These questions bring us to the current climax in the civil rights movement and the Negro revolution, which stands in such curious juxtaposition to the present climax in the Vietnam war. Technically, the two have no relation to each other, except that the same nation is experiencing them at the same time with capricious effects.

The climax in civil rights is not merely the triumph of democratic justice. It is a climax of two forces. The first is the gradual escape by talented individuals from the closed society of our Negro minority. The number of able Negroes now holding high office testifies to their ability in public affairs as well as to a growth in racial tolerance. In the case of elected officials, it also indicates the political power of universal suffrage. Certainly it is significant that today we have a Negro Cabinet member, Negro Justice of the Supreme Court, Negro U.S. Senator, and Negro mayors in two major cities (Gary, Indiana, and Cleveland, Ohio).

To be sure, neither this trend nor the increasing recognition of Negroes in the arts and athletics, can possibly be defined as a "Negro revolution" (unless by that we mean rapid change in the evolutionary processes of a genuinely free society). The phrase more aptly describes the concerted movement of Negroes to assert their rights, particularly the efforts of young people to use every possible peaceful strategem—from sit-ins to court action—to eliminate discrimination in public places.

The second force that has reached a climax is marked by the terrible symbols of violence and arson in the city ghettos. This eruption, the cause of much concern among both Negro and white civil rights exponents, has also been falsely considered a part of the "Negro revolution." In reality, it is the explosion of despair and irresponsibility within the segment of the Negro community that is unemployed and often unemployable because of the rapid expansion of industry and technology in our society.

These people in their poverty have been deprived of any skill that an increasingly technical culture demands. Their outburst of hopelessness calls to mind the Luddite violence of the early nineteenth century, when impotent workmen smashed the new labor-saving machines. Both situations demonstrate that impotence may be the cause not of revolution, but of a very uncreative response to new techniques beyond the workers' control. Karl Marx defined this inability to create a revolution as the impotence of the *Lumpenproletariat*. Our predicament now is that in our bourgeois paradise, we have few creative or even revolutionary workers; we have only the ragged proletariat of unskilled Negroes, and we must realize that our racial situation confronts us for the first time with a situation similar to that described by Marx. In the past, the industrial workers of the Western democracies were not driven to Marx's revolutionary desperation, for they had the skill and wisdom to organize labor unions, to bargain collectively, and if need be, to strike. Their collective economic power altered the whole shape of an industrial culture, making it immune to the apocalyptic Marxist vision. It also showed that social justice in an industrial culture requires that the political power of the vote be augmented by some form of collective economic power.

True, the Negro minority has the power of the boycott to enforce its claims, and Martin Luther King used it most effectively to abolish segregated buses in Montgomery, Alabama. While this gave the Negro revolution a needed impetus, one has the uneasy feeling that there are simply not enough economic tools in Negro hands to effect real social change. Demonstrations for open housing have proved partially effective. But it is the absence of any weapon resembling the strike that makes the Negro so dependent upon government help in achieving his objectives in housing, education and job training.

We are, in short, in a unique historical situation. The baneful consequences of a closed society for the Negroes has deprived them of those instruments that white industrial workers used both politically and economically in an open society to achieve justice for their ranks. To meet the challenge, the government launched its war against poverty—including programs to raise the educational level of deprived children and provide untrained youngsters with skills.

The Administration, I believe, was honestly committed to these programs and has been consistent in all its commitments to social welfare and civil rights. But here the Vietnam war comes into juxtaposition. The President needs a tax surcharge to pay for the astronomical costs of the war. Yet the chairman of the House committee in which all fiscal and tax bills must originate is certain there will be no new tax program unless the Administration cuts its budget. The Great Society policies are thus imperiled.

The collision between the Negro problem and the Vietnam war began with a coincidence: 1954 was the year of the Supreme Court decision, in a sense the beginning of our Negro revolution; it was also the year of the Geneva Conference, where France finally capitulated to the three budding nations of its empire in Indochina. It was relatively simple to ordain the neutralization of the princely states, Laos and Cambodia, at Geneva. But Vietnam was a different matter since Ho Chi Minh, the father of Vietnamese unity, was a fiercely nationalistic Communist, and the country had a number of staunch anti-Communist leaders as well, motivated by both religious and class considerations. Our first step into the "quagmire" was our offer of financial assistance for the migration of this anti-Communist minority to the South.

Our involvement deepened when we helped set up the "democracy" of President Diem, whom we hailed as a "Churchill of Asia." We did not give due consideration to the implications of the strident Mandarin and Catholic biases of the Ngo family and its aides in a country with a substantial Buddhist population. While Buddhist peasants were largely apolitical, their monk-leaders were inclined to hate the Catholic landlords as much as the Communists. Ultimately the Diem regime perished in a bloody coup, led by the army.

Significantly, the date of the Diem overthrow is celebrated as a national holiday. It may be equally significant that South Vietnam has since been ruled by a series of military governments, the current one more securely established because two members of the junta have been elected President and Vice-President, in accordance with a new constitution enacted by a General Assembly. The wife of one of the defeated candidates complained to our ambassador that the government was keeping her husband in confinement without trial. Yet the election has been billed in our nation as the final validation of the principles of democracy for which we are paying such a high price.

We have vainly called to Communist governments, indeed to all and sundry, to help bring Hanoi to the conference table. But Hanoi is adamant in its refusal. Meanwhile, we and the rest of the world debate whether bombing or no bombing would be more effective in achieving the desired conference—from which we ask nothing but a "peace with honor," albeit a peace that must assure the attainment of our objectives.

We have insisted upon two objectives for our military presence in what I see as a civil war that we inadvertently strayed into. One is the Wilsonian ideal of the right of self-determination and self-government. We have failed to consider the possibility that Western democracy is not a viable option for a peasant culture in which both religious and class differences cannot be democratically resolved. Moreover, the Vietcong in the South are the fiercest of terrorists, able after all to wreck any attempts at a "united front" government.

Our second objection is based upon our sense of responsibility as the hegemonic power of the non-Communist world. We must contain and resist the expansive ambitions of Chinese Communism, we argue, even though our actual operations drive Vietnam more and more into dependence on that ancient enemy. True, our military presence in Southeast Asia may have been effective in influencing the military leaders of Indonesia to thwart the

Communist coup, prepared secretly with President Sukarno's connivance; but with that event our military presence has ceased to be influential in Asia.

These ideological confusions and contradictions throw much light on the cost a great nation pays for covering up an original miscalculation. We are paying a tremendous price, in billions of dollars and the blood of American boys, merely to avert the catastrophe of being pushed out of Asia by a little nation using guerrilla tactics. President Johnson was not the author of our gradual stumble into the quagmire. But he is certainly responsible for the military build-up, calculated to save our imperial prestige in Asia. Ironically, our physical destruction of the small nation we are intent upon "saving" seems to be simultaneously reducing our prestige in Asia and the whole world.

Perhaps two morals should be drawn from our pathetic involvement in this civil war in Asia. First, the "consensus" needed to reconcile the nation to this war must surely be based on idealistic democratic motives and upon a tough-minded concern for our imperial prestige. But, second and more important, the necessary consensus is bound to create domestic dissension among the exponents of democratic justice. Too many people feel that a redress of the social injustice to our own Negro minority is necessary *now* and must not be thwarted by our capricious involvement in a foreign war.

This calculation is increasingly made not only by Negro civil rights workers or militants, but by their white colleagues among our students, the faculties of our universities and the leaders of our religious communities. This attitude has no resemblance to the old isolationism. It is based on moral scruples—not on patriotic complacency or irresponsibility toward the ills of a poor world.

[1968]